JAMES LOUIS PETIGRU

JAMES LOUIS PETIGRU

Southern Conservative,
Southern Dissenter

William H. Pease and Jane H. Pease

University of South Carolina Press

© 2002 by William H. Pease and Jane H. Pease
Original cloth edition published by the University of Georgia Press,
1995

Paperback edition published in Columbia, South Carolina, by the
University of South Carolina Press, 2002

Manufactured in the United States of America

06 05 04 03 02   5 4 3 2 1

Library of Congress Cataloging-in-Publication Data

Pease, William Henry, 1924–
   James Louis Petigru : Southern conservative, Southern dissenter /
   William H. Pease and Jane H. Pease.
      p. cm.
   Originally published: Athens : University of Georgia Press, c1995.
   Includes bibliographical references and index.
   ISBN 1-57003-491-5 (pbk. : alk. paper)
   1. Petigru, James Louis, 1789–1863. 2. Lawyers—South Carolina—
Biography. I. Pease, Jane H. II. Title.

KF368.P44 P43 2002
340'.092—dc21
[B]   2002073320

Title page illustration: James Louis Petigru, painted by his daughter
Caroline Carson in 1885(?) from memory and an 1860 photograph.
(University of South Carolina School of Law)

In memory of
Margaretta Pringle Childs

with admiration for
her dedication to justice,
her love of history,
and
her knowledge of her native state

CONTENTS

Illustrations

ACKNOWLEDGMENTS

Like all authors, we owe many debts of gratitude to those who have helped us in a variety of ways. We probably never would have begun a Petigru biography had Alice Wakefield and Angus Murdoch not organized a bicentennial celebration of his birth and had not Margaretta Childs and Lee and Cheryle Drago encouraged us along the way. But even those friends might not have convinced us had we not once lived for three months in the building that James Petigru had built for his law offices, but which in 1973 was the home of the late Misses Charlotte and Edith Smith. Those months fed not only our curiosity but also an occasional fantasy about the man who had trudged up the steep steps to the second-floor offices, in one of which we made our temporary home as we first tried to fathom antebellum Charleston.

Because we are novices in legal history, we have called on many who know the field well for expert advice. Prime among them are the late Judge Randall Bell and Professors Norma Basch, Randall Bridwell, James Ely, Paul Finkelman, Kermit Hall, Herbert Johnson, Pamela Robinson, and Marylynn Salmon. Other colleagues came to the rescue when we asked them for assistance. Stanley Engerman helped us figure out Petigru's finances in 1990 dollar equivalents. William McFeely and August Meier provided information conveniently available in their universities' libraries. Robert Olwell ferreted out information from the alumni files of Mount Saint Mary's College. The late George Rogers made interpretive suggestions rooted in his comprehensive knowledge of South Carolina history. And Michael O'Brien far exceeded customary professional courtesy not only in leading us to several collections containing Petigru manuscripts but also in providing notes on Petigru references in collections so unlikely we should surely have missed them otherwise. A number of South Carolina lawyers delved into their own recollections to help us reconstruct the recent fate of the Petigru legend. Among them were Nathaniel Barnwell, Lewis Burke, Gedney Howe III, Harry Lightsey, Jr., and Ann Sterling. And Robert Rosen not only talked with us at length about the legend but lent us his own records of the Petigru Society. Dr. Jonas Brachfeld helped us assess the medical histories of both James and Jane Amelia Petigru. Finally, Randall Bell, Edmund Lee Drago, Paul Finkelman, Kermit Hall, David Moltke-Hansen, Jon Wakelyn, and an anonymous reader all read the entire manuscript and gave us most helpful commentary, which has saved us from many errors, made us clarify obscurities, and generally improved the text.

None of this, of course, would have produced material sufficient for a book had not libraries made both manuscripts and printed sources available. Most of the manuscripts came from the South Carolina Historical Society, the South Caroliniana Library of the University of South Carolina, the Southern Historical Collection of the University of North Carolina at Chapel Hill, and the Library of Congress. The University of South Carolina Law Library provided the reports that allowed us to trace Petigru's work in state appeals courts, and the South Carolina Department of Archives and History made available lower court and other relevant public records. Betty Taylor of the University of Florida Law Library helped us explore federal court records through the Lexus and Westlaw computerized indexing systems. Michael Phillips and the Robert Scott Small Library of the College of Charleston did yeoman service in garnering an array of both primary and secondary sources through interlibrary loan. Unfortunately, while staff members at many other institutions gave generously of their time and talents, space limitations allow us to thank here only those few upon whom we imposed at greatest length: Joseph Cross, Harlan Green, Herbert Hartsook, Stephen Hoffius, Charles Lesser, Richard Shrader, and Allen Stokes. Our affiliation as Fellows at the Institute of Southern Studies of the University of South Carolina and as Associates in History at the College of Charleston has facilitated our work in a number of ways.

Finally, we could have worked neither so efficiently nor so long in Columbia and Chapel Hill had not Constance and the late Carl Schulz and David Moltke-Hansen been such generous and tolerant hosts.

The following institutions have generously given us permission to quote from manuscripts in their collections: the Alabama Department of Archives and History, the Amelia Gayle Gorgas Library of the University of Alabama, the Charleston Library Society, the William R. Perkins Library of Duke University, the University of Georgia, the

Huntington Library, the Library of Congress, the Historical Society of Pennsylvania, the University of Rochester, the South Carolina Historical Society, the South Caroliniana Library of the University of South Carolina, and the Southern Historical Collection of the University of North Carolina. For permission to quote from copyrighted material we thank Princeton University Press and Yale University Press. We acknowledge the courtesy of the Greenwood Publishing Group in allowing us to use the portions of our essay "Law, Slavery, and Petigru: A Study in Paradox," which appears in Randall M. Miller and John R. McKivigan, eds., *The Moment of Decision: Biographical Essays on American Character and Regional Identity* (Westport, Conn.: Greenwood, 1994). To all of them we are most grateful.

The following institutions have given us permission to reproduce images from their collections: the Collection of City Hall, Charleston, South Carolina; the South Caroliniana Library, McKissick Museum, and School of Law, all of the University of South Carolina; and the South Carolina Historical Society.

JAMES LOUIS
PETIGRU

ONE

The Legend

In the great Civil War
He withstood his People for his Country
But his People did homage to the Man . . .

—*Monument inscription, grave of James Louis Petigru,*
St. Michael's Episcopal Church, Charleston, South Carolina

Caught between an intense intellectual commitment to a system of justice to which the United States Constitution was essential and the physical and social realities that molded personal and public life in his native South, James Louis Petigru trod a serpentine course. Consequently, the most persistent theme of his life and of the legends it generated is ambiguity. Sometimes, especially in his politics, he was forced to choose between the commitment and the reality. More often, and most markedly in his legal career, he found ways to merge the two or to circumvent the conflict. As a result, when he died in wartime Charleston, this longtime Unionist who never hid his scorn for the Confederacy was given a funeral in which his fellow townsmen, government dignitaries, and almost all the city's Confederate officer corps paid him tribute. This they did when hostile federal troops were a scant twelve miles away. But only a month later, when the Loyal National League met in New York to mark the second anniversary of the bombardment of Fort Sumter that had begun the bloody war, it too praised Petigru.[1] That a man who dared to stand alone against passionately committed fellow citizens, who attributed the war they had begun to madness, and who drew warm praise from the enemy still commanded veneration at home confounds simple logic. That he embodied, on the one hand, an idealism that transcended the emotions of both sides, and represented, on the other, principles distinctive of each section that even he could not reconcile allowed partisans on both sides to lionize the man. Northerners venerated his loyalty to Union, Constitution, and, yes, country. Southerners prized his sense of honor, his manly independence, his courageous pursuit of justice for the weak, and, yes, his gracious dignity bespeaking a patrician culture.

Once the war was over, the ambiguities that marked Petigru's life gave rise to conflicting legends, to each of which the diverse experiences of his seventy-three years lent substance. How the content and meaning of the Petigru legend evolved as succeeding generations applied it to the concerns of their own times only continued the narrative of changing priorities that had molded the seasons of Petigru's life from youth to maturity to old age.[2] The flexibility of the mythmaking that followed his death poses paradoxes that a biography of the man must address.

In the months immediately after his death, southern eulogists played on Petigru's service to his community, stressing especially his professional expertise. The directors of the Bank of Charleston, who commended his contributions to "the dignity and impartiality of our courts," only repeated what other fellow citizens had long said. The trustees of the College of Charleston voiced familiar themes as they expressed final gratitude for the "force of intellect" and "noble disinterestedness" that had made him a valuable "friend of education." Memorialists for the Charleston Bar Association reiterated familiar tributes when they praised the "legal mind" and "love of truth and justice" that had put Petigru on a par with Supreme Court justices John Marshall and Joseph Story.[3] Northerners addressed Petigru's political dissent from the loyalty to community values so vaunted by his neighbors. General Winfield Scott, who had known him as a fellow Whig, wrote Edwin Stanton, Abraham Lincoln's secretary of war, that Petigru was, when he died, the "greatest moral hero of the age." And William Tecumseh Sherman, who had once been stationed in Charleston and had been a frequent visitor to Petigru's home, believed that "there is not an officer in my army but knows that Mr. Pettigru [sic] stood almost alone a Rock against which the Waves of Treason beat in vain, but swept all that was near and dear to him into ruin."[4]

Not surprisingly, once the war had ended family members hastened to meld both themes. Caroline Petigru Carson, who alone of her father's family had remained loyal to the Union and abandoned her native state, erected a monument over his grave that bore a lengthy inscription she wrote with the help of several northern friends of her father. Enjoining "Future times" never to forget the man who had "confronted Life with antique Courage" and "held his conscience higher than . . . praise," it described a "Jurist, Orator, Statesman, [and] Patriot . . . Unawed by Opinion, Unseduced by Flattery, Undismayed by Disaster."[5]

Filiopietistic though they surely were, both text and monument soon became a public shrine accepted as a dispassionate assessment. Carson's attempt to convince former Massachusetts governor and senator Edward Everett, another admirer of her father, to write his biography, had come to naught. As a result, the first biography was written not by a northern Unionist but by Petigru's old college chum, Confederate loyalist William Grayson. Published in 1866, after Grayson too had died, it was nonetheless free of wartime rancor. If it made some few criticisms—that its subject, for instance, had an "irritable" temper—it differed little from the graveyard epitaph. Whatever Petigru's defects, they were "lost in the broad light of his numerous virtues." Subsequent biographies, compiled largely from family letters by kinsmen Joseph Blyth Allston in 1899 and James Petigru Carson in 1920, were no more critical.[6]

Such bland exercises in personal friendship and family pride are predictable. Less so are the uses to which the Petigru legend was shaped to forward sectional reconciliation. Although a former law student recalled in his old age a conversation in which Petigru had expressed active opposition to slavery, it was only after Reconstruction had ended that Petigru came to exemplify a course that many southerners, viewing the shambles of defeat, wished they too had followed. In an effort to bond with them, the *Philadelphia Evening Express* urged Rutherford B. Hayes, only days after his inaugural in 1877, to learn from Petigru's example. Southern men with the "character and self-respect" to serve national interests best were, like that unique Carolina loyalist, "not to be bought. . . . The modern American Radical cannot comprehend this," but a president who would reunite the country must.[7]

In subsequent years, southern men with similar goals followed suit. As the South Carolina Bar reorganized itself and as its members evolved a new rationale to deal more effectively with postwar realities, they turned with fair frequency to the Petigru heritage. In 1882, Carolinian Alexander Lawton, addressing the American Bar Association, spoke pointedly to the northern lawyers who had assembled at fashionable Saratoga for their annual convention. He emphasized the values his southern colleagues shared with them and suggested that a more sympathetic understanding of the Old South would be the first step in the process of national reconciliation. Building his remarks around a familiar story of a poor boy from a respectable family who, by hard work, self-discipline, learning, and personal integrity had become a successful attorney and a great man, Lawton made of Petigru a Horatio Alger hero. The story he told demonstrated the compatibility of the Old South's cultural gentility with the professional diligence required to face harsh economic realities: perfect ingredients for the road to reunion.

A model of the Puritan work ethic, Petigru had known that "he *must* make bread as a lawyer, and not as a charlatan, even though starvation should stare him in the face." But he also successfully trod "the 'primrose paths' " of cultivated leisure—albeit most often "at the midnight hour [when] he had already satisfied the demands of that jealous mistress, the law." During the Civil War, Lawton continued, Petigru had never condoned the "lawlessness which breaks off all habits of submission and support to government." Through good times and bad he had remained a "gentleman," "the product and outgrowth of that peculiar phase of Southern civilization which has probably now disappeared forever."[8]

Then, expanding his canvas to include that civilization as a whole, Lawton addressed North-South differences in the most emotionally appealing way possible. He admitted that his region had not generated "great cities, or marvelous material growth"; that it had not produced "literary or scientific works of a permanent character." It was rather a "social civilization" whose "radiating centre was the home; its chief inspiration the social affections and kindly emotions."[9] Those social values, so well exemplified by Petigru, could only forward renewed southern participation in the reconstituted United States.

During the years that followed, when flags seized by victorious opponents on Civil War battlefields were returned to their regiments, when Confederate and Union veterans began to hold joint reunions, and when freedmen's rights once more became the responsibility of the states, the Petigru legend continued to serve sectional reconciliation. It stirred old memories only to reshape them to new purposes. In 1882, the same year Lawton addressed the American Bar, Charleston mayor William A. Courtenay and onetime South Carolina governor Andrew Magrath commissioned a bust of the attorney who now symbolized their ideal of civic virtue.[10] Two years later an elderly Yankee provided the *Atlantic Monthly* with a romantic reminiscence of an 1860 Charleston visit, relating in his dotage an interview with the patriotic Unionist whose "snowy" hair was still black when he died and in an office that in no way resembled Petigru's. Closer to reality were the memories exchanged by middle-aged and aging Charleston gentlemen in their clubs, where they talked with some frequency about the Petigru who had earlier graced their city's social life. One recorded in his journal an extended discussion of that "stern and uncompromising" patriot, whom he compared to the Roman statesman Cato and about whom he could "fill volumes" with Petigru stories still current in 1898. Many of those stories were the same ones Judge James Cothran, a Confederate veteran, had told the Abbeville Literary Club in 1883 about the "intellectual athlete" "who . . . stood towards his brethren of the bar like Saul . . . among the prophets—a head and shoulders above all others."[11]

This particular Petigru legend probably peaked about 1890, the same year the Charleston Bar sent to the state association in Columbia the large portrait that Caroline Carson had painted of her father in the late 1880s. In formal ceremonies it was presented to the chief justice of South Carolina, who had it hung in the courtroom over which he presided. Philippe Verner, a young lawyer who was present, wrote Petigru's sister that the portrait was "an inspiration to the young, and an example to the aged of pure patriotism and loyalty to truth."[12] By calling Unionism "pure patriotism," Verner hinted that the Petigru legend served not just the cause of reconcilation between North and South but the reconciliation of at least some South Carolinians to Petigru's politics, to a belief that wisdom had lain not in secession, war, and inevitable defeat but in the Unionism that Petigru had expounded.

Ironically, the reconciliation about which Verner wrote was eased by yet another. During and after the 1890s, northerners failed to challenge constitutional revisions and new legislation in southern states that undid what remained of Reconstruction by disfranchising black voters and intensifying racial segregation. In 1891 the Honorable Joseph D. Pope, addressing the law students graduating from the University of South Carolina, called on the Petigru heritage to justify even this latest "reconciliation." Pope had studied law under Petigru and believed that his teacher had been "the greatest private citizen" the South had ever produced. But, turning preference into presumed fact, he very much

Bust of James L. Petigru, commissioned by Charleston mayor William A. Courtenay, executed by A. E. Harnisch, and erected in Charleston City Hall, August 13, 1883, with the following inscription:

James Louis Petigru, Jurist, Orator, Heroic Man.
Born May 10th, 1789; Died March 9th, 1863.
"Shall construction and implication be resorted to
in defiance of the Charter? Forbid it Heaven!"
"The visions of hope have fled and the fire of youth is extinct.
But such as it is, I lay this offering of age on the altar of justice."
[Petigru's last words in court in the sequestration cases, 1862.]
IN MEMORIA AETERNA ERIT JUSTUS.

(Collection of City Hall, Charleston, South Carolina)

doubted that his hero would ever have consented to "the enfranchise-
ment of the recently emancipated slave, as well for the slave's own
good as for the good of the victorious North, and for the good of the
vanquished South." Petigru, Pope asserted, had certianly hated slavery.
But he had hated it "not in its domestic aspects, but as an institution."
Never could he have hated "the master who in that relation fed and
clothed and sheltered the slave; who humanized him, who civilized
him." To enfranchise those same slaves, however, would threaten the
South with the fate of Haiti.[13] Pope thus reshaped the Petigru legend to
justify emerging American imperialism and to make its hero a spokesman for the White Man's Burden—to "civilize" and "humanize" all
dark-skinned people. Pope's further insistence that Petigru had favored
limited monarchy over republican government, an allegation Petigru
himself had refuted when it was first made by a British journalist in
1861, suggests the scope of the liberties that legend makers took in the
first fifty years after his death.[14]

With his ideas already remodeled to suit the concerns of the new
century, it is not surprising that Petigru's name was also invoked to
buttress American patriotism during the First World War. Yet it was
the older version of the legend that offered solace to Woodrow Wilson.
Denounced by powerful senators for his treaty making at Versailles and
attacked for the vapid idealism of his League of Nations, the president
felt himself as isolated as Petigru had been in Civil War Charleston. He
envied the legendary Carolinian, who, "unawed by opinion" and despite his support for "the abolition of slavery," had retained the friendship and respect of his political opponents. On a particularly bleak
March day in 1919, the president talked with his doctor about Petigru's enduring friendship with Robert Hayne: "Though they differed it
never interfered with their friendship." Even the Civil War was unable
to sever that bond, Wilson said, observing with astounding inaccuracy
as to date and place that they were buried side by side in St. Michael's
graveyard.[15]

More revealing of the new and contradictory meanings that the
Petigru legend was made to bear immediately after World War One
were two public addresses. In mid-June 1919, elderly Charleston lawyer Joseph Barnwell spoke at the dedication of the University of South
Carolina's new law school building, Petigru College. The name had
been chosen, Barnwell said, because the antebellum lawyer best represented extraordinary legal expertise combined with professional integ-

rity, a merging much needed at a time when "cynical indifference to truth and equal boldness in refusing to carry out contracts" marked the practice of law. But the old lawyer went on to address a third "crying evil" as well, the failure of state courts to punish lynching. Only a constitutional amendment making lynching a federal crime, Barnwell asserted, could restore public order and civil decency. He sought that amendment "in the name of Petigru," and in Petigru's own ironic style he continued, "Let us hope, if such amendment pass, it will be before burning is established as the approved punishment for crimes and even misdemeanors."[16]

Only two weeks earlier, on Memorial Day, John P. Thomas, president of the South Carolina Bar Association, had addressed a joint meeting of the Georgia and South Carolina bars. Speaking less than two years after the Bolshevik Revolution, at a time when many Americans believed that only vigorous efforts to suppress Communists at home would save their country from a similar fate, Thomas emphasized Petigru's loyalty to the United States. Petigru's rejection of secession and his refusal to cast his lot with the Confederate States of America provided a worthy model for contemporary Americans, who should now put down "fanatical minorities, prompted by new and untried theories of government and society and inimical to the spirit of American ideals, whether under the guise of Bolshevism, I.W.W.ism, or any other ism, whose followers wave the red flag of anarchy."[17]

Taken together, Barnwell's and Thomas's addresses mark a bifurcation that distinguished the Petigru legend after 1919. Yet then as later, the dividing line between these vastly differing viewpoints was blurred. For Barnwell, Petigru symbolized society's need for law and order to protect a minority endangered by an unrestrained majority. For Thomas, Petigru was equally a pillar of law and order, but in his view the minority needed to be restrained and controled, and dissent confined to a small and shrinking group. Given the thrust of the rest of his speech, Thomas's praise for Petigru's defense of Reuben Smalle, "a helpless tramp from the North, supposed to be an Abolitionist,"[18] whom some slaveowners had treated to lynch law, is downright perplexing.

Whether because the Petigru legend had become so murkily diffuse or because southerners sought escape from the economic realities of the Great Depression, commemorations of the antebellum Unionist during the 1930s had little political or social meaning. An assortment of articles in South Carolina newspapers described his Charleston law office and the upcountry Petigru family plantation near Abbeville. But if they served any ulterior purpose, it was to support the preservation of historic buildings, a movement already well under way in Charleston.[19] Drawing upon similar nostalgia for a vanishing past, Carolina-born DuBose Heyward, best remembered as the author of *Porgy*, made Petigru a significant character in his 1932 Civil War novel, *Peter Ashley*. Primarily a romance of the antebellum South brought to ruin by the war, *Peter Ashley* portrayed Petigru as a "staunch and philosophical Unionist," an isolated voice of reason whose message was relevant, but only to the rose-colored provincialism of the Old South.[20]

Then, in 1936, the year *Gone with the Wind* was published, the South Carolina Bar Association once again heard an address about Petigru. Judge Rion McKissick dealt neither with politics nor constitutional issues, however, but confined himself largely to amusing anecdotes. The stories he told illustrated personal characteristics, also mentioned in most previous Petigru speeches to the bar. The antebellum attorney was still the man of inviolate personal and professional integrity, fiercely loyal to his values and ready to defend them against overwhelming opposition, but McKissick went on to wax romantic about Petigru's family life, his loyalty to his father and brothers, his devotion to his sisters and his saintly mother. It was a theme foreshadowed when Barnwell commended the old lawyer's dedication to his invalid wife, whom Petigru had "petted as though a young beauty to his dying day."[21] And, in 1940, Helen Hennig, in her *Great South Carolinians*, returned—with more fervor than accuracy—to the theme of Petigru's ideal marriage.[22]

But as white southerners faced challenges to segregation in the 1950s and 1960s, some of them brought the public Petigru heritage back into focus. Liberal lawyers and civil rights advocates drew inspiration for their own struggles against racial discrimination from Petigru's willingness to represent African Americans and alleged abolitionists. J. Waties Waring, the controversial Charleston-born federal judge whose landmark 1947 decision ended the all-white primary in South Carolina, and who, even before the 1954 *Brown* decision, had ruled that separate schools were inherently unequal, enlisted Petigru's example for much-needed moral and psychological support.[23] Even the *Charleston News and Courier*, which had long been harshly critical of Judge Waring, celebrated the one hundredth anniversary of the attack on Fort Sumter by reprinting an old article from a New York paper extolling James Petigru as an exemplar of toleration when times were rife with hatred.[24]

Not surprisingly, then, when journalist Sally Edwards wrote a young people's biography of Petigru in 1970, she made his life a text to encourage both toleration and desegregation. More than a hundred years earlier, she told the young Carolinians who were largely her intended audience, this Unionist had stood his ground without disparaging his opponents. He had shown her ancestors and theirs both what Carolinians "did right" and what they "did wrong" without ever doubting that they were a "goodly, great, and decent people." Now, Edwards admonished, her contemporaries must try for a similar balance so that they could accept the changes in social institutions that would end "racism and repression and 'separate but equal' hypocrisy."[25]

For some South Carolinians who came of age in the 1960s and 1970s amid the controversies associated with the civil rights movement and the Vietnam War, Petigru symbolized still more heroic dissent. In 1970 some law students who considered themselves liberal and a few who deemed themselves radical organized the Petigru Society to focus their efforts to make immediate changes in the generally conservative University of South Carolina, from which Petigru had been graduated a century and a half earlier. Like other student organizations at that time, the society challenged traditional restraints, although, compared with more nationally visible groups, their goals were limited and their means subdued. They secured student representation on faculty committees and thereafter successfully pressured faculty and administrators to end requirements that law students wear coats and ties to class. They opened up the guest speaker program to divergent views. They visited undergraduate colleges throughout the state to recruit African-American and women law school applicants, who would, they hoped, eventually change the composition of their state's bar. Their program, their style, and their goals reflected what Petigru meant to members of the society named for him. As the state's onetime leading lawyer, he represented their own aspirations to professional expertise, especially as trial lawyers. They admired his political support for unpopular causes in the face of nearly universal opposition. And they were drawn to his idealism, a trait of youth, which in Petigru survived the demands of making a living as an attorney.

Nonetheless, subsequent events bled the meaning from the Petigru legend that their program enshrined. In 1972, when its founding members graduated, the Petigru Society disappeared. Their attempt, in association with the student bar association and the law school faculty, to call the newly completed law building Petigru College was blocked by trustees and deans. First there was a reluctance to rename the old law school building, known since 1919 as Petigru College. Subsequently, administrators seeking a major gift from a donor, for whom the building could then be named, rejected the proposal unless the Petigru enthusiasts could raise such a sum themselves. More than twenty years later, the law center still remained a nameless structure.[26]

Meanwhile, historians who came to maturity in the same social and educational milieu as did the protesting law students questioned Petigru's reputation for liberal reform. Weighing his political writing and the opinions of contemporary politicians rather than his legal career and his repute among lawyers, they concluded that Petigru was a political conservative, an advocate of the status quo, even an ossified Federalist, whose political ideas were so out of step with his own times that he was already irrelevant in the early nineteenth century. Lacy Ford, interested primarily in southern radicalism, portrayed Petigru as a "Conservative in a radical age," an "*arriviste*" peevish in his dealings with the planter elite to which he aspired, a politician isolated by his rigid and anachronistic views even from fellow Unionists, and a man whose public activity was motivated largely by the self-serving "desire to create a bright political future" for himself.[27] In his 1986 intellectual history of *The Metaphysical Confederacy*, James Farmer dismissed Petigru out of hand as a man who "had so isolated himself that he had been assigned the role of admired eccentric—the exception who was so singular that he could be tolerated without fear."[28] Whether or not the naming of the new Petigru Law Library in the recently restored Charleston County Court House in 2000 represented a shift in opinion or simple historicism is difficult to judge.

Had Petigru's life been all of one piece, wholly unambiguous, it would have sparked no legends. It is because he was a man loyal to his region and its culture yet a critic of its politics and ambivalent about its economics that the multiple legends offer insights into his own times as well as a warning against reading the present into the past.

TWO

—⋯—◄⁑◉⁑►—⋯—

Becoming a Lawyer

That one man could generate so diverse and persistent a legend as did James Louis Petigru is little more remarkable than that the son of a marginal backcountry farmer could come to occupy so central a place in the aristocratic Carolina low country among the wealthy planters and businessmen who were its power brokers. But the very improbabilities of Petigru's life make it a fascinating reflection of the time and place in which he lived. Not only did he make his way in antebellum Charleston, a commercial city within an agricultural slave state within a nation of steadily growing economic diversity, Petigru also balanced the critical intellectual demands of a cultural heritage that simultaneously professed faith in a divinity that foreordained each person's fate and asserted that individual freedom was a God-given right. At the same time the conflicting expectations of family, friends, and foes often deepened his understanding of his world's diversity. Taken together, external forces of time, place, and people interacted with his own hopes, talents, and emotional needs to create a life of continuing change and development.

James Louis Pettigrew (for so his father's family spelled it) was born May 10, 1789, in the northwest corner of South Carolina near Abbeville.[1] The Ninety Six District, where he lived as a child, had a long history of frontier violence, disruption, and conflict. Because courts and public officials were concentrated in distant Charleston, the district's citizens responded to the increased lawlessness generated by the French and Indian War with vigilante justice. In the late 1760s the residents of Long Canes, where Pettigrew's grandfather, James Pettigrew, had recently settled, organized irregular and extralegal citizen groups, called Regulators, to combat thievery, murder, and rapine with means no less violent than those of the criminals they pursued. When the American Revolution broke out in 1776, backcountry insecurity was further exacerbated. Continued Indian warfare, the failure of law enforcement, and the adoption that year of a new state constitution that left the backcountry white population greatly underrepresented in comparison with the large slaveholders of the low country all intensified the sense of isolation among the thinly settled frontier's residents. Finally, in 1780–81, when backcountry Carolina suffered the fiercest fighting of the war, the last remnants of order collapsed. The early post-Revolutionary years did not bring much improvement. In a section whose male population had been decimated, whose livestock and farm implements had been stolen or destroyed, whose remaining property owners faced a debt crisis of untoward proportions, and whose dire economic circumstances spurred crime, vagrancy, and widespread social unrest, general mayhem remained the order of the day.[2]

Admittedly, some families, like the Calhouns, Pickenses, and Nobles, not only survived but fared well, consolidating their already substantial resources during the 1780s. The Pettigrew family, however, did not. James Pettigrew, who had arrived in the Long Canes area on the Little River in 1768, was part of the same Scots-Irish migration southward along the Appalachians that in its earlier stages had introduced his more prosperous neighbors into the area.[3] But Pettigrew, who had already resettled twice—once in Virginia, once in North Carolina—before he arrived in Long Canes, quickly lost his first South Carolina land claim. In 1773 he took up another in the nearby Flat Woods section, and there he made a go of it. At his death, eleven years later, he left his wife, Mary, the use of three hundred acres, two slaves, two horses, and two cows, property that after her death passed to their sole surviving son, William.[4]

William Pettigrew, born in Virginia in 1758, was still in his teens when the Revolution began. During the early stages of the fighting he had been a reluctant soldier, miserably homesick when forced to take part in sporadic Indian skirmishes. But in 1779 he volunteered and served under General Nathanael Greene, though he distinguished himself neither by notable action nor officer's rank. Nearly nine years later, in 1788, William married Louise Gibert. The next year, after his father's will had finally been proved, he inherited full ownership of the property that James had left for Mary's support, and which William had worked for himself since his mother's death three years earlier. When the couple's first son, James Louis, was born in May 1789, William's property put him somewhat above the level of most of his backcountry neighbors, three quarters of whom in 1790 owned not a single slave.[5]

Despite his new responsibilities, William did not settle down to diligent husbandry. Stuck in the semiwilderness of Flat Woods, he continued the diversions of his bachelor years, preferring hunting, fishing, and horse racing to cultivating an isolated farm. Not surprisingly, he soon fell into debt and by 1800 had lost all his property. Thus diminished, the Pettigrews, with three children of their own and the child of Louise's sister, who had died not long after she gave birth, moved to nearby Badwell, the Gibert family farm.[6]

Although young James was caught up in family tensions between the Giberts and the Pettigrews, he put down roots at Badwell, quickly absorbing Gibert values and standards. Despite the disgrace of his father's improvidence, the move to Badwell gave James the psychological and social security he had previously lacked and provided the whole family with decidedly improved material and economic circumstances. His mother's father, Jean Louis Gibert, a well-educated French Protestant minister, had come to South Carolina with his Huguenot congregation in 1764, settled with them in the Ninety Six District, and founded New Bordeaux on the Little River. Not only a steadfast pastor, Gibert, who had experimented with silk manufacturing and operated a general store, was able, at his death in 1773, to leave a comfortable estate for the support of his wife and three children. Far more extensive than James Pettigrew's property, it included ten slaves, between fifty and eighty head of cattle, nine horses, a substantial house, and the Badwell farm.[7] Shortly after Jean Louis died, his widow moved to Charleston and there married a fellow French immigrant, Pierre Engevine, apparently a retail merchant. When she died in 1783, Engevine took Louise, now fifteen, her younger sister, and an older brother back to Badwell.

That brother, Joseph Gibert, who now owned Badwell, was a somewhat eccentric soul who had trained to be a physician but never practiced his craft.[8] A determined bachelor, he undoubtedly had little interest in being joined by a sister with four youngsters in tow. And his reception of William Pettigrew was clearly icy. "He would have wished," so one of the five Pettigrew children subsequently born at Badwell recalled, "that my mother should separate from my father on the ground that he could not provide for her wants." The Pettigrews not only stayed together, however, but regularly added to their family until

Louise was forty-five. Her "refusal to yield to the wish of her brother" understandably "brought about a coolness between them."[9]

Uncle Joseph kept his emotional distance. James's father, on the other hand, proved a great problem for his oldest son. "Endowed with good humor, with gaiety, [and] a pronounced taste for books," William Pettigrew could be fun to be with. As a model of adult male behavior for his sons, however, he was less satisfactory. He understood "nothing of business" and lacked "penetration and perseverance," with the result that his resources diminished "whilst his family increased."[10] Worst of all, he was an alcoholic whose behavior was unpredictable and whose proclivities for "a drink of grog"[11] crowded out other childhood memories of him. Although William's children all consequently developed behavioral patterns common among the children of alcoholics, the three oldest sons each responded quite differently to their father's problems. John, the second son, became a ne'er-do-well, the black sheep, a drunkard even less responsible than his father. Thomas, only two years younger, straddled; though he avoided his brother John's fate, he also had a drinking problem that frequently got him into trouble. James tried to compensate for his father's deficiencies by assuming family responsibilities well before he was ready for them. When he first arrived at Badwell in 1800, a husky eleven-year-old, he at once became a full-time laborer. By the time he was thirteen he and his brothers, whose efforts he oversaw, did most of the farm work despite the presence of Uncle Joseph, step-grandfather Engevine, and his own father.[12] Rather than being alienated by this experience, James became deeply attached to Badwell, which always remained for him the symbol of family continuity and the means by which he could fulfill the obligations he believed were his.

But young James's world was not all work. A bookish lad who preferred reading and dreaming to hunting and fishing, he made the most of his father's well-chosen library. It was his mother, however, who oversaw his early education and directed his reading toward the classics, most especially Plutarch's *Lives*. Here the young frontiersman encountered the men of ancient Greece and Rome, complex and sophisticated people whom the ancient historian depicted as neither complete heroes nor total villains.[13] That balanced presentation gave James a way to think about himself and his kinsmen and to grapple with the reality of life at Badwell. It was a far better preparation for life than his occasional attendance at nearby short-term country schools.

James's systematic education began when he was fifteen and, in October 1804, went off to Willington, a tiny village five or six miles from Badwell, where Moses Waddel had just opened an academy that already had attracted pupils from all parts of the state. Educated at Princeton under the tutelage of its famed president and teacher, John Witherspoon, a Presbyterian cleric who mingled Calvinist theology with a civic humanism well suited to the new Republic, Waddel intermixed character building with instruction in Latin and Greek.[14] Although the formal schoolroom was a log cabin and study periods were more often than not conducted in forest clearings, and despite an unchanging menu of cornmeal and bacon, Waddel insisted that his pupils cultivate self-discipline, integrity, and even the social graces as well as their minds. His academy was therefore as important to James's self-image as to his intellectual growth. Moreover, the schoolmaster was in all likelihood the first adult male whom James admired enough to emulate, and Waddel repaid the compliment, asking him to stay on as a teacher after he had finished his two-year course.[15]

James and his mother, however, had set their sights on South Carolina College. Chartered in 1801, the college, which had opened only the year before, in 1805, was expected by its Federalist sponsors to bring the sons of low country planters and the offspring of settled backcountry farmers together in order to produce a well-educated and cohesive political leadership for the state.[16] So, either to regain the social status of their Huguenot father or simply to prepare the most promising Pettigrew son for a better life, Uncle Joseph Gibert contributed part of the college tuition, as he had Waddel's fees, while Louise Gibert Pettigrew borrowed the rest from a prosperous neighbor.[17] In December 1806 Pettigrew set out for Columbia and college.

Having more than satisfied entry requirements in Latin and Greek, arithmetic, and English grammar by his study at Willington, Pettigrew entered college as a member of the sophomore class. Always pressed for funds, having to work and live off campus much of the time, he nonetheless stood second and then first in his class as he progressed through a traditional classical curriculum supplemented by mathematics (algebra through trigonometry), science (physics, chemistry, and astronomy), and studies in the Christian tradition, culminating in moral philosophy. He also joined a debating society—the Clariosophic —a standard component of early nineteenth-century higher education. Here Pettigrew learned to think on his feet, to develop his own ideas in rational discourse, and to respond to challenges from his peers. The topics set for debate, while often trivial, provided him with opportunities to apply insights and concepts garnered in the classroom to contemporary issues seldom considered there. The student debaters thus sharpened their understanding of the world in which they would live their adult lives. And here Pettigrew began a lifelong fascination with politics and political theory, assessing the impact of the French Revolution or weighing the merits of property qualifications for legislators. Here, too, in debates over capital punishment for debtors and compensation for jurors, his later preoccupation with law and justice took shape.[18]

The college lived up to its founders' purposes, as its eighty students—many of whom became judges, governors, congressmen, church leaders, or college presidents—learned to know each other. Pettigrew soon became intimate with scions of the great coastal plantation families.[19] His closest friend—and intellectual competitor—was William Grayson, who grew up near Beaufort and whose inherited estate allowed him to live most of his life there as a nonpracticing lawyer and minor poet. Coming from a background of plenty and security, Grayson little sensed the personal discomfort that Pettigrew's relative poverty imposed. Despite his social graces and his intellectual acumen, which charmed both his peers and his seniors, the backcountry fellow was never quite comfortable. His country clothes so embarrassed him that he refused dinner invitations lest he appear a rural bumpkin. So deeply ingrained was that discomfort that only when they were both in their seventies did he finally tell Grayson about his single altercation with Waddel, who had punished him severely and, he thought, unjustly for fighting a fellow student who had taunted him about his homespun garb.[20]

Pettigrew's sensitivity about appearances underscored his constant fear that his father's fate might become his own. Well after he had earned professional prestige and secured his social position, he rejoiced to discover a Pettigrew genealogy whose evidence "that we are so respectably descended" surprised him. Well before that discovery, however, and very shortly after his graduation in 1809, James Pettigrew had become James Petigru. The wellborn Mary Boykin Chesnut later jested about his "Huguenotting" his name, but for Petigru the spelling change signified no mere social climbing.[21] By it he announced his re-

jection of the Scots-Irish frontier culture of his father for the education
and relative security of his mother's family. Implicitly he also signaled
his rejection of his father and the disgrace his drinking had brought on
the family.

For all that, however, Petigru was no dour ascetic. Never a teetotaler,
he enjoyed his wine and, some critics thought, often drank beyond
moderation. He himself enshrined in family lore the tale of a youthful adventure in which he got thorougly soused. And many years later
he apologized for having overindulged and gone off with a pair of his
brother-in-law's overshoes after drinking his "good liquor till I did not
know what I was doing." Nevertheless, as an adult he generally followed
the rule that "no one . . . ought ever to get drunk and fall down, or not be
able to preserve the proprieties of life. He should know when he has as
much as he can carry or ought to drink." The dangers of not knowing,
to which brothers Jack and Tom, who repeatedly injured themselves
and their families by their excesses, unhappily attested, stalked him
throughout his life.[22]

Necessity, experience, and his devotion to his mother had so strongly
ingrained a sense of family responsibility in Petigru that he might easily
have returned from college and settled down to the drudgery of farm
life. But he was saved from that, though not from the need to support
his parents and siblings, by the intervention of his uncle Thomas Finley.
A longtime friend of William Pettigrew as well as his brother-in-law,
Finley warned his nephew that should he return permanently to the
backwater of the marginally productive Badwell, he would face "inevitable ruin," in which he and all his family would "sink together."[23]
Thus convinced that he must strike out on his own, Petigru chose to
teach, the option Waddel had offered him three years earlier. He had
already gained some experience at the Columbia Academy, where he
had taught to support himself while he was in college. Now, with a college degree in hand, he set out for the village of Eutaw, where he had
been offered a job. Either Willington or Columbia would certainly have
provided more stimulus to his "zeal for study" than did this isolated village midway between Columbia and Charleston but almost fifty miles
from either. Yet, for six months he was the master of a small school
there and a boarder in the home of the local minister. With little else
to do in Eutaw, he contended with the likelihood of intellectual vege-
tation, the dissolution of his mind, and the dissipation of his education
"by regular gradation, without the annoyance of passion or eccentricity

of mind."[24] His plight and the dreariness of the village aroused compassion in Daniel Elliott Huger, a local planter who took an interest in the promising young teacher some ten years his junior. He introduced Petigru to other planters in the area and thereby opened to him "the best houses," including Whitehall, whose excellent private library provided intellectual diversion and whose young heir, Thomas Heyward, became his friend. When he left Eutaw, Petigru, who was still not sure what he wanted to do with his life, had acquired in Huger a powerful mentor.[25]

In June 1810, Petigru, with Huger's help, used his Eutaw experience to land a job as assistant teacher at Beaufort College and made arrangements to prepare himself for admission to the bar by reading law with William Robertson, a local attorney. Though very much a small town, Beaufort was the social hub for the planter families who had grown rich cultivating rice and Sea Island cotton along the southernmost Carolina coast. Consequently, Beaufort College—really only a secondary school—enrolled between thirty and fifty students, whose fees made possible Petigru's $900-a-year salary. All in all, his position there satisfied him. He earned enough to support himself comfortably and still help out at home. Furthermore, he loved teaching and had fun with his students. He especially enjoyed the late months of 1811 when, after the college's president died, he managed the whole school himself.[26]

Indeed, Petigru might well have remained an academic had he been appointed the new president of Beaufort College. But the trustees chose New Englander Martin L. Hurlbut, a teacher accustomed to the rigorous standards of the Phillips Academy in Andover, Massachusetts, who was both older and more experienced. When he arrived on the scene, Hurlbut was appalled at the disorder he found. The school's once handsome and expensive building resembled "a heap of ruins," its trustees seemed incompetent, and, just as bad, the loose style of his assistant teacher had created "a condition far from being agreeable." So, although Petigru stayed on for a few months, until mid-1812, learning much about teaching and discipline from this Williams College–educated Congregational minister, who soon became a fast friend, he was glad enough to leave and pursue his alternative career in the law.[27]

In 1812 Petigru completed his legal studies with Robertson and was admitted to the bar. The next year he was admitted to practice in the equity courts. Still, he always regretted giving up the classroom for the courtroom because, as he observed late in his life, his "natural temper and the tendency of [his] mind were altogether alien from the law." His success as an attorney really came, he commented wryly on another occasion, from overcoming "the fact that I had no vocation for it."[28] In any event, he began his career as a lawyer in Coosawhatchie, the court town of Beaufort District, where he now lived, and his first years were mightily discouraging. For the first three he wrote not a single brief, and his small income came mainly from teaching law students rather than from practicing law. Like Eutaw, Coosawhatchie was a rough frontier village whose one hundred residents in winter were reduced to one during its malaria-ridden summer.

Early on, lawyering did not look very promising, but Petigru's alternatives were limited. He lacked the capital to become a planter, the interest to pursue medicine, and the faith required to follow the ministry. And there were virtually no other vocations that would utilize his most valuable asset, his education. Furthermore, memories from his early years probably pushed him toward the law more than even he realized. His childhood had undoubtedly been filled with tales of the frontier mayhem and vigilante justice that had wracked the South Carolina backcountry before, during, and after the Revolution. Countering these stories, Plutarch's *Lives* had weighed the lives of heroes and villains in the scales of wisdom, prudence, honor, and especially justice. "Justice," that historian had written when considering Aristides the Just, "makes the life of such as are in prosperity, power, and authority the life of a god, and injustice turns it to that of a beast." The mature Petigru never forgot youthful lessons of this sort. Addressing the South Carolina Historical Society late in his life, he pointed to South Carolina's pre-Revolutionary Regulator movement as a warning that where there was no effective legal system the inevitable result was either "want of justice," or the use of "lynch law," or both.[29]

Finally, Daniel Huger exerted a powerful influence. It was he who had urged Petigru to study law and had helped arrange his move to Beaufort to enable him to do so. When Petigru was admitted to practice, Huger made him a professional associate and introduced him to the larger legal fraternity of the state. His sponsorship enabled the popular young lawyer to move ahead rapidly. When he was only twenty-seven, the state legislature, in which Huger sat, elected Petigru solicitor (state prosecutor) for Beaufort District. Three years later, in 1819, Huger, now a judge, arranged a prestigious Charleston law partnership for his protégé.[30]

As it turned out, the Coosawhatchie years gave Petigru the experience he needed to move ahead rapidly in his career, while his sociability allowed him to combine friendship with professional advancement. He renewed his ties with John Trezevant, a Willington schoolmate who became his first law partner. William Grayson, his old college chum, was a fellow novice with whom Petigru could discuss law as readily as literature and love. By mid-decade, with Petigru's practice at last flourishing, it had become a standing joke that in virtually every important case in the Coosawhatchie court he represented one side and his close friend William D. Martin, the other. When he left for Charleston in 1819, almost on his thirtieth birthday, Petigru had acquired professional experience and an easy court manner and was used to the advantages of being a big frog in a small pond. He made his charming farewell in doggerel verse, spoofing himself and others among the "Hosts of Lawyers" who gathered in the Coosawhatchie Courthouse "when justice holds her semi-annual sway." His humor in describing it confirmed that this chapter of his life, in which he had, with whatever doubts, chosen his occupation and begun his professional career, had lived up to his expectations.

> My grief in parting's more than I can bear
> Or cleverly express, it is a pity
> That friends should part; but of your famous City
> I must now take my leave, and you shall say . . .
> Here lies a hapless youth, his years were few,
> But when he drew a picture, drew it true.[31]

While he was beginning his law practice, Petigru had also married and begun a family. He had first flirted with Jane Amelia Postell in 1812, while he was still teaching at Beaufort, but his real interest at the time lay with two other young women. He first actively courted a Miss Chisholm, who turned him down. The only record of this romance is a single sentimental poem in which Petigru compared his love to the beautiful aloe and ended with the cloying plaint that it depended upon Chisholm "whether, doomed to endure like the aloes, my love, / Must resemble its bitterness too." Unsubstantiated family lore says that the young lady subsequently regretted both her indifference at the time and her suitor's failure to renew his quest. The second woman to spurn his suit was Mary Bowman, who, as a matter of practicality, preferred a rich widower to an impoverished young lawyer. So, in 1815 Petigru again turned his attention to Jane Amelia, whose rumored engagement to another suitor, and thus her presumed inaccessibility, may have made him the more willing to court her. In any case, when he discovered the competition, Petigru wrote Grayson wondering whether he actually did or did not love her. Scanning his owned mixed emotions, he concluded, "Had she loved me or had I thought so I should have been exposed to that conflict, from which Tragedy has drawn so many touching events, in the strife of reason & passion." So he remained calm when the affair seemed ended, despite his belief that he had been imposed on—but whether by Jane Amelia or his own emotions is unclear.[32]

Nonetheless, within the year, on August 17, 1816, James Louis, now twenty-seven, and Jane Amelia, aged twenty-one, were married. To on-lookers the marriage between Louis and Amelia (as they called each other, apparently because James and Jane were already the names of a Postell brother and a Pettigrew sister) looked propitious. Jane Amelia was a beauty whose "somewhat willful or capricious mode of address . . . no one could . . . resist." Her father, James Postell, was a well-off Coosa-whatchie planter who had sent his daughter to Julia Datty's highly esteemed school for young ladies in Charleston. All in all, the Postells were a more prestigious family than the Pettigrews. Her grandfather, Colonel James Postell of Abbeville, was both a Revolutionary War hero and a planter. Moreover, in marrying Jane Amelia, the still property-less lawyer acquired by their marriage settlement joint use and control of her ten slaves.[33]

Probably no one foresaw the potential misfortune inherent in the traits Jane Amelia shared with her fun-loving father-in-law, William Pettigrew. Family members did contrast her high spirits and sophistica-tion with the pious seriousness of her mother-in-law, but these charac-teristics were especially attractive to her new spouse. Indeed, he shared them; but he also curbed them by the same Huguenot restraints of hard work and self-denial that had enabled him to build his mother a new house at Badwell with his first earnings. All, however, seemed idyllic in the early years of their marriage. The young Petigrus spent their first

James L. Petigru miniature, painted by Charles Fraser in 1834. (From Alice R. Huger Smith and D. E. Huger Smith, *Charles Fraser* [Charleston: Frederic Fairchild Sherman, 1924])

winter in the home of friends; then they rented a house where, a little more than a year after their wedding, their son Albert was born. And at last they built a house of their own in Coosawhatchie.[34]

By the time he reached thirty, Petigru's career and his family were both well launched. His marriage seemed to resemble the ideal he later defined for his sister, one in which the wife devoted "herself heart and soul to promote the good of her husband."[35] In his friendship with

Daniel Huger he enjoyed the patronage of a powerful mentor eager for his success. And he had built a reputation that extended beyond his immediate peers to those who could do much for an ambitious and talented man. Facing his next decade, he reached out for more visible success.

The Petigru who moved to Charleston in 1819 already combined up-country bearing with low country manners. Five feet ten and a half inches tall and big of frame, he nonetheless moved lightly and with a distinctive determined gait. His broad forehead and high cheekbones topped a square face framed by dark hair and lighted by eyes that read meaning in the faces of others as quickly as they sometimes betrayed their owner's sense of the ridiculous. Courteous to persons of all ranks, his manners were always "hearty," "often impulsive," and sometimes, at least as his grandson remembered them, "hilarious." He never quite fit the stereotype of the southern gentleman. He danced like a bear, avoided oratorical flourishes, and, especially in the courtroom, came straight to the point. A lawyer's lawyer, respected for his knowledge and logic, he was also a superb performer whose sudden changes of mood and outbursts of humor brought witnesses up short and carried juries before him. Then, just as he scored a major point, he would whip out his gold snuffbox with a dramatic flourish, sneeze, and abruptly conclude.[36]

For all his talents, Petigru still found Charleston a professional challenge. He began as the junior partner of the already politically powerful James Hamilton, who had just the year before taken over the extensive practice of Colonel William Drayton on the latter's appointment as city recorder, or municipal judge. In his new position Petigru regularly faced the state's most experienced and prestigious lawyers, men well accustomed to pleading in the formal courtrooms of the eighteenth-century statehouse. Nonetheless, his first two years as junior partner were more stultifying than intimidating. While top-notch lawyers in the city were reputedly making as much as $20,000 annually, Petigru was not "overburdened with business." He devoted a major portion of his time, as he had in his early years in Coosawhatchie, to wide reading and intensive study to improve his legal expertise. For steady income he kept his post as solicitor for Beaufort District. But his participation in the big private cases, which brought his partner fees as large as $9,000, was relatively rare. Within three years, however, he made the grade.

He handled more important cases, appeared more frequently before the appeals courts, and grappled more expertly with the complexities of equity law, all the while building a bread-and-butter counselor's practice. Accordingly, when Hamilton left the firm in 1822 to serve in Congress, Petigru took over the business handily; and a few years later he added Lewis Cruger, Hamilton's brother-in-law, to the firm as his partner.[37]

By then, Petigru was happily established in the city in which he was to spend the rest of his life. The merchants and businessmen who dominated the economy of the state's major port and its commercial and banking center needed legal services more varied and often more interesting than the planters and farmers who had formed his rural clientele in Beaufort District. Nor were new professional demands the only excitement to which urban living introduced him. When the cotton crop began to flow into the city each November, ships from New York and Boston, Le Havre and Liverpool crowded the harbor, their captains and supercargoes eager to load the bales piled high on the wharves. After Christmas planter families arrived for the Charleston social season, which peaked in February with balls and horse races, nightly plays and concerts, and a constant round of private parties, dinners, and visits. And the summer social season again enlivened the city and the nearby islands where beaches and seasonal homes beckoned. Whenever prominent politicians, scientists, writers, or other luminaries came to town, the city's leaders supplemented public business with private entertainment. So, despite the economic doldrums of the 1820s, those who had come to Charleston from elsewhere in the state sensed in its cosmopolitan flavor and fast pace an atmosphere more exhilarating than anything they had previously experienced.

The Charleston of Petigru's day was confined physically to the small peninsula between the Ashley and Cooper rivers that comfortably accommodated a maximum population of 40,000 inhabitants, a city small enough that one could easily walk to any destination in less than an hour. Even so, lawyers generally chose to live no more than a few blocks from the courthouse and established their offices closer still. Thus, even though at first Petigru moved his growing family from one rented house to another, he was never more than a twenty-minute walk from his law office in St. Michael's Alley, itself less than two short blocks from the courthouse. And when in 1828 he finally bought a house at the corner of Broad and Friend streets, his residence was almost as close.

It was a sensible arrangement for a man driven by his work. When Petigru was not out of town, Charleston's geography defined the rhythm of a daily life that intermingled work and home. In the morning he walked to the market, some six blocks from his home, returning with the day's fresh produce and meat in time for a nine o'clock breakfast with his family. By ten he was either at his office or in court, where he stayed until two or three in the afternoon. Then he returned home for dinner, frequently bringing friends and colleagues with him to enjoy conversations as wide-ranging as his table was ample. By four, Petigru customarily returned to his office, where he tussled with writs and court documents, answered his mail, and was always ready to lay aside his pen and papers to discuss law with his student clerks or to chat with colleagues about philosophy, literature, or politics. Generally by ten o'clock, but often later, he walked home, had a snack, and went to bed. It was a good life, and Petigru enjoyed it, though he occasionally became impatient with the drudgery of the law. Work was, for him, a bulwark against the temptations that had ruined his father's life. "One may," he wrote a friend's son in 1819, "keep bad company [and] engage in dissolute pleasure and be amused for a few years, but if he live to be thirty or thirty-five"—Petigru was then thirty—"he will be wretched." More than forty years later he gave the same advice, more elegantly phrased, to his teenaged grandson, impressing on him "that the only thing worth living for is to become wiser and better."[38]

Part of Petigru's own growing wisdom came from his increased familiarity with public life. In 1822 he was chosen by the legislature to be the state attorney general. Doubtless politically powerful friends guaranteed his resounding victory over all his competitors, but his record as solicitor for Beaufort District was also a major factor. As attorney general, his duties extended far beyond the courtroom. He reviewed proposed legislation for its substantive as well as its technical ramifications, served as the governor's legal adviser, and acted as the state's lawyer in enforcing contracts and tax collection.[39] In addition, he was ever more visible in the state courts, for as attorney general he not only conducted all appeals court cases involving the state but also prosecuted the state's cases in the Charleston District, South Carolina's largest. In this latter post, Petigru carried a heavy load of criminal cases. Overwhelmingly these involved crimes against persons rather than against property. In his final year as attorney general, for instance, he prosecuted twenty-three cases in the Court of General Sessions:

seventeen of assault and battery, three of assault with a deadly weapon. Only two involved theft; only one, a forgery.[40]

Most of these criminal cases were, from the standpoint of law, routine and thus did little to sharpen Petigru's definition of the public interests it was his offical duty to forward. But three of the nine appeals of criminal convictions he handled do suggest subscquent themes of his career. In two he opposed appeals by masters who had been convicted of killing their own slaves. In each, Petigru blocked motions for new trials, convincing the panel of judges before whom he argued that murder of a slave was still murder, "the highest offence which an individual can commit against his fellow man." Even though the penalty for such a homicide was only a fine and the forfeiture of future office-holding, it was, he contended, essential that the crime be punished for what it was.[41] Just as these two cases enforced the admittedly limited protection the law gave to slaves' lives, they, along with a third in which Petigru sustained the conviction of a landowner who had forcibly evicted a tenant farmer before he could harvest his crops, undoubtedly helped create his subsequent reputation for protecting the rights of the disadvantaged.[42]

In those civil cases in which individuals had fallen prey to the misbehavior of public officials, furthermore, Attorney General Petigru consistently threw the weight of his state office on the victim's side. It surely occasions no surprise that when a sheriff left his accounts in disarray, or when another sheriff resolutely refused to turn over official records to his elected successor, or when a militia official absconded with regimental funds, the attorney general prosecuted the offenders.[43] But other cases intended to restrain governmental conduct in the interest of private property rather than of state authority suggest an underlying preoccupation with controlling the power of public officials. For instance, Petigru prosecuted an overly avid patrol for having seized horses from slaves who legitimately possessed them (the animals belonged to the white man for whom the slaves were working). In another case he prosecuted road commissioners who not only did their jobs sloppily but, after having failed to notify the persons legally obliged to furnish labor, fined them for failing to provide it.[44]

Indeed, in Petigru's eyes, even the most destitute and disreputable citizens deserved protection from official misconduct. Charles Chitty, a justice of the peace and the first South Carolina official ever tried for barratry, had kept his Charleston office among sailors' dives: taverns, brothels, and gaming houses. There he had not only demanded bribes from those who sought his services but exacted double fees by stirring up a countersuit for each complaint that came before him. Indignant that anyone would so abuse public office, Petigru fumed when Chitty sought to excuse his "prostitution of the dignity and character of a magistrate" by alleging that the madams and bartenders who testified against him were too morally corrupt to be credible. "One who goes into Elliott-street to commit an offence," said the attorney general, "must expect to be tried upon evidence from Elliott-street." And so Chitty was, and found guilty, and denied his appeal, and stricken from the roll of attorneys, and imprisoned for two months, and fined $200.[45]

Still, much of the attorney general's role was discretionary, and he entered many otherwise private cases when he perceived state or public interest to be at stake. Some of these cases dealt with issues that later lay at the very core of Petigru's politics. As attorney general he was expected to uphold the state's authority, and in most cases he did so. He successfully defended the legislature's right to levy a surtax on plantations where no white person was resident. He resisted private challenges to state laws governing real estate transactions and to administrative procedures for recording them. He successfully defended the use of eminent domain to extend public streets and roads. He forced elected militia officers to recognize that their primary duty was to the state rather than to their fellows in individual militia companies. He asserted the governor's power to appoint state officials and demand compliance from those he had dismissed from office.[46]

But three times while he was attorney general Petigru encountered implicit or explicit conflict between state and federal power. Each case involved issues rooted in slavery. Each he handled differently. In none did he address the peculiar institution head-on. The least complicated case addressed less an issue of state authority than the authority of the United States Army, during the interregnum marking Florida's transfer from Spanish to American rule, to seize potentially rebellious slaves recently brought into the territory. An English trader had imported several such slaves into Florida in 1820 and sold them to a planter near the Georgia border. When the slaves threatened insurrection, the army impounded them in Fort Fernandino, where one was killed when he attempted to escape. The dealer, who had not yet been paid for the slaves, then sued the post commander for the dead slave's value as well as for costs incurred by the whole group's detention. But because Captain Mathew Payne had by then been transferred to South Carolina, the case was tried in that state's courts. Despite the trial judge's instructions that the military had the authority to act as it did, the jury found for the slave dealer in a verdict reflecting local commitment to the sanctity of a slaveholder's property interest over suppression of a threatened slave servile rebellion—at least if it was far away.

In the appeal, heard in January 1824, South Carolina Attorney General Petigru and United States District Attorney John Gadsden convinced the appeals court to overturn the jury's verdict by arguing that the army's action was justified on two grounds. First, importing West Indian convicts into Florida had imperiled the safety of Americans in Georgia and, by extension, South Carolina. Second, federal law not only required military officers to suppress the illegal foreign slave trade but authorized them to seize those apparently being brought into the United States as slaves even before they had arrived.[47]

That Petigru's support of federal authority exceeded the immediate requirements of that case seems likely in the light of his deliberate failure to have represented the state's interests in the *Elkison* case in the spring of 1823. In that case, Henry Elkison, a Jamaican seaman who had been jailed under South Carolina's recently passed Negro Seamen's Law, which required incarceration of all free black sailors whose ships docked in the state, sought a writ of habeas corpus from the federal circuit court. Presiding was United States Supreme Court Associate Justice William Johnson, a native Charlestonian, who handed down an opinion finding that the state law violated both international treaty and the federal Constitution. Indeed, he noted explicitly that "state officers," Attorney General Petigru included, themselves believed the law unconstitutional and had therefore "shown every disposition to let it sleep." Yet in fact, Johnson also let it sleep in a Marshall-like ruling denying the writ because no federal law empowered him to issue it.[48]

Johnson's opinion on the law's unconstitutionality so angered the community that local newspapers refused to print it. But Petigru's abstention from this case, in which the private South Carolina Association provided lawyers eager to defend state law, attracted no further notice.[49] Accordingly, there is a touch of irony in the third case, in which Petigru confronted competition between state and federal sovereignty. In 1829 he not only sustained state power against federal privilege but attempted to subject Judge William Johnson himself to its strictures. The judge, claiming exemption as a federal official and under federal law, had refused to pay the fines imposed by state law on slave owners who failed to perform patrol duty. While the court report is mute regarding Petigru's argument, it may be inferred from Judge Charles Colcock's summary of the disputed issue: "whether the state has . . . a right to impose this duty, however irksome and incompatible it may be." Nonetheless, the appeals court avoided confronting the issues of state and federal sovereignty and excused Johnson from serving in the unpaid night guard, which policed the slave population after dark, because those with greater duties should as a matter of principle rather than law be exempt from lesser ones.[50]

Within the context of these cases, Petigru's apparent lack of involvement in or commentary on the Vesey affair of 1822 may not be surprising. On May 30 a slave informant warned his master that Denmark Vesey, a free black carpenter, and Gullah Jack, a slave and reputed sorcerer, were planning a slave insurrection. It was not until June 14, however, that the city authorities were convinced that a conspiracy existed to organize country and city slaves into military units, seize arms from arsenals throughout the city, kill their masters and public authorities, and hold the city until they could seek freedom in Haiti. In rapid response, some 131 blacks were arrested. Of them 93 were tried in closed court sessions that condemned 35 to death, aquitted 15, and either ordered or proposed that the rest be transported out of the state.

Surely as the law partner of James Hamilton, who was Charleston's intendant (mayor) during and immediately after the abortive slave insurrection, Petigru was well aware of these proceedings. He did not, however, appear as counsel in any of the trials, although slave owners retained other leading Charleston lawyers to appear as defense attorneys for their accused slaves. And because it was the same legislative session that made him attorney general that considered Governor Thomas Bennett's condemnation of Charleston's hasty and closed-door trials of the conspirators, Petigru had nothing to do with either the governor's message or its subsequent rejection. Indeed, the only clue to what his response might have been in 1822 is an observation he made to a Georgetown magistrate seven years later when a similar uprising was rumored in the northeastern corner of the state. "I am afraid you will hang half the country," he chided General Joseph Allston. "You must take care and save negroes enough for the Rice crop. It is to be confessed your proceedings have not been bloody yet, but the length of the investigation . . . alarms us with apprehension that you will be obliged to punish a great many."[51]

Petigru's failure to take public stands on controversial issues associated with slavery in the 1820s—the Vesey affair, ever-tightening legislative restrictions on free blacks, or the new South Carolina Association's vigilantism against any perceived threat to slavery—has several possible but no demonstrable explanations. Perhaps he was so busy with his own career that he had no time for politics beyond the demands of his work as attorney general. On the other hand, in South Carolina as elsewhere in the early Republic, law was commonly a stepping-stone to public visibility and elective office. So perhaps his own ideas and political allegiances were still in flux.

For whatever reason, Petigru participated little in elective politics or local government of any kind during the 1820s. He did, it is true, draft petitions for his fellow townsmen to sign in support of constructing a railroad from Augusta to Charleston. But other than that his public activity was always immediately related to the law or to his post as attorney general. For instance, the legislature appointed him to a commission charged with codifying the state's criminal law. The commission, however, bogged down in political maneuvering and died before it could produce a report. In any case, Petigru's interest in legal reform was professional rather than political, as he made clear when he supported the 1824 reorganization of the state's appeals courts, which addressed his concerns as both the state's attorney general and a private practitioner. The new law created a single bench for both law and equity appeals and thereby eliminated the chaos that conflicting opinions from the somewhat overlapping jurisdictions of the old two-court system had produced. In addition, because the new appeals bench was quite separate from the courts of original jurisdiction, it eliminated the possibility that the judge who heard a case at the lower levels would be called upon to review on appeal his own earlier rulings and instructions to jurors.[52]

Radical democratizers, however, found such limited reform insufficient and called for a codification of all law, which they hoped would make lawyers superfluous, and the abolition of equity courts, which would curtail judges' power to make law. In 1829 Petigru reacted to their proposals in a long essay in the *Southern Review*. His elaborate defense of equity began with an assessment of law courts. In cases tried there, the jury determined the facts and the judge advised the jury on the common law that applied. In a simple society, these common law courts sufficed. But as society grew more complex—as business structures became more elaborate, as private property took on a multiplicity of forms, and as contending parties found themselves in something other than simple adversarial positions of plaintiff and defendant— equity courts were devised. In them a chancellor or judge probed complicated evidence without aid from a jury and, if no specific common or statute law applied, rendered decisions designed to produce fairness and justice. But Petigru believed that South Carolina's equity courts had so expanded their jurisdiction that they now encroached upon the law courts and introduced judge-made law not only when it was totally unnecessary but when, in fact, it was prejudicial to justice itself and a threat, by its unpredictability, to the very defense of private property.

The solution, Petigru argued, was not to abolish equity jurisdiction but to restrict it to those cases alone in which common law provided no reasonable alternative. With such an arrangement, the current five chancellors could be replaced by a single individual who actually understood equity and who, being but one, could be well paid. By drawing the boundaries between case law and equity more clearly, the pernicious "blending of Law and Equity, which would relax the rules of law, and increase the discretion of the judge," would be nipped in the bud, and equity court decisions would become more predictable. Thus the chaos created by the several chancellors, "each ruling according to the bent of his private way of thinking" and thus creating a "vague and arbitrary" system, would be eliminated.[53]

Petigru's prescription for curbing the state's bloated equity system reflected a variety of factors that together defined the principles undergirding his legal and political thinking. Perhaps in response to the uncertainties that had plagued his childhood, he insisted that both law and government had to act within rational and constitutionally prescribed limits in order to ensure an orderly society in which individuals' natural rights to life, liberty, and property were secure. His fear of unrestrained power, furthermore, made him support republicanism just as it made him mistrust majoritarian democracy. In court, a jury of one's peers was essential for just verdicts, but equally essential was a well-educated bench capable of explaining the relevant law to the laymen on the jury. If in all this, Petigru was unwilling to back radical changes in the law, he was ready to challenge illegitimate authority, whether exerted by judges who presumed to make law or by legislators who passed laws exceeding constitutional limits on their power.

If clear logic, calm reason, attention to basic principles, and dedication to fairness and justice were the hallmarks of Petigru's legal thought and practice, the personal traits that informed his everyday experience and shaped his emotional life were often markedly at odds with his classical education and cerebral inclination to be moderate in all things. Away from books, free of stimulating intellectual conversation, and unimpeded by the constraints of courtroom decorum, Petigru was often hot-tempered and sometimes downright rash. When he was a beginning teacher at Eutaw, he had once picked up a rambunctious student and pushed him out of the classroom through an open window. As a young lawyer he had stopped a fight at the Coosawhatchie Courthouse "by lifting one of the combatants bodily by the collar and the waistband of his trousers," carrying him to his office, "seating him without ceremony in the centre of the floor," and there admonishing the miscreant to "keep the peace." This temptation to respond immediately and directly to offensive persons persisted into Petigru's old age. At seventy-three he threatened a careless and impertinent railroad employee with a thrashing, though in that instance the threat alone proved sufficient.[54]

It was probably the same impulsive drive to confront those for whom he had no respect that brought Petigru close to a duel in 1826. However much low country gentlemen might frown on frontier fisticuffs and eye gouging, and however much liberal reformers tried to curb the notion that an offense to personal honor justified a dawn encounter at twenty paces with pistols drawn, legal proscriptions against duelling had little effect in Charleston, even on lawyers. The erstwhile hill country boy become urban gentleman accepted that form of violence when civilities broke down between him and Benjamin Fanieul Hunt, Esquire. Hunt, born and educated in Massachusetts, had settled in Charleston, where he had earned a reputation as an able but somewhat unsavory attorney whose "rash and overconfident" style, as Judge John Belton O'Neall later characterized it, made him in the 1820s the city's most successful courtroom lawyer. Whether it was Hunt's sharp practice, his reliance on obscure legal technicalities, or his frequent victories for sordid clients that sparked the personal antagonism between Hunt and Petigru is moot. Whatever its exact cause, the friction between the two men rubbed raw until, in the late summer of 1826, Hunt challenged Petigru. The preduel rituals were well under way when personal tragedy intervened, and Hunt, sensitive to his opponent's plight, withdrew his challenge.[55]

On September 11, 1826, eight-year-old Albert, the Petigrus' firstborn child, lost his balance while playing on the third-floor banister and fell some thirty feet straight down the stairwell. The servants left in charge had ignored the little boy's antics. Neither of his parents was at home when he fell. And after the accident nothing could be done to save him. Only once did he briefly regain consciousness before he died thirty-seven hours later. The hopes that Petigru had vested in his favorite child were dashed. Stunned, he sat silently for hours with a close friend. Finally he was able to write his sister Jane, telling her what had happened and assuring her that at long last his tears had stopped. But for the rest of his life Petigru observed the anniversary of Albert's death in his room, where he meditated and grieved alone.[56]

Petigru had barely finished his tortured letter to Jane when news of a second loss arrived. On September 14 Louise Gibert Pettigrew, James's mother and the emotional anchor of his childhood, had died at Badwell. The two deaths, within hours of each other, seemed to shatter his sense of ongoing family stability and threaten his hopes for the future. Yet, characteristically, he found what solace he could by assuming new responsibilities for his kin. His mother's will left Badwell in trust to James for the support of her husband and her unmarried children.[57] Three of the latter were adolescent girls, whom Petigru would not leave in his father's care. So he and Jane Amelia, already devastated by Albert's death, enlarged their household to include the three attractive teenagers: Louise, aged sixteen; Adeline, aged fourteen; and Harriette, aged twelve. Far less sympathetically, James dispatched his alcoholic brother Jack to the West in a vain hope that the challenge might force him to change his dissipated ways. His youngest brother, Charles, he placed in a Charleston school that would prepare him to enter the military academy at West Point. For brother Thomas, who had already begun his naval career, Petigru could do little but press for his promotion in the officer corps.[58]

Doubtless it was the arrival of his young sisters that prompted Petigru to purchase a summer house on nearby Sullivan's Island in 1827 and the next year to buy the commodious house on Broad Street in which the family lived thereafter. But their arrival also fueled the emotional turmoil that had begun with the two family deaths. Jane Amelia, aged thirty-one and the mother of three young children (aged two, four, and six) who were themselves coping with the loss of their elder brother, now confronted three teenagers, who competed with her and her own children for Petigru's attention.[59] She resented especially Petigru's fondness for Adeline, who, like her sisters, changed the spelling of her last name to match his and then Huguenotted her Christian name to Adele. A much courted belle who, in 1832, wed the wealthy rice planter Robert Francis Withers Allston, Adele was, according to her sister Harriette, "the darling of [Petigru's] heart." Indeed, her marriage was, for her brother, a self-confessed "sacrifice," for which he compensated by having her portrait painted and hung conspicuously in his home.[60]

Had James been home more of the time to preside over this family cobbled together out of tragedy, things might have gone better. But as his law practice expanded he was more frequently on the road, riding the circuit of trial courts or appearing before Columbia sessions of the appeals court. Spurred on by the need to support a family suddenly doubled in size, he also stayed later in his office when he was in Charleston. Not surprisingly, his marriage, which had begun almost as an idyll, gradually began to deteriorate. The fairly usual pattern of a child born every other year stopped,[61] though Jane Amelia did have at least one abortive pregnancy after Albert's death. Indeed, that miscarriage may have precipitated the debilitating ill health from which she suffered for the rest of her life. Severe headaches increased her dependence on the opiates she had first taken as an adolescent to relieve menstrual cramps. By the mid-1830s she regularly used the morphine that doctors had prescribed for a variety of ills, including the pain associated with bearing four children and, later, the agony she suffered from a serious facial neuralgia. And so, like many other nineteenth-century women, she was soon addicted, made so by the medical practice that was common before the age of nonnarcotic painkillers.[62] However innocently begun, Jane Amelia's addiction triggered a marital pattern in which she and her husband played the roles—but reversed the genders—

that his parents had played in their marriage. In turn, *their* children's lives were shaped by the tensions and expectations that this pattern imposed on them.

When Petigru turned forty in 1829, he could look back with satisfaction at his rise in his profession. He could also take pride in his standing among Charleston's social elite. Soon after he had bought a pew in St. Michael's Church, in 1829, he had been chosen a vestryman of that most prestigious Episcopal congregation. His circle of friends included the city's intellectuals, editor and novelist William Gilmore Simms, and that self-conscious exponent of belles lettres, Hugh Swinton Legaré, among them. In an era of splendid dinner parties, Petigru was noted for his Sunday afternoon feasts, to which he invited visiting dignitaries as well as local politicos and clerics.[63] Finally, he had settled down as a homeowner and commanded an income sufficient to support his expanded family. By decade's end, Petigru had achieved the goals he had set when he had come to Charleston twelve years earlier.

It was now time for this ambitious man to turn elsewhere, to mark out new areas of accomplishment. Typical of his time, place, and status, he looked to politics and the opportunities that passage of a high protective tariff in 1828 had created. The rise of new factions in his agriculturally oriented state—one determined to nullify that tariff, the other equally determined to block nullification—reoriented old allegiances and opened the way for new men aspiring to public leadership. But true to the conservative legal and political principles he had come to espouse, Petigru chose not the faction that threatened things as they were but the one committed to the established order.

THREE

Becoming
a Politician

That James Petigru chose to fight the Nullifiers rather than join them reveals commitments far deeper than a simple decision to enter elective politics. Any prominent Carolinian would have found it difficult to avoid participating in the acrimonious and nearly revolutionary conflict that followed the passage of the 1828 tariff, which was almost universally perceived as a tax on cotton exports that would benefit only northern manufacturers. For Petigru it was impossible. His close friend, former law partner, and by 1830 governor of South Carolina, James Hamilton, led the Nullifiers. Petigru's mentor, Daniel Huger, resigned his judgeship in 1830 to rally the Unionist opposition to nullification. Petigru, however, was not torn by these conflicting personal ties. He did not waver, as even John C. Calhoun once had, between national and state loyalty. Nor did he pause to weigh which faction was more likely to open the way to office and power. Nullification, to Petigru's way of thinking, was a revolutionary challenge to legitimate authority, an assault on orderly government, an abandonment of constitutional restraint. Accordingly, he rejected it outright from the beginning.

That decision reflected both personal experience and theoretical commitment. During his student days Petigru had absorbed the religious conservatism of the Calvinist theology that had permeated Moses Waddel's academy as well as the political conservatism of the Federalists, who in their waning days had made South Carolina College their last bastion. Then, while he taught at Beaufort College during the preliminaries to the War of 1812 he was exposed to a more vibrant, commercially oriented federalism by its Yankee president, Martin Hurlbut, whose sharp critique of the predominantly Republican politics of South

Carolina and its planter class gave Petigru an outsider's perspective.[1] Nonetheless, his conservatism's deep southern roots bound him to the politics of an older generation whose identification with established low country rice plantations rather than the dynamic westward expansion of cotton culture shaped their economic views. But Petigru's federalism was minimally a matter of economics, despite the mentorship of aristocratic rice planter Huger. Rather, he was more strongly drawn to the legal principles that Old Federalist Henry W. DeSaussure had embodied in the South Carolina Constitution of 1790 and in the state's equity system, which he had molded during his long tenure as chancellor. To Petigru's way of thinking, those principles mirrored exactly the premises upon which Chief Justice John Marshall had based his argument that it was the federal authority created by the United States Constitution that ultimately guaranteed the sanctity of private property and the inviolability of contracts.[2]

Petigru early recognized, however, that his own relatively moderate positions could be tarred by association with the old guard. How much he tried to avoid the Federalist label is demonstrated by an almost apocryphal scene played out in front of the Beaufort District Courthouse. An irate youth taunted him with a barrage of abuse, calling him first a rogue, then a rascal, and finally a "damned Federal." Petigru kept his temper until the last charge. Then he promptly laid his accuser on the ground. Asked why he had ignored the first maledictions, Petigru responded with some truth: "I incur no injury from being abused as a rogue, for nobody believes the charge; but I may be thought a Federalist readily enough, and be proscribed accordingly."[3] This was more than a matter of public image, for an essential ingredient of his admitted conservatism was the balance of moderation that came from his legal philosophy. Responding to criticisms of the equity courts, he advocated neither their retention as they were nor their abolition but proposed modification to correct their abuses. He defended juries as a necessary check on judges' power just as he defended an independent judiciary because it provided an essential check on legislative and executive power. While he was attorney general, he entered private cases both to limit governmental authority when it infringed on individual rights— usually that to private property—and to uphold that authority—even when it curtailed such rights—if it was exercised in the interests of public health and safety.

Even his moderate federalism, however, set Petigru at odds with his own generation, who by 1830 were the middle-aged sons of fathers who had won glory in the American Revolution. With a sense of having missed an opportunity that would not be repeated, they sought an achievement to equal their fathers'. But little Revolutionary glory clung to Petigru's father. Nor had William Pettigrew's sons inherited the wealth or status of their backcountry peers who now sought radical change—men like Vice President John C. Calhoun and state senator Andrew Pierce Butler. For the Pettigrews, the Revolution had meant the loss of security, and its aftermath had added nothing to their property or their repute. So James Petigru was little drawn to the revolutionary lure of planter-polemicist Robert Turnbull's 1827 "Brutus" letters, with their defiance of federal authority. In what soon became the Nullifiers' bible, Turnbull asserted that the sovereign states had retained the right to limit federal power, even to challenge the federal Constitution. To Petigru, this was arrant nonsense. It was the Constitution alone that had curbed the social, economic, and political disorder produced by the Revolution and its unruly aftermath. And Turnbull's resurrection of Thomas Jefferson's 1798 Kentucky Resolutions, which justified the nullification of federal law, further offended Petigru, who had little use for "St. Thomas of Cantingbury."[4] But he equally scorned Turnbull's praise of high federalist plans for New England's secession, which had been voiced but defeated in the 1814 Hartford Convention. Like most Carolinians, Petigru certainly opposed high tariffs on imports at a time when the state's economy languished in the wake of the cotton market collapse of 1825. But unlike those radicals who urged the state legislature to declare the 1828 tariff null and void, he looked to the orderly governmental processes embodied in the Constitution rather than a revolutionary challenge to set that bad law right.

His preference for orderly change made Petigru question even how much the American Revolution had accomplished. Although he justified it as a necessary revolt against arbitrary and concentrated power, he thought its achievements would have been temporary had they not been consolidated in a constitution that protected against future abuses of power by dividing sovereignty between state and federal governments and by imposing an orderly hierarchy of authority that "retrenched the prerogatives of the State to make the national government supreme within its proper jurisdiction." Consequently, large slave owners whose claims to exercise unrestrained "power and liberty" challenged "the established order of things" were in his eyes "Jacobins" whose politics threatened the plantation society they claimed to defend. Indeed, it was this elite class, not their slaves, who endangered social and economic stability. Perhaps reflecting his inbred upcountry resentment of low country aristocrats, Petigru feared that the nullification these great planters now supported would lead South Carolina back to the same concentration of power against which the American Revolution had been fought.[5]

Petigru was well aware of the irony implicit in his views. He anticipated that Union men would universally be called Federalists because popular opinion held that men "cannot be conservative without being federal." He knew as well that there was some truth in the charge. Many of his Unionist allies, most visibly Daniel Huger and William Elliott, were well-known Old Federalists. But despite the Federalist taint, in 1830 upcountry Abbeville District like low country Beaufort returned Unionists to the legislature, even though both districts were home to major Nullifier leaders. Charleston, the low country capital, was almost evenly divided between supporters and opponents of nullification. Indeed, among the planters claiming residence in the city there were almost as many Unionists as Nullifiers.[6] And, still more ironic, political reality required that Unionists ally themselves with Andrew Jackson, that rampant Democrat who also, as president of the United States, personified federal power.

The tariff that Congress had passed in May 1828 was initially proposed to protect and thus aid the development of infant American industries. But it was soon made hostage to that year's presidential election campaign. The rationale for the Tariff of Abominations supported by John Quincy Adams and his New England clique is still subject to dispute. Bloated with excessive rates as some congressmen added protection for their districts' special interests and others proposed exorbitantly high levels simply to kill the bill, the tariff boomeranged. In its final version it astounded the administration, dismayed many—but not all—Jackson supporters, and so enraged the South Carolina legislature that it denounced the tariff in formal resolution and published an "Exposition and Protest," expounding the theory of nullification, which had been secretly drafted by John C. Calhoun, Jackson's running mate in the fall campaign. All that only thickened the political stew.

In 1829, after the election fever had passed, several attempts were made to revise the tariff. Still, Congress took no final action. The stalemate that followed only increased a rancorous dispute that became increasingly sectional. Dramatizing the issues at stake, in January 1830 Senator Daniel Webster of Massachusetts confronted Senator Robert Y. Hayne of South Carolina. Supposedly debating Senate action on western land policy, they argued in reality about the Constitutional definition of federal sovereignty and the powers, implicit or explicit, it had reserved to the contracting states. In fact, they were debating the legitimacy of nullification and the threat of national fragmentation that it posed. Their fundamental differences were pithily summed up at a Jefferson Day public dinner held that April in a Washington hotel. President Andrew Jackson, with his customary brevity, proposed a toast to "Our Union: It must be preserved." Vice President John C. Calhoun responded: "The Union, next to our liberty, most dear"; and then added sotto voce, or so some who sat near him said, "May we all remember that it can only be preserved by respecting the rights of the States and by distributing equally the benefits and burdens of the Union."[7]

That confrontation followed South Carolina's representatives when they came home from Washington. On the Fourth of July Senator Hayne and Congressman William Drayton were guests of honor at a large public banquet in Charleston. Hayne had already made his position clear in his debate with Webster. Now it was Drayton's turn to stake out his ground. This he did by opposing both high tariffs and nullification and pledging himself to work for tariff revision during the next session of Congress. Choosing to work through established institutions, he warned his audience against any actions that would, by fracturing the Union, cause civil strife.[8] Nullification, it was now clear, encompassed more than differing sectional interests of North and South and a power struggle between Washington and South Carolina. It had become the central political dispute at home.

So it was that as the fall elections of 1830 approached, their tone was sharply different from that of the 1828 election. Even before the Independence Day banquet, Unionist and Nullifier factions had begun organizing for the Charleston City Council elections in September and the state elections a month later. At the head of the Union party were Daniel Huger and James Petigru; at the head of the Nullifiers, Robert Hayne and James Hamilton.[9]

James Hamilton, despite their former partnership and persisting friendship, seemed almost the exact opposite of James Petigru. Small of stature, socially graceful, born to wealth, he had taken up the law more as a preparation for politics than for its own sake.[10] By 1830 he was a skilled and experienced politician who measured success more by votes won and lost than by issues opposed or defended. He found it impossible to understand why Huger and Petigru would ally themselves with Old Federalists like James R. Pringle, whose support for John Quincy Adams and Henry Clay had lost him all support at home despite his patronage-rich post as collector of the Port of Charleston. As reasonable men, they should, like Hamilton, himself, keep their eyes on building the popular majorities who would vote their leaders into power and act accordingly. As Hamilton surveyed the situation in 1830, South Carolina was, with the possible exception of Charleston, already in the Nullifiers' camp. And so, as he wrote another states' rights supporter, he could only deplore the "erroneous move" by which Huger and Petigru must ultimately be destroyed in the contest "*between* the Genl. Govt. & the St[ate]." His former law partner, by refusing to compromise "on some ground . . . short of absolute submission," had "fairly passed the Rubicon & joined the forces of the enemy on the opposite Bank." That enemy Hamilton scornfully, albeit with reasonable accuracy, defined as the "Rail Road party[,] Merchants on East Bay[,] Yankee Traders[,] French[,] all the U[nited] States office holders and the timid *par excellence* and moderates of native origin."[11]

What Hamilton passed over in all this were the problems he faced as he tried to reconcile differences among his many political allies. While he forwarded nullification at home he was also courting Andrew Jackson through the good offices of Martin Van Buren, Jackson's secretary of state, praising the president's opposition to internal improvements as commendable opposition to federal usurpation of state power. At the same time he courted Jackson he also cultivated Old Hickory's archenemy Nicholas Biddle, from whose Bank of the United States he continued to borrow heavily on credit extended most generously to the president's opponents.[12] But Nullifiers did not monopolize such shenanigans. Many Unionists, Petigru among them, who had voted for National-Republican candidates, supported Henry Clay's American System, and backed Biddle's national bank were now allied with the principal opponent of all three, Andrew Jackson.[13]

Amid such conflicting political currents Charleston citizens went to the polls in September 1830, clutching partisan tickets that blurred party lines and obscured ideological differences. Indeed, almost half the candidates for municipal offices on the Union ticket appeared as well on the Nullifiers' list despite Unionists' open condemnation of the opposition's only platform—to call a state convention to consider nullification. Petigru's name, however, appeared on only one ticket. He was just beginning his active political career and was the clear-cut Unionist candidate from the Second Ward for a seat on the city council. It was well known, furthermore, that he would have nothing to do with nullification. He won by a comfortable margin and joined a city government whose Unionist majority comprised exactly half of the wardens (councilmen) together with James Pringle, who had been elected intendant.[14]

This city election, however, was of little consequence except as a test of Unionist voting strength, for only the state legislature, not city officials, could call a convention. Consequently, Petigru, encouraged by his handy victory in his first electoral contest, promptly resigned his attorney generalship to accept his party's nomination to run for the state senate. As he wrote his old friend Grayson, he had, in the style of the day, "resisted stoutly and bawled lustily for help" but had been so pressed to run that "nothing was to be done but take my place in the team." But the avidity with which he campaigned and his eagerness as a party warhorse belied that disclaimer. His efforts this time, however, were in vain. Contesting a senatorial district that extended beyond the city limits and into the outlying suburbs, where he was less well known, Petigru narrowly lost the election, garnering 1243 votes against his opponent's 1268. But before the year ended, and with the legerdemain of political caprice, his close friend Hugh Legaré, like Grayson a lawyer as well as a litterateur, was elected to succeed Petigru as attorney general. Legaré therefore resigned his seat in the lower house, and Petigru ran to replace him in a by-election, which he won with 55 percent of the votes cast.[15] But it all took time; and the new representative, who did not win his seat until mid-December, thought it scarcely worth the effort to travel the 120 miles to Columbia by jouncing stagecoach just to sit in the house for the few remaining days of the session.[16]

Thus the first year of Petigru's intense political involvement closed successfully at the polls—but generated little positive action elsewhere. Nonetheless, his hopes ran high. Nullifiers in the legislature had lacked the votes to call a state convention to void the tariff. Unionists had pulled enough votes in the Charleston elections to claim that they represented the majority there. But on both sides the leaders knew that a shift of a hundred votes from one side to the other could reverse the situation.

As 1831 opened, political debate seemed less fierce. Reasonable men, Unionists and Nullifiers alike, anticipated that Congress would resolve the tariff crisis. So it was not until well after Congress had adjourned in March without taking any action that factional feuding again flared. Just as they had in 1830, Unionists and Nullifiers began the year's campaigning at partisan Fourth of July celebrations, where each faction turned patriotism to the business of enlisting new recruits. From the Unionists' point of view, at least, the difference between the two galas favored them. William Dukes, a Charleston cotton factor, boasted that his associates had displayed restraint and dignity throughout. The opponents of nullification had marched sedately to the Scots Presbyterian Church in downtown Charleston, there observed the anniversary of their nation's birth, then paraded with similar restraint the six long blocks to the large vacant lot where they consumed an appropriate banquet. "I never expect to see again such an assemblage of talent and respectability," Dukes noted with great satisfaction. By contrast, although the Nullifiers managed a solemn procession to the Congregational Circular Church for their celebration of the Revolution, revelry soon replaced discipline. When they reassembled for their outdoor rally and banquet it was "under a splendid Pavillion," from which mere boys of "8 to 12 years old [were] carried on the backs of servants, completely insensible from drink," while their "*dead drunk*" seniors staggered and swore up and down the public streets. To men of Dukes's persuasion it was "a complete exemplification of that depravity which the foul doctrine of Anarchy and Nullification is calculated to end in." [17] For many young men, however, Nullifier anarchy was a lot more fun than Unionist respectability.

If the Nullies were more successful in luring new and previously uncommitted voters, the Unionists pulled a significant coup two weeks later when their party commandeered the president's popularity. At a large meeting they "nominated Genl. Jackson & pledged him their support!!!" Hamilton was indignant that his Nullifiers had been outmaneuvered and left with no viable presidential candidate. Surely they could not endorse Henry Clay, whose American System promoted protective tariffs. And no state other than South Carolina showed any eagerness for John Calhoun's candidacy. The only remaining alternative, he confessed with chagrin, was to have the legislature, which cast the state's ballot in the electoral college, cast a blank one.[18]

But the Unionists had their own tactical and strategic dilemmas. During the summer Benjamin F. Hunt, Petigru's old courtroom nemesis but a prominent Unionist notwithstanding, wrote and circulated a campaign pamphlet that actually supported protective tariffs—a position as repugnant to most Unionists as it was to all Nullifiers. Although Petigru conceded that it was written "devilish well," he thought that having no pamphlet at all would have been preferable, for in stepping "over the line" of political prudence Hunt had done more harm than good.[19] It was a harm Petigru tried to evade if he could and confront only if he must as he went on the stump that fall, addressing crowds in large towns like Columbia and Georgetown and smaller audiences in rural outposts like Black Oak in St. John's Berkeley Parish. Through it all he cajoled and encouraged his handful of coworkers as they traveled together by stagecoach or on horseback and camped out in the crowded inns and dingy hotels that he already knew too well from riding the court circuit.[20]

As the campaign heated up, Petigru's legal expertise too was pressed into service. In September he and United States District Attorney Robert Gilchrist argued a case before the federal district court in Charleston in which the supremacy of federal law was the implicit issue. Three Charleston lawyers—Alexander Mazyck, Isaac E. Holmes, and Thomas Gadsden—had deliberately created a test case by refusing to pay the bonds they had posted for duties owed on two parcels of imported goods. Confident that a Charleston jury permitted to consider the tariff's constitutionality would disallow it, and therefore find for the Nullifier defendants, Petigru and Gilchrist steered clear of constitutional issues. With favorable rulings from the federal judge, they managed to hold trial arguments to questions of evidence and extracted a favorable verdict. Restricted to considering only whether the defendants had imported the European commodities and whether their bonds had been properly drawn, the jurors had little alternative but to find against them.[21]

A clear-cut victory in court, however, did little to balance another Unionist defeat at the polls. Running for office at the same time that the *Mazyck* case was in court, Petigru was defeated for reelection to city council by a margin of one hundred votes. This time the entire Nullifier slate, with every candidate on it committed to their cause,

triumphed.[22] But although the Nullifiers now controlled Charleston's
municipal government, Petigru still held a seat in the South Carolina House of Representatives. So, in late November he went up to
Columbia to attend the 1831 session. Although living in the capital for
weeks at a time meant forgoing the amenities of home, it did have
its rewards. It was customary for leaders of each party to live in the
same boardinghouse. There Petigru and his Unionist messmates enjoyed mutual support as they shared information about upcoming bills
and mapped a common political strategy. Doubtless they also chat-
ted informally, and Petigru especially enjoyed the camaraderie of his
old Beaufort friend William Elliott, the knowledgeable conversation of
former United States minister to Mexico Joel Poinsett, and an unusually close period of companionship with Daniel Huger.[23]

Little of the legislature's routine business had anything to do with
either union or nullification, and most of Petigru's activity in the state
house involved minor and transitory issues: supporting appropriations
for the state lunatic asylum and the purchase of John J. Audubon's
ornithological works, opposing new regulations on the law courts and
a comprehensive tax.[24]

At least two legislative issues, however, attracted considerable attention back in his home district. In the first, Petigru attempted to mediate
a struggle for control of the Medical College of South Carolina between the school's sponsor—the South Carolina Medical Society—and
its faculty. After negotiating with the society's spokesman, Petigru, a
member of the legislative committee appointed to adjudicate the affair, drafted a compromise bill that he believed satisfied both sides
and which the legislature adopted. Later the Medical Society decided
that the new provisions favored the faculty at the society's expense
and took the matter to court. When the lower court decision was appealed, Judge John Belton O'Neall, writing for the majority, ruled that
the act Petigru had drafted was unconstitutional because it altered a
state charter, which granted the Medical Society the right and privilege to found and conduct a medical college. O'Neall's ruling, which
looked back to John Marshall's decision in the *Dartmouth College* case
(that the terms of a charter, like those of any other contract, might be
altered only by mutual consent of the contracting parties), undoubtedly disconcerted Petigru. As a politician he had overlooked what as a
lawyer deeply committed to Marshall's constitutional theory he ought
to have caught. After all, during his eight years as attorney general he

had vetted all proposed legislation for its constitutionality. But political pressure from others and his own preference for compromise had led him into a practical accommodation that violated both his legal and his political principles.[25]

In the second issue, his compelling political commitment, unqualified by any proclivity to compromise, drove Petigru to mastermind the campaign to remove Thomas Cooper from the presidency of South Carolina College. Appointed a professor in 1820 and shortly thereafter made president, the English-born physician, lawyer, and scientist had created controversy almost from the day he began his tenure. His inability to stem student revolts made parents anxious. His proposals to eliminate equity courts and simplify all other law irritated lawyers. His deism, strongly laced with anticlericalism, offended the clergy—especially Presbyterians, on whom he was particularly harsh. His radical Jeffersonianism galled even many Democratic-Republicans. Finally, his early and avid support of nullification made him offensive to Unionists, who feared that he used his privileged position as the college's president to propagandize a captive audience and imbue the state's future leaders with a dangerous disregard for the Constitution.[26]

An apparently unrelated turn of events in 1831 gave antinullification legislators their best chance to unseat Cooper. A religious revival swept through the Carolinas and settled with particular tenacity in the Beaufort area. With an eye to his own political agenda, Petigru responded to Grayson's report of its effect: "You say that in Beaufort you are all trying to become every day more religious and more States rights. The connection between the two pursuits is not so obvious at first sight as it becomes on closer inspection."[27] It was that fortuitous connection that gave Petigru an unanticipated opportunity to dislodge Cooper.

When the legislature assembled that fall, Petigru and his fellow Unionists forced Nullifiers to choose between their acclaim for Cooper's politics and their dismay at his anticlericalism. Leading the attack, Petigru, who personally scorned the excesses of revivalism, went straight to the defense of religion. He accused Cooper of seeking "to bury in one common ruin the whole Christian Clergy and the institution of religion." He denied that legislative action would infringe on the good doctor's convictions, for it was as citizens that "men are by the [state] Constitution protected in their religious opinions." "That clause of the Constitution," he continued, "certainly could not be construed to mean, that we should employ as the Teacher of our children, a man who openly and zealously sought to overthrow the fabrics of Religion." Petigru then vigorously supported the bill to remove Cooper from the college presidency.[28]

He lost. The legislature refused to do more than order the college trustees to investigate the charges, and the trustees cleared Cooper. Yet Cooper's was a Pyrrhic victory, for only a year after his vindication, in 1833, pressures generated by sharply declining enrollments and persistent student indiscipline forced his resignation.[29] Although Petigru subsequently equated religious with political freedom, he had quite openly played on religious sentiments for political purposes in his opportunistic strategy to rid the college of its offensive president. Believing that Cooper's irreligion underlay the college's decline, he never revealed the least discomfort with having thus intermixed politics and religion.

The war against Cooper, like Petigru's endorsing a second term for Andrew Jackson, illuminates the politics of the possible in which he engaged throughout 1832. It was strategy rather than substance that produced, in December 1831, Unionist legislators' enthusiastic praise for Old Hickory in terms designed once again to preempt his popularity for their cause. Their resolution, which rang with idealistic verbiage about the "independent and manly" Andrew Jackson, whose "worth and merit," like his "virtue and patriotism," made him the prime exponent of "national honor," reflected Petigru's pragmatic conversion to Machiavellian policies. "It is impossible for us to break ground on Presidential topics," he later wrote former South Carolina congressman William Drayton. "The Gen. is against the Nullifiers who are enemies that we regard the worst and hatefullest of their kind. Unless we can act with the Nullifiers we must support the President."[30]

Thus oriented, the Unionists faced their crucial year, seizing every available strategy that might help them carry the national, state, and local elections of 1832. They launched their campaign early. In January, forty-eight Carolina Unionist dignitaries, Petigru among them, addressed an open letter to the "People of South Carolina," setting forth their program. Their action was designed, like their endorsement of Jackson, to steal their opponents' thunder. They opposed any and all protective tariffs. They endorsed the "Jeffersonian" doctrine that it was the people of the individual states, not the American people collectively, who had delegated power to the federal government. They even referred to the natural rights assumption, enshrined in the Declaration of Independence, that a higher law entitled each state to resist fundamental abuses of power. But when they turned specifically to the Tariff of 1828, which they labeled a clear abuse of power that went well beyond the legitimate federal right to levy tariffs, imposts, and duties, they asserted that there were already adequate legal provisions for correcting the abuse of constitutional restraints. It was the responsibility of the people and the state, the letter insisted, to exhaust all legal means to restore the balance between state and federal power. The first such means was effective use of the ballot box. Then, if the Congress so elected still failed to revise the tariff, Carolinians must next look to the federal courts to test the tariff law's constitutionality. To pursue this sane, conservative course, the letter concluded, the people must support the institutions and the men who upheld and knew how to use legitimate authority; they must defy the hotheads who would plunge their society into chaos by nullification and other unconstitutional actions.[31]

The presidential election was critical to the Unionists' strategy, not because they were dedicated to any one presidential candidate but because in South Carolina, where the legislature rather than the voters chose presidential electors, the election of state assemblymen and senators was shaped by the voters' presidential preference. If pro-Jackson sentiment could be turned to electing a Unionist legislature, the voters would also have chosen a legislature that would block a nullification convention, which only the legislature could call. It was therefore positively dangerous that many Unionists in 1832 still preferred the locally unpopular Henry Clay to Old Hickory. Petigru was furious when this National-Republican faction, which had never been able to carry even commercially oriented Charleston, let alone the whole state, met in April to choose delegates to a Washington convention of Clay's friends. He tried to convince James Haig, the Charleston lawyer who had presided over the whole unfortunate procedure, to rescind the endorsement. He warned Haig that if his associates did not reverse their course, the Union party would have to disavow the Clay men and their actions. The Unionists' only hope for victory, Petigru insisted, lay in their own union; support for Clay was not only impractical in itself but was likely to ensure a Nullifier victory.[32] Thereafter the Clay faction fell silent.

Through all this maneuvering, Petigru was never a genuine Jackson enthusiast. He even suspected, in the fall of 1832, that the president was "more than half a Nullifier himself." Nonetheless, when Carolina Unionists convened in June, Petigru again urged cohesion around Jackson and political compromise within their own ranks. As the chairman of the committee that produced both the meeting's agenda and its address to the public, he proposed yet another stratagem to diffuse support for nullification. Overwhelmingly the June gathering pledged itself to call a regional convention of all southern states should the December session of Congress adjourn without revising the tariff downward.[33]

That openly opportunistic move to capture Nullifier votes by implying consent to nullification if a convention of several states adopted it infuriated Unionist purists such as lawyer-reformer Thomas Grimké. Any such convention, whether of a single state or many, would breach the Constitution. Indeed, proposing action by the whole South was inherently more dangerous than proposing nullification by a single state. But Petigru, who two years earlier had dismissed Grimké as a "monopolist of martyrdom," was prepared to utilize any tool that came to hand if by so doing he could fend off the revolution he so feared. It was no idle fear, for James Hamilton had signaled the possibility of armed revolt in May when he ran successfully for the post of commanding general of the Fourth Brigade of the South Carolina Militia without even bothering to surrender his gubernatorial office.[34]

With peace increasingly fragile, Petigru well understood the need for self-restraint among his followers and his own responsibility for their behavior. He also acknowledged the Unionists' weakness compared with the strength of the Nullifiers' organization. "I agree," he wrote William Elliott early in August, "that the times would justify it in us to meet club with club, but, can we," he pointedly noted, "get a gang to oppose robbers, as easily as robbers unite in gangs?" As the month progressed, gangs were clearly ascendant. And as Charleston grew ever more tense, came ever closer to violence, other Unionists expressed similar concern. John N. Barillon, a justice of the peace, described "the most terrible political excitement" and feared that "there will be some *very serious* business before the Elections are over, and [that it] would not occasion any surprise that many persons were *slain.*" He himself would "go to the polls *prepared,*" and "if I am assaulted I shall defend myself to the *uttermost.*" And cooper Jacob Schirmer recorded in his diary "a dreadful disturbance" on September 2, which almost triggered "a fight between the 2 political parties" after Peter Staunton was found dead in Queen Street. Staunton had, so the coroner, a Nullifier stalwart, reported, fallen from an upstairs window in the Union party headquarters, where those willing to sell their votes were locked up and plied with liquor until they could be marched to the polls.[35]

City elections took place in this ominous atmosphere on September 1 and 2. It was, planter John Grimball later exclaimed in his diary, an occasion of "horrible corruption which . . . walked unblushingly in the open day, throughout our streets." When the votes were counted, Nullifiers could boast a victory significantly greater than the one a year earlier, and Unionists were stunned by their total rout. Admitting to fraud, violence, and voter enthusiasm run riot on both sides, Petigru was still more upset that political excess affected official conduct. He found the coroner's report on Staunton an "awful warning of the temper of revolutionary tribunals" when the courts were swayed by a "poisoned" public mind. Worst of all, he feared that nothing could be done to rein in the partisan poison.[36]

Two weeks later, however, leaders of both sides signed a formal agreement to prohibit late night meetings, abandon free liquor, shun bribery, and cease locking up unreliable supporters. But shaken though they were by the prospect of impending mayhem, these same leaders were driven even harder by the high stakes to be won or lost in the state elections. Unable to resist the pressure, they soon broke the truce. One of the first to be caught doing so was Petigru, whose name was conspicuous on the truce agreement. Speaking at a rally that lasted until well after the agreed-upon curfew, he responded to the subsequent finger pointing with too many excuses. He had been absent when the new rules, to which a friend had signed his name, were drawn. Though he approved the restraints the new rules were intended to impose, he was not aware of the 10:00 P.M. curfew set on all political meetings. He had, he continued, delayed speaking until important latecomers arrived because it was only civil to do so. Innocent of intended offense himself, he justified the event still further by insisting that the meeting had been orderly, indeed decorous, despite the hour and so really complied with the spirit of the anticorruption pact.[37]

The last assertion may indeed have been true; but the federal and state elections held on October 8 and 9 were neither orderly nor decorous. The Unionists, Petigru wrote Hugh Legaré, now the United States chargé d'affaires in Brussels, "were beset at Seyle's [public meeting rooms] night after night by a disorderly mob and obliged to arm . . . with bludgeons and march out in files." On one occasion, after a gala supper, the two parties met face to face. As the Unionists left their hall, the Nullifiers, marching up the street in the opposite direction, "began to throw stones and one of them aimed a brick" at Petigru. It glanced off his shoulder and struck Bernard Bee, a Nullifier chieftain, a bruising blow on the cheek. However poetic the justice, the incident increased Petigru's fears for the future. "We could have cleared the street and it would have been policy to do so, but doubtless the parties would have met the next time with muskets." [38]

For all that, the state election returns dashed the Unionists' hopes. Petigru, who had run to retain his seat in the state house of representatives, lost, as did the entire Union slate, by a little more than a hundred votes. In fact, he had pretty much conceded defeat in advance. Sure though he was that the Nullifiers would again resort to bribery, and resigned when the Nully-controlled city government allowed the unqualified to vote, he nonetheless supported the Unionists' decision not to buy votes in this election. [39]

However much Petigru had expected the outcome, the nullification convention that it guaranteed was deeply upsetting to him. There was no further way to block it. James Hamilton, still governor until his term expired the following month, promptly called an extraordinary session of the newly elected legislature for October 22. When it met, it mandated yet another election to choose delegates to the convention, which it scheduled for November 19. The rapid pace of events, added to the scope of their recent defeats, unhinged the Unionists altogether. In Charleston, as in most of the state, they fielded no candidates in the election for convention delegates. As a result, when the delegates assembled to consider an ordinance nullifying the tariff, only a very few Unionists—Daniel Huger among them—were seated. But even a more sizable minority opposition could not have stopped the Nullifier steamroller. Hamilton, who had been succeeded as governor by Robert Hayne, chaired the convention. Within five days the delegates adopted an ordinance that nullified the Tariff of 1828 and its unsatisfactory 1832 revision, barred federal officials from collecting customs duties in state ports after February 1, 1833, and required all state officials to take an oath of allegiance to South Carolina. The ordinance also prohibited any legal action contesting its terms from being tried in a federal court. Finally, anticipating that the federal government might use force to collect customs duties in South Carolina ports, the convention openly threatened secession. [40]

Shortly before the state elections, and well before Hamilton's call for a special legislative session in October, the Unionists had already settled on their next step. They too planned a statewide meeting of their own supporters to respond to the nullification convention. Once again Petigru prepared the resolutions, and once again he pitted prudence against rashness, flexibility against rigidity as he confronted not the threat of nullification but its accomplishment. The resolutions that the Unionists' convention endorsed in early December were mostly familiar ones. The platform was simple opposition to nullification, without support for any particular tariff policy. Focusing on constitutional rather than economic issues, this December conference, like its predecessor, proposed an all-southern convention, but this one was expressly designed to consolidate support for the Union. The delegates adopted Petigru's draft resolutions that supported their political agenda with extensive legal arguments.

Petigru had already enshrined their substance in earlier partisan documents. Now he sharpened and clarified the arguments for a more pointed attack on the Nullification Ordinance. The United States Constitution, so his and the convention's reasoning went, contained absolutely no provision for a state to void a federal law. An attempt to do so was tantamount to endorsing revolution. As Petigru had written in an earlier address to the "People of South Carolina," it was "monstrous to contend that the framers of the Constitution did not invest the General Government with full power to execute their own laws, or that without such a power Union can exist." And so, although they conceded a theoretical possibility of secession, the delegates denied that a state could legitimately use nullification as a step toward achieving it. And they condemned altogether the "direct collision" any attempt to secede would produce "between the authorities of the states and those of the Union."[41] Finally the resolutions of the December meeting concluded with total scorn for the Nullification Ordinance, which was "nothing more than a declaration of the will and high determination of the ruling powers of South Carolina, to which our obedience is commanded in the language of despotism."[42]

Samuel C. Jackson, a visiting Boston cleric, recorded the resolute tone of South Carolina's Unionists facing the reality of the Nullification Ordinance: "Mr. Pettigru [*sic*] of Charleston, a most distinguished lawyer," read the convention's official report, which Jackson thought was "a manly & able document, yet calm & temperate." Jackson was, however, unaware that behind that apparent calm lay backstage maneuvers to avoid a direct collision with those "ruling powers." "It was understood," Petigru reported privately to Legaré, "that if we would not resolve to disobey the ordinance, but confine ourselves to the impeachment of it, the Legislature would not enforce the test oath [of allegiance to the state] nor levy the 10,000 men which are to form the standing army of Carolina."[43]

Petigru's hope that this implicit compromise signaled the Nullifiers' willingness to "blink the Ordinance" was, however, badly misplaced. Both sides began at once their preparation for war. The Unionists looked to Washington, where President Jackson was kept well informed about South Carolina affairs by Joel Poinsett, who chaired the Unionist five-man committee of correspondence within the state. That committee, which included both Petigru and Daniel Huger, had "without the knowledge of what [the federal] government might do" already begun "organising all the means of resistance in our power." Very shortly, however, the group was guided by a steady flow of information from Washington channeled through South Carolina's Unionist congressman, William Drayton, who was serving out the last weeks of his term.[44]

Even before these arrangements were in place, President Jackson had assigned Major General Winfield Scott to take charge of all federal forces in South Carolina. Holding the whip in one hand, he extended the olive branch in the other by following up with a message to Congress on December 4 urging a conciliatory revision of the 1832 tariff. A week later, he made it clear that that was the limit of his concession. On December 10, the same day the Unionist convention met and issued its resolutions, the president issued his "Proclamation to the People of South Carolina," declaring that nullification was an impractical absurdity and "disunion by armed force, . . . *treason.*" A month later, the president again went to Congress to request specific authority to use armed force if it was necessary to collect federal revenues in South Carolina. As February 1, 1833, approached, the date when the ordinance against federal tariff collection would take effect, Charlestonians prepared for the worst. Poinsett reported to Jackson that the Unionist committee had organized "a legion . . . composed of the young and I hope & believe the brave," who with other armed civilians would add 1200 effective fighters to troops already stationed at the federal forts surrounding South Carolina's major port. On the other side, Nullifiers, who already controlled most of the state's militia, went ahead with plans to raise an additional 10,000 men.[45]

Even in December Petigru had shuddered at the Nullifiers' steady march toward armed confrontation: "I believe a great number are amazed as in waking from a dream, to find what they considered one of the simplest things in the world is going to turn out the parent of war, prostration of commerce and a Military Government." What did it matter if the "War and Revolution party" were "a decided minority" even among the Nullifiers? They still had "an ascendancy which gives them an absolute control over the weak minds of that numerous class who are afraid or ashamed to think for themselves." Others, who also felt themselves at the "centre of a dormant volcano," shared Petigru's anxiety. Poinsett pondered the consequences of enmity among kin: "There is scarcely a family wherein some member is not in the opposite ranks, and it is certain in such a contest father would be arrayed against son and Brother against brother." Mitchell King, a Scottish-born and widely traveled lawyer and another stalwart of the Union cause, warned still more bleakly that civil war among Carolina whites would lead inevitably to "servile war" of slaves against masters.[46]

Finally, however, the tension broke. In mid-January, reports of a pending congressional compromise on the tariff reached the state and gave the Nullifier-dominated legislature a graceful opportunity to pull back. On January 21, 1833, just ten days before Jackson's threat to use armed force would have taken effect, the South Carolina legislature voted to suspend the Nullification Ordinance. Then, on March 11, with the new compromise tariff safely enshrined in law, the nullification convention reconvened to rescind its ordinance voiding the previous tariffs. But to reassert its power to nullify federal law the convention then declared that the act permitting use of armed force to collect federal taxes that Congress had adopted simultaneously with the new tariff was without effect in South Carolina.

For Petigru, the ending of the crisis by a compromise that preserved constitutional order was arguably a political triumph and certainly a personal relief. But long months of stress had taxed him to his physical and psychological limits. Not only had he been in the thick of party organization, electoral battles, and partisan argument, he had carried as well an increasingly heavy professional workload. During the early 1830s the number of cases he argued before appeals courts and the proportion of them that he won both climbed substantially. As a result, he bore office and courtroom burdens greater even than those he

Charleston Courthouse (top) and City Hall (bottom), from
"View of Charleston, 1872," a lithograph by C. Drie.
(South Carolina Historical Society)

had carried during his peak years as attorney general. Additionally, his practice dealt increasingly with equity cases, whose preparation was usually more extensive and whose presentation was generally more complex than ordinary law cases. By September 1832, when the critical state election campaign had demanded that he speak here, consult there, exhort elsewhere, he had had to admit that he was simply too tired to keep it up. If he were "independent of the shop," he wrote a Beaufort Unionist, he could "take the field in earnest."[47] But he was not, and his family obligations necessarily kept him in the shop.

This double load took its toll. Shortly after the compromise tariff was passed in March 1833, Petigru's friend and colleague Mitchell King observed that although Petigru was "the same noble[,] generous, witty, able and delightful being . . . , a shade comes occasionally over his spirit, and mingles with his moods a bitterness which has been engendered by these bitter times." Finally, in June, Petigru collapsed. He was involved in a particularly contentious case, pressing the claim of a physician to whom the South Carolina Medical Society had denied a license to practice because, so they alleged, he was of "mixed" blood. The outcome turned on the caste of Dr. John Schmidt, Jr.'s, maternal grandmother, who had migrated to the United States after the Haitian revolution. Suspicions that her grandson had black ancestors stirred the community prejudice that Petigru strove to defuse by challenging as hearsay the scanty evidence on which the grandmother's heritage of miscegenation and thus her grandson's exclusion from the medical profession was based. Already "very sick, growing weaker and losing ground," Petigru summoned the energy to deliver an emotionally charged speech to the jury that won a favorable verdict for his client. Then he succumbed to a painful illness. Although he played it down, Petigru's friends were alarmed. "We really were afraid for him," King wrote Legaré, "[and] we all advised him to relax for the summer."[48]

Taking their advice, Petigru traveled to the North for the first time. He sailed by packet from Charleston to Old Point Comfort in early July, then journeyed inland to Virginia's famed White Sulphur Springs, a health spa much favored by Carolinians. Although he rested there for barely a week, enjoying the company of his old friend Alfred Huger (a planter cousin of his mentor) more than the presumed benefits of the waters, his health improved so swiftly that by July 12 he had traveled on to Washington. There he met and talked with President Jackson, his ally of necessity, and found that "the old gentleman looked better than

I expected." Jackson made some political observations and inquiries, and then expressed regrets that Petigru "was going to stay so short a time."[49]

Though his audience at the White House flattered him, Petigru hurried northward, trying to see it all in a single trip. He was an enthusiastic tourist in Philadelphia and New York, where he met a number of distinguished Yankees and enjoyed as well the company of fellow southerners who, like himself, had fled the summer heat. So well did he feel and so elated was he by travel that he went from New York to Boston by way of Niagara Falls, then widely regarded as one of the great natural wonders of the world. To his sister Adele he described what he saw as "altogether the land of romance."[50]

The high point of Petigru's tour was Boston, which he reached in late August. Even though he suffered a bad cold, which "greatly dampened my pleasures both in staying at home and going abroad," he reveled in the land of high thinking and plain living. Harvard president Josiah Quincy not only invited him to the college commencement, a veritable Cambridge festival, but "distinguished me very much and took me to the Commons" afterward to dine with the "Governor, Senators, Judges and all down to the Freshmen." It was a wonderful occasion for this erstwhile upcountry farm boy, and vastly different from his own college experiences. He could "almost fancy that the old times had returned and the Puritans with them" when, "as dinner was over and grace was said[,] a psalm was sung to the tune of the 'Old Hundred.' "[51]

By the time Petigru left Boston in early September he was fully recovered. On the way home he stopped in Washington to visit his youngest brother. Charles, now a West Point graduate stationed at the Washington Arsenal, reported to their sister Adele that "brother is in fine health, better than he has been for many years."[52] It was a good thing, too, for Petigru would need all the strength he could muster when he came home and had to face a seething political strife almost as fierce as the one that had undermined his health the year before. Nullification per se was past, but the partisan rancor it had generated was not. Those who had earlier confronted each other over the tariff now battled over the oath of state allegiance, authorized by a section of the 1832 Nullification Ordinance that had not been rescinded.

Because the oath could be required of all officeholders, although it applied at present only to militia officers, Unionists understood that it could be used to exclude them from public life altogether. Consequently they promptly challenged it in two cases, which by March 1834 had reached the state court of appeals. The upcountry case of *McDaniel* v. *McMeekin* was, by then, already overshadowed by its low country equivalent, *McCready* v. *Hunt.* The latter case, because prominent lawyers had been engaged to represent each side, promised the most rigorous test of the oath's constitutionality.[53] The circumstances were straightforward. Edward McCready, a newly elected militia officer, had refused to take the oath. Colonel Benjamin F. Hunt, commander of the Sixteenth Regiment of the South Carolina Militia and Petigru's old antagonist, had then denied him his commission. McCready had at once sued for it in an action that Hunt sought as much as he because both men were in fact Unionist opponents of the oath. Since the participants had agreed that whoever lost would appeal, the lawyers on both sides recognized that the lower court's decision would be of little consequence. Therefore neither plaintiff nor defendant presented full arguments before Judge Elihu H. Bay, an open Nullifier, who predictably refused to issue the writ of mandamus that McCready sought. So McCready appealed to test the oath's constitutionality; and his lawyers, Thomas S. Grimké and James L. Petigru, developed arguments that were as much political as legal.

The oath, both lawyers contended in somewhat overlapping presentations, violated the 1790 South Carolina Constitution because it both altered the oath there required of elected officials and contravened that constitution's prohibition against any religious test for officeholding. Both lawyers also challenged the putative authority to require a new oath specified in the Nullification Ordinance, averring that the ordinance itself was "repugnant to the Constitution of the United States."[54]

In support of these positions, Grimké made two additional points. First, he said, any citizen of South Carolina was, by that very fact, a citizen of the United States who therefore owed allegiance to both entities. The federal Constitution defined the nature of that dual allegiance by making the Constitution and federal law superior to the constitutions and laws of the several states. Any law, therefore, that required loyalty to the state alone must be invalid. Second, Grimké argued that any "test of opinion, compared with some fixed and known standard," whether political or religious, was a "test oath," and as such it violated South Carolina's own constitution.[55]

Responding to Grimké, R. Barnwell Smith (who in 1837 would change his surname to Rhett to satisfy the terms of a bequest), acting

in his official capacity as South Carolina's attorney general in defending Hunt, a militia officer pursuing his official duties, rejected the very
idea that allegiance could be divided or dual in nature. Then, asserting
the states' rights argument that sovereignty lay solely with each state,
he maintained that the Nullification Ordinance was as legitimate an
expression of that sovereignty as the 1790 South Carolina Constitution.
There could, therefore, be no appeal to the state constitution to over-
ride an action permitted by the ordinance. In sum, Smith argued, at
neither the federal nor the state level was there a constitutional issue.

It was left to Petigru to close for McCready. He returned to the constitutional issues that Grimké had raised, but his tone was markedly
different. Grimké had ended his speech with an apology to those to
whom he might have given "an instant of pain."[56] Petigru built relent-
lessly to a climax from which he allowed no retreat. He stated as a self-
evident truth that all government was limited by individuals' natural
rights to life, liberty, and property. He postulated that state and federal
constitutions made up a hierarchy of public authority and legitimate
power. Having thus stated the same fundamental assumptions that had
guided his actions as South Carolina's attorney general, Petigru continued his argument by establishing the state appeals court's authority
to judge whether or not the loyalty oath was constitutional. Asserting
John Marshall's judicial review argument that in the United States "the
judiciary is made co-ordinate with the Legislature" and that both are
subordinate to the constitutions that give each its powers and responsibilities, Petigru tackled the South Carolina legislature's proclivity to
concentrate power in its own hands. Against that practice he stressed
the court's obligation to check the very legislative excesses that made
judicial review essential not just to balance governmental power but to
protect a citizen's individual right to be secure from unconstitutional
intrusions. In no case was such a test of a law's constitutionality more
essential than when a law implicitly prescribed a point of view and
thus violated the most basic "freedom of an individual." Letting the
law stand would endanger the survival of republican government when
in cases like McCready's a law threatened not just a single individual's
freedom but "the rights of many thousands of the people of this country
to be accounted free."[57]

Continuing, Petigru analyzed the oath as an infringement on individual liberties protected by both state and federal constitutions. Characteristically exploring the historical sources of law, he discovered the

origins of all oaths of allegiance in the feudal practice whereby the serf swore unlimited fealty to his liege lord. To impose such an oath on a nineteenth-century American, Petigru charged, was to regress from republican citizenship to monarchical subjugation, to forge "a chain which none but the royal hand can hold, and which the subject can never shake off." South Carolina had cast off whatever remained of those chains in its 1790 constitution, which forbade oaths of religious conformity, for, as far as Petigru was concerned, there was no difference between a religious oath and a political one as a test for officeholding. Both were vestiges of monarchies that had been molded by the wars of the Reformation, which had made "all test oaths . . . political, not religious, in their objects." When church and state were one, he explained, it made no difference which kind of oath was used, for either imposed complete subjection to the ruler, who headed both. But in South Carolina, where state and church were separate, imposing any loyalty oath, and especially one requiring allegiance less to the state per se than to a particular political position, was no different from "acknowledging an absolute supremacy, in subscribing to a declaration that Gov. Hayne is supreme head of the church upon earth." [58]

It followed that an oath of allegiance to the state—when *allegiance* was understood to be "only another word for the right to nullify" —made it the "equivalent to abjuration of allegiance to the United States." In short, the South Carolina oath placed state law above the federal Constitution, despite the additional verbiage with which legislators had garnished the act that demanded it. It made no difference that legalistic language had been added to the first version of the oath to require paramount allegiance to South Carolina only so long as a citizen remained a resident of the state. That was mere subterfuge. No better was requiring obedience to federal law only so long as its "control over [its] citizens" was not delegated elsewhere, for the very wording created an intended "ambiguity" worthy only of contempt. "Among all the abuses of power," Petigru thundered, "a certain pre-eminence is due to the singular wickedness and enormity of the wretch who caused the laws to be promulgated in such a way as to be purposely unintelligible." [59]

Then came Petigru's peroration. In it he unleashed his fear of unlimited democracy, his mistrust of an unrestrained majority. Individual liberty, he said, could not rely on republican virtue alone to shield it from incursions, for even in a republic people were "liable to be transported with passion, blinded with folly, corrupted with vice, and yet more with power—maddened with faction, and fired with the lust of domination." Only a system of law, limited by constitutional bounds and enforced by government, could guarantee the rights of a minority. When the "ordinary Legislature" of a state exceeded constitutionally imposed limits to grasp at "dangerous and paracidal power," as had South Carolina's in imposing a loyalty oath, the only remaining protection for individual rights lay with federal authority as it was defined by the Constitution. Fortunately, Petigru concluded, that Constitution was the ultimate authority, "and the laws of the United States, made in pursuance thereof, are the supreme law of the land. . . . What idea a man may have of a law, higher than a supreme law, I know not."[60]

The three appeals court judges did not hand down their decision until May. The majority limited themselves to finding that the loyalty oath violated the state constitution. Taking notably narrower grounds than Petigru had argued, Judges John Belton O'Neall and David Johnson, in separate but concurring opinions, ruled that the Nullification Convention lacked the power to impose this or any other oath because its authority was limited to the tariff issue that it had been specifically called to address. While they agreed that citizens owed dual allegiance to state and nation, they skirted the question of federal supremacy altogether. By contrast, Judge William Harper's dissent explicitly confronted federal supremacy, but only to deny it. As for individual civil liberties, Harper, an ardent Nullifier, held that the state had an uncontested right to require conformity from all state officers, who must execute and enforce "*every* act of the sovereign authority of the State."[61]

The decision satisfied few. Charleston Nullifiers vented a "rage" that "far exceeded" Petigru's expectations. Unionists continued to debate the wisdom of "going to law about the test oath." Each side sought another round that would give it the definitive victory. Nullifiers publicized their intention to amend the state constitution to remove any impediment to reenacting the oath of allegiance. Petigru, though he thought that it could "hardly be regarded as unconstitutional," believed that reimposition of the oath would certainly be an "insult" to Unionists and would effectively exclude them from "civil privileges." But so long as it did not "derive its authority from the ordinance" of nullification and amounted to nothing more than a "mere declaration of 'allegiance to the State,'" he could see no effective defense against it. Rural Unionists were considerably more militant, threatening either to emigrate—or to follow Daniel Huger's "chivalric sentiments" and fight it out.[62]

As it turned out, it was not in the backcountry but in Charleston that violence flared. As the 1834 state elections approached, political rhetoric again grew hot. While established Nullifier leaders Hamilton and Hayne now equivocated about the meaning of allegiance, wishing, as Petigru thought, "to keep on the windy side of the law and on the blind side of Demos," their would-be successors recklessly stirred the passions that would guarantee another victory. On election eve, a crowd hove bricks through the windows of a downtown Union party clubhouse and beat up the men who emerged. Then, on the first night of the two-day election, a more menacing mob gathered around Union headquarters on the edge of town. Some of the occupants, doubtless anticipating further violence, were armed. Before long, they peppered the jeering crowd with duck shot, wounding six men. Enraged, their fellows rushed to the nearby arsenal to demand arms for self-defense. The captain of the city guard refused to yield to their demands. But it was only the arrival of ex-governor Hamilton and Governor Hayne that kept the crowd from more bloodshed. Hayne soothed them with promises of a subscription for the wounded, Hamilton, with assurances that electoral victory would bring just and full revenge. Having calmed his own men, and proceeding under a flag of truce, Hamilton then arranged a "treaty" with Dr. Samuel Dickson, "the most prominent gentleman" at the Union headquarters. Partisans on both sides went home in relative safety, but a great tragedy had only narrowly been avoided. Petigru was sure that "had the Nullifiers renewed the attack there would have been a great deal of bloodshed." Worse still, he feared that now Union men were "more excited than the Nullifiers."[63]

While Petigru shuddered at the passions let loose, Hamilton, who shared his anxiety, was moving toward compromise. Even at the convention that repealed nullification, in March 1833, he had urged reconciliation. Mitchell King, a distinctly unsympathetic Unionist, believed that "after all the adulation he [Hamilton] has received from his infatuated admirers, the Bayard of the South, the soul of honor, the mirror of Chivalry, is sick, very sick of the game." And Petigru rather cynically observed that Hamilton no longer courted a popular following but now left "the defence of nullification . . . to the train bands of editors and pot house politicians and patriots in search of office."[64]

Unlike Petigru, Hamilton was a highly skilled politician who looked first to strategy and tactics. By 1834 his sights were set on reentering the national arena as part of the emerging anti-Jackson coalition. But he knew that to do so he had to retain a power base in his home state. With this in mind he had run for a seat in the state senate and won a sweeping victory in the election that simultaneously ousted Petigru from the lower house in what was his worst electoral defeat. Those results told both men that political opponents of a test oath had no hope of defeating a new oath law in the legislature. But the armed encounter on election night also warned both of an excitement so intense on each side that efforts to amend the constitution to permit such an oath might well leave the state "knee deep in blood." [65] That contingency propelled moderates on both sides toward compromise and made even the fully committed reconsider the alternatives.

In this mood, Unionist legislators from around the state asked Petigru to come to Columbia in early December to help them develop their strategy. Their goal was simple enough: to block the anticipated constitutional amendment and the oath it would permit. After talking with them as well as with Unionist leaders in Charleston, Petigru concluded that Union men would refuse to take any oath of exclusive allegiance to South Carolina and that many would resist it fiercely, whether it was constitutional or not. This he conveyed to friends and foes alike. Sensing an impasse, legislators from both parties then invited him to address a joint session of the state house and senate. Addressing this deadly serious situation, Petigru spoke without subterfuge. He warned Nullifiers that the proposed constitutional amendment would leave one-third of the state's white population unrepresented because no Unionist would take an office for which the oath was a prerequisite. Moreover, if a constitutional amendment legitimizing an oath was adopted, it would foreclose any challenge to the oath in the courts. The Unionists would thus be left with no legal or constitutional outlet. Driving his message home, Petigru concluded by observing that armed defiance was illegal and unconstitutional.

His opponents assailed Petigru bitterly for the stark picture he drew. Yet he had cooled a few heads. The very next day Hamilton made a conciliatory speech in the senate, and the day after that David McCord, a Nullifier representative, publicly pressed Petigru to propose a compromise that Unionists would find acceptable. In response Petigru organized an impromptu committee of five Unionist leaders, who hammered out the terms with which they could live. Any act requiring an oath must include official notice that swearing allegiance under it would in no way alter the allegiance a citizen owed to the United States. Moreover, it must omit any provision that would make refusing to take the oath treasonable. Finally, the committee insisted that political attacks on the state's judiciary, most of whose members were Unionists, must stop.

The initial response to these proposals was openly hostile and thoroughly alarmed Petigru. Discouraged and perplexed, he returned to his hotel room, wondering what he should do next. There he found Hamilton waiting for him. Fearing that his former partner had come only to talk about legal or plantation business, Petigru accordingly waited for him to take the lead. Before long, Hamilton made clear his intention to talk politics. Petigru replied that they "had come to the brink of the precipice," and that the fall over the edge was now "impossible to avert." Hamilton, agreeing that the situation was desperate, voiced enough genuine concern that Petigru "ceased to doubt his absolute and unconditional desire of peace." Then the two old friends methodically reviewed the painful political questions that divided them and pondered all conceivable outcomes. Finally, Hamilton pledged himself to work for Petigru's three proposed conditions as the only way out of the morass. Those proposals did at least spare the Nullifiers the embarrassment of an outright retraction. And resolving the crisis coincided with Hamilton's broader political agenda. To Petigru the outcome was almost too good to believe. "The rank and file was really in pursuit of a test oath—and . . . no man but Hamilton could possibly bring them to bear the dose which they were now to swallow." Although he retained doubts about his former partner's sincerity, their "very long talk" had convinced him that Hamilton was now ready to play the statesman rather than the demagogue, "to work as hard now for peace as ever he did for nullification. . . . And so he did."

The two men left the hotel together, Petigru to report to his associates, Hamilton to call a legislative caucus of his party for the very next morning. Even Hamilton's timing was prudent, for, as Petigru noted almost jovially, it avoided "the disadvantage of contending with John Barleycorn, a most potent auxiliary to Nullifiers of an afternoon." So, soberly, Carolina retreated from the precipice. Both houses of the legislature adopted Petigru's proposals by large majorities. In watering down the oath, they defused the issue. Hamilton reported to Petigru when the compromise was completed, "We have triumphed!!" But it was the politician rather than the peacemaker who continued, "Our Rank & file . . . in this most heated conflict . . . stuck manfully to the old Leaders, & it is due to your party to say that they redeemed their pledges in the handsomest possible manner."[66]

Petigru was deeply grateful—but he was not ecstatically triumphant. He hoped that eventually his state would return to its customary pattern, "just warm enough to keep up the distinction between a majority & a minority." But he knew that it would be "a long time before parties will be so reorganized as to obliterate the traces of the old lines between nullifiers and friends of the Union."[67] The years that followed proved him right on both counts, but in ways that dismayed him. The lines between Unionists and Nullifiers did indeed disappear, but only because Unionists themselves virtually vanished. And the distinction between majority and minority measured increasingly only a difference over the timing of secession.

More immediately Petigru writhed as the promised protection of an independent judiciary melted away. In 1835 the legislature once more reorganized the courts, abolishing the three-judge Court of Appeals that had decided the *McCready* case and returning the court structure to very nearly what it had been before 1824. From 1835 to 1859 South Carolina had no separate appeals bench. All the trial court law judges sat as the law appeals court, and all the chancellors as the equity appeals court. The only novelty was a measure to avoid the confusion that conflicting decisions from two appeals courts had caused before 1824. A new Court of Errors, on which the law judges and the chancellors sat together, would resolve by majority vote whatever legal contradictions they had created separately.[68] That there was a political motive in all this was abundantly clear. The two appeals court judges who had constituted a majority in the *McCready* case were separated, John Belton O'Neall becoming a law court judge, and David Johnson, a chancellor. But throughout the debate that the reorganization generated, Petigru held his peace, fearful lest anything he might say would only further antagonize the enemies of an independent judiciary. Uneasy with the "natural instability of the democracy," he mused privately that his opponents in the legislature wanted "a tub for the whale, and if nothing else is at hand the leaders will have to toss the judiciary overboard, or amuse the monster with some new lie."[69]

The abolition of the separate appeals court with its bench of highly qualified judges affected Petigru's legal practice far more than it did his political life, for by 1835 his political career had peaked. Although he continued to occupy the "first rank at the bar," and many thought he had "the best practice . . . of any lawyer" in South Carolina, his standing as a politician was minimal.[70] True, he had demonstrated that he could enunciate theory, develop strategies, and even ignore legal niceties when elections hung in the balance. But his Calvinistic faith in human frailty and his deeply rooted fears of disorder made him as suspicious of majoritarian democracy as he was of the often demogogic aristocrats who kept South Carolina firmly under their own control.

Petigru held that informed reason was the best means to control individual passions and therefore espoused an ideal politics in which well-educated leaders informed a rank and file ready, like good juries devoid of prejudice, to hear and assess the evidence and to vote accordingly. Neither leaders nor the rank and file could safely be trusted with power if unchecked by the other. Necessary though it was to protect individual rights and maintain legality, power must always be restrained. Deploring the governmental structure of his own state, where few judicial checks or executive balances reined in the general assembly, which elected both the judges and the governor, Petigru looked to the federal Constitution as the sole protection against the otherwise unrestrained power of the South Carolina legislature. In so thinking, he cut himself off from the politics of his state. An ambitious man, scarcely "indifferent to opinion" or "careless of office," he was neither able nor willing to cut his personal beliefs to fit a popular political style.[71]

His political colleague and longtime fellow Unionist Benjamin Perry saw all this and called Petigru simply "a Federalist of the old school." His former law student Robert Barnwell Rhett, an ever more ardent secessionist, attributed Petigru's political failure to his being "a bad courtier of the people." Both men agreed that however perceptive Petigru was as a political theorist and legal thinker, as a practical politician he was sadly inept. But neither addressed the fundamental shift in South Carolina politics that would eventually smother the development of a two-party system and leave no role for those whose commitment to Union and federal Constitution cast them as threats to their state's economic priorities. Thus did Petigru's unwillingness to refashion a conservatism he had shaped largely in jurisprudential terms make him a dissenter in a society most of whose values he shared.[72]

FOUR

Becoming
an Entrepreneur

As the nullification controversy gradually wound down, James Petigru came to realize that a meaningful career in Carolina politics would never be his. Restless at the "want of novelty" in his professional life and ambitious for something more than mere success, he contemplated the options open to him. In his mid-forties, with twenty years of legal practice behind him, he savored the bitterness that a former student had summed up by observing that "the history of every lawyer at our bar has been—ten or fifteen years of intense application in preparing for the arena & the prize when won scarcely worth possessing."[1] But what choices did he have? He could, of course, simply change his location, leave Charleston to practice law in a bigger arena. Alternatively, he might become a judge, especially if he could gain an appointment to the federal bench. Or he might desert the courts altogether and turn his attention to totally different pursuits, ones that might produce a fortune sufficient to support life as a man of leisure and amateur scholar.

Deciding to make a major change is never easy, and for several years Petigru mulled over his options. In October 1832, when it seemed likely that nullification would lead to disunion, Petigru wrote Hugh Legaré that if "in fact . . . the Union is severed my mind is made up to quit the negro country." But he really didn't know where to go. New York was likely his first choice, for two years later he advised Legaré to settle there on his return from Belgium. In 1835 Petigru was less specific than that when he confessed to Francis Lieber, then a newly appointed professor at South Carolina College, that "if I were young and had to choose my own career I would cast it in [the] North. American life and action are there."[2]

But he was no longer young and had already established his career. So even though thirty years later he would regret that he had not left the South, his choice to stay seemed reasonable in 1834. Moreover, at the time it appeared quite possible that, as a Carolina Unionist, he might be appointed to the United States Supreme Court. William Johnson, whom Thomas Jefferson had made an associate justice in 1806, had just died in office, and Petigru's recent conspicuous defense of federal law brought him favorable consideration as a candidate to fill the spot that political wisdom assigned to a southerner. Distinguished lawyers and Unionist politicians petitioned Washington on his behalf. They described him as "one of the most learned, able and eloquent Lawyers in the Union," a jurist blessed with a great "variety and depth of . . . learning & Knowledge," a man marked by the "soundness of his Judgment," a person endowed with "integrity and honor of the highest order." Joel Poinsett, former congressman and future secretary of war, corraled out-of-state political support for his friend, assuring Congressman Charles Ingersoll of Pennsylvania that as a legal scholar Petigru compared favorably with Chief Justice John Marshall. More opportunistically, another supporter noted that his politics were "of the orthodox order."[3]

Ironically, however, that orthodoxy worked against him, for the president was too shrewd a politician not to realize that Petigru and most of his Unionist colleagues—Poinsett was a clear exception—were not Jacksonian loyalists. From the start, Petigru, sensing the importance of this obstacle, doubted that the appointment would be offered to him. He long insisted that Legaré was "the only one . . . fit to fill the place," either because he had studied law at Edinburgh or because this impoverished heir of a prestigious low country family had better political connections than he. In any case, Petigru concluded in a letter about his own prospects, "I don't think it is the will of God, and have certain information that it is not [Vice President Martin] Van Buren's."[4]

Yet privately he wished for it. A seat on the Supreme Court would satisfy his personal ambitions as nothing else could. But he wondered whether he should accept it if it was offered. Common sense told him he could not afford to. His extensive family obligations argued against surrendering a fine income as a Charleston lawyer for a judge's salary equal to only three quarters of his current earnings. On the other hand, he yearned for the intellectual rewards and new life a Supreme Court appointment would bring. So, as he admitted to Legaré, although he "ought to refuse it," he would, "for reasons too many to need mentioning . . . not probably have the wit to do so."[5]

In the end, however, the choice was made for him. President Jackson appointed a loyal political supporter, Congressman James Wayne of Georgia. By the process of elimination, then, Petigru was left with only his third and least appealing option. It was, however, also the most practical choice for a man little given to practicality. Once, when simultaneously exasperated by the Jacobinism he saw in nullification politics and the irrationality he detected in religious revivalism, he had exploded. "I am sick and weary of all this flummery; I long for a little common sense. I must get me a taste for money. Avarice is the most innocent kind of excitement for a man who has reached 'the middle ages.' "[6] He called it avarice, and yet he chose it. With a certain desperation Petigru settled down in 1835 to make money.

Whether he did so in response to the psychological pressures common to men who at mid-life realize they have not fulfilled their youthful aspirations or simply in practical recognition that his own prodigality and his family's extravagance already overtaxed his financial resources is unclear. What is clear is that throughout the 1830s family expenses expanded while family satisfactions diminished. Jane Amelia, whose exuberant spirits and personal beauty had first attracted him, had after twenty years of marriage become a frequently querulous and quarrelsome woman. The repercussions of Albert's death and the arrival of James's sisters had probably triggered the change. In any case, she clearly resented the beauty and liveliness of the adolescent girls—first her sisters-in-law and then her own daughters—who attracted the attention she craved for herself. Doubtless her emotional distress contributed to her growing dependence on addictive drugs, so that by the mid-1830s she lived the life of a semi-invalid, had become extremely short-tempered with servants and relatives alike, and brooded on every minor disability as a sign of the dropsy or stroke she believed was imminent. Her housemates, not surprisingly, found her very difficult to live with.[7]

Some of them at least some of the time questioned the severity of Jane Amelia's illnesses, from which she frequently experienced amazing recoveries when interesting diversions beckoned. Three times during the 1830s she spent whole summers in the North, participating enthusiastically in the resort life of Newport and Saratoga, socializing with other southerners in New York City, and shopping lavishly wherever she was.[8]

During those periods she consumed notably less morphine. But as soon as she returned to Charleston she resumed her invalid's couch and her medicines. As her nineteen-year-old daughter Caroline observed of her mother's sufferings, "There seems to be no end to them; as soon as she gets better of one thing she is attacked by another."[9]

Petigru naturally rejoiced in Jane Amelia's temporary remissions from invalidism and intensive drug dependence. But he was also sorely tried by the costliness of her sojourns. In good times he could afford them—even though they might cost as much as a sixth of his annual professional income. But when times turned bad and creditors pressed hard, as they did in the late 1830s during her second and third trips, he resented Jane Amelia's traveling as a "lamentable thing for me." And when he had to accompany her to "hotels and watering places," where there was nothing else for him to do but loiter away his time, he felt "like a fish out of water." He was uncomfortable in the idle, fashionable world his wife and daughters so enjoyed. He would much rather have relaxed in the hospitality he found in the Milledgeville home of Governor George Gilmer of Georgia, where there was "no parade—no show—no silver forks." And best of all, there he enjoyed the genuine "heartiness with which his little wife welcomes anyone that has the good fortune to be her husband's friend."[10]

Much closer in style to Mrs. Gilmer than Jane Amelia was Petigru's sister Jane, who had in 1827 married John G. North, her brother's former law student. When North's sudden death in 1836 left his young widow with three daughters and an estate too small and too encumbered to support them, Petigru characteristically stepped in to help. He met the immediate crisis by seeing that John's tangled business affairs were settled and arranging Jane's return to Badwell, where, for the rest of her life, she ran the family farm, struggling unremittingly to make it at least minimally productive.[11] As the years wore on, James's fondness for Jane and his own attachment to Badwell led him to finance improvements that enabled her to eke out a livelihood from the place.

First, however, James had encouraged his sister to undertake a school at Abbeville, thinking that by teaching she would be "far happier and far more usefully employed than in your present situation or any other within our reach."[12] But when she found that local supporters had little use for the demanding curriculum she hoped to offer, and when, in 1837, William Pettigrew died, James turned Badwell's resources and their management over to her. Thereafter Badwell became James's most frequent vacation spot, a retreat from work and a refuge from domestic discord—for Jane Amelia hated the place and refused to go there. Over time, too, Jane North became her brother's particular confidante. To her more than to anyone else he poured out his personal woes, professional satisfactions, and political views.

No other sister was so close to the man they all called simply "Brother." Yet all acknowledged James as the head of their family— in one way or another its spokesman, its defender, and its conscience. Mary, who never married and never lived anywhere else except Badwell, seldom communicated with Brother and was the most emotionally and intellectually removed from him. Louise, the oldest of the three who had moved to Charleston after their mother's death, had in 1829 married Philip Porcher, a Charleston real estate and slave broker and minor planter. Though the Porchers lived in the city, the brothers-in-law never formed close ties; so, though James and Louise frequently visited back and forth, their spouses rarely did. But James's ties with his sister Adele, even after her marriage to Robert Allston, never lost the intensity that had developed when his three younger sisters had come to live with the Petigrus in 1826. Indeed, Allston, a wealthy Georgetown planter who ultimately became governor, was a fast friend of Petigru, who remained his attorney and occasional political adviser despite their sharp differences about nullification and South Carolina's course thereafter. Finally there was sister Harriette, who in 1836 married Henry Lesesne, a law student of Petigru's who subsequently became his partner. Although Harriette was almost as openly critical of Jane Amelia as Louise was, the Lesesnes spent considerably more time in the Broad Street house. Indeed, during their first year of marriage they lived with the Petigrus. Almost always they were close neighbors. But whether they were near at hand or seldom seen, Petigru kept track of his sisters and their affairs. He worried about Jane North's finances, Louise's children, Adele's relative isolation, and Harriette's constant ill health, and he never surrendered his self-assumed but broadly accepted role as his sisters' guardian.

His sisters, however, were by no means his greatest familial responsibility. Not surprisingly, his own children caused him considerable concern and, not infrequently, anguish. After Albert's death, in 1826, Caroline got the greatest share of paternal attention. Schooled in Charleston until she was fourteen, she was then sent off to Miss Binsse's prestigious school for young ladies in New York, where she excelled academically.

By the end of her first year she was "at the very head of the school," in part because she had been so well prepared at home in English and history and in part because she had rapidly learned at Miss Binsse's to speak French with a "readiness & accuracy" that her father envied. Proud that his older daughter was "very clever, & wins golden opinions of all who see her," Petigru urged her to stay on for a second year. But Caroline, who was both high-spirited and homesick, balked. New York was "a most horrible place" with its cold and snow. And Madame Binsse, with her constant scolding, was not much better. Moreover, her Mama, who sided with Caroline, went up to New York in June 1835 "bent on bringing her home." In a pattern typical of the next ten years, Petigru gave in to Jane Amelia's determination. "Fifteen," he admitted somewhat embarrassedly to Jane North, was "not an age to finish one's education and in taking her from school I do wrong, and do it knowingly."[13]

But take her he did. And though he set out courses of reading for her when she returned home, Caroline was before long swept up in the social concerns of a Charleston belle. Her coming of an age to be courted was celebrated by an elaborate eighteenth birthday party, where she reportedly outshone all others. On that occasion, so her aunt Harriette said, she replaced her mother as the family member pressing on the front ranks of fashion and society. But although Jane Amelia surrendered her place on the dance floor to her daughter, she did not alter the difficult "circumstances" at home to which Caroline had quietly to submit.[14]

Caroline did not, however, succumb at once to her mother's pressure to marry well and soon. She repeatedly rejected the young swains who wooed her. Then, without warning, she accepted their neighbor William Carson, who at forty-one was twenty years her senior. Startled by a marriage proposal from an apparently confirmed bachelor more of the mother's generation than the daughter's, Petigru nevertheless refused to advise his daughter when she sought his opinion of the match. It was a strange dereliction of duty, for Petigru was well aware not only of the barely concealed hostility between daughter and mother but also of Caroline's consequent reliance on him for emotional support. Moreover, this was the same man who had voluntarily assumed so much responsibility for his sisters' fate. Certainly he had misgivings about the match. His very surprise when Caroline told him signaled his intuitive fear that so great a difference in ages, added to Carson's previous life as a man about town, would undo the advantages that Jane Amelia saw in his reputed wealth and his large Cooper River rice plantation, Dean Hall. Yet Petigru said nothing. And Caroline married.[15]

Well before Caroline's marriage, however, the two younger children had learned that only by defying parental authority could they steal some of the limelight that otherwise shone on their sister. Each grew up in the shadow of an older sibling—handsome but mischievous Daniel, in that of Albert, whose early death had almost canonized him at home; and husky, dark Susan, in that of her beautiful, bright, and blonde older sister. Left behind during those summers when the rest of the family journeyed north, these youngsters were also sent off to school in the heat of Charleston summers while everybody else vacationed on Sullivan's Island. Not surprisingly Sue and Dan quickly became rebels.

By the time he was fourteen Dan was a serious discipline problem at home and at school, although his father still had hopes that he would improve with age. But when, at sixteen, Dan "mutinied" against an attempt by his latest Charleston schoolmaster to administer physical punishment, Petigru decided that the only solution was to send him off to boarding school. He looked for a school where the seemingly un-controllable youth would be removed from all familiar influences and finally found it in Mount Saint Mary's College, an isolated Catholic school hemmed in by the Catoctin Mountains of northwestern Maryland.[16]

That very remoteness, however, presented logistical problems. For all his determination to straighten Dan out, Petigru was reluctant to disrupt his professional obligations to escort his only son to Emmitsburg. "I will have to go with the boy myself," he wrote grudgingly to Legaré, "and tho it will be very inconvenient I must try to do it."[17] So when Legaré, then a congressman, offered to meet Dan in Baltimore and take him inland to his new school, Petigru speedily agreed. At the same time, however, he had reservations, for he feared that when the clerics who ran the school actually met Dan and tested his academic competence, they would deny him entry. So he asked Legaré to take the boy on to New York should that unhappy event occur. There he should put Dan in the charge of yet another friend, who had volunteered to place him in some school until his father could "make arrangements to dispose of him permanently."[18]

Underlying all these plans was Petigru's emotional difficulty in coping with Dan and his fear that the lad would repeat the family pattern from which he himself had struggled so hard to escape. His reference to disposing of Dan "permanently" echoed, in fact, his brusque treatment of his ne'er-do-well brother Jack, whom he had exiled from Badwell, sent west, and refused to aid until he should reform. That there were similar problems as well in the Postell family only made matters worse, for Jane Amelia was as apprehensive as her husband when she contemplated her two brothers who refused to work or support their families and a third who was "lost entirely." She believed that Dan desperately needed strict discipline to avoid a similar fate—but it was a discipline from which she excused herself because of her "wretched" health. "I am," she confided to a cousin, "able to do nothing, but pray to God for my children." [19]

Although Dan survived two years at Emmitsburg with gentlemanly passes in most subjects except Latin, Mount Saint Mary's College did not turn him around. As soon as he went on to Princeton, he resumed his old ways, and in 1842 he was suspended for disobedience, intemperance, and cutting chapel. So he returned to Charleston. There he halfheartedly studied law—much in the style of another young man whom his father described as a "convert to the utilitarian theory, so far as it favors indolence and pleasure," one whose studies were adjusted to "how little learning" he needed to know rather than how much.[20]

Sue, the youngest child, was as ungovernable as her brother. Sporting her father's temper as well as his appearance, she lacked his self-control. Although she shared his passion for books, she read only novels. Blessed with wit and imagination, she used both to alienate acquaintances rather than make friends. Self-willed, she would gain her own way regardless of how much she hurt others. Like her siblings, she attended Charleston's best schools, ending up at Mme. Talvande's famous institution for young ladies, where she did reasonably well. Then she too was sent north, to be finished at Mme. Guillon's classes in Philadelphia, which she later characterized as oppressive and a waste of time. Like Caroline she therefore returned as soon as she could to the intriguing world of belles, beaux, and courting. But unlike Caroline she clashed openly with her mother at home, shocked the rest of the family with extravagant behavior, and generated all kinds of gossip around town. Jane Amelia thought the only solution was to marry her younger daughter off quickly—and, if possible, to money.[21] Her father, on the other hand, paid little attention to his wife's matchmaking. It may indeed have been that his own tangled business affairs in those years not only diverted his attention from his younger daughter, except for those tense occasions when he tried to rein her in, but also made Jane Amelia especially determined that her daughters should avoid the financial disaster with which their family was increasingly threatened.

With his children grown and his wife ever more testy, Petigru devoted less and less time to a home that offered him so little joy. His flourishing practice demanded that he spend most of the time either in his law office or in courtrooms—not just in Charleston but throughout the state. Following the pattern common to American judges and attorneys of the time, who often lived less than eight months a year under their own roofs, he spent much of his time on the road. Even when he was in Charleston he was "harrassed with business" at the several courts whose terms overlapped in the busiest months from January to May. Equally demanding of time and energy was his office work, for not only was he singularly conscientious about the details of his cases, he also believed that he must be prepared for all eventualities and that "the only way of being prepared is to see to everything that is done."[22]

Over the years Petigru had a series of partners. But it was not until Henry Lesesne joined him in 1840 that he was willing to delegate any of his own accountability. By that time, however, his firm was handling 20 to 25 percent of all the civil cases heard in Charleston's district courts, so even with a trusted partner Petigru was kept on the go. Apologizing to Legaré for the paucity of his letters and perhaps nostalgic for a more relaxed past when he had had time at the end of the day to talk philosophy as well as law, he declined to "attempt any defence on the score of my being pulled and haled from the Judge to the Jury, and the office to the court from morning till night. Often [I dine] in St Michaels Alley [at the office] and seldom [get] home till 10 o'clock."[23]

After 1840 Petigru did try to curtail his practice by limiting his out-of-town caseload to appeals court cases and by giving up criminal law altogether. Yet even so he was pressed to his limit. He traveled regularly to try difficult cases in Edgefield and Abbeville in the northwestern section of the state, in midland Sumterville and Camden, in Walterborough just west of Charleston, and in Beaufort District, where he still had a large practice. So in 1850 he tried to cut back still more, making it a rule (with a few exceptions) that he would not appear in an out-of-town lower court for less than a $500 fee. But nothing could reduce his frequent trips to the state capital, where, in addition to Charleston, the appeals court sat and where United States district and circuit courts frequently held their sessions. Even though travel became somewhat more comfortable after 1842, when the South Carolina railroad was completed between Charleston and Columbia, the journey took more than ten hours and was quite taxing. And even in the 1850s much of Petigru's travel elsewhere was still in bouncing stagecoaches over miserable dirt roads frequently mired in mud.[24]

In addition to traversing his own state, Petigru occasionally represented clients in federal and state courts elsewhere, most frequently in Georgia, where he had been admitted to practice in 1833. Moreover, when he was not in court he spent considerable time lobbying both South Carolina and Georgia legislators on behalf of clients. Indeed, for ten years during the 1830s and 1840s, he went almost annually to Milledgeville, then the Georgia state capital, where during their regular sessions he pressed on members of the Georgia legislature a claim deriving from the *Chisholm* v. *Georgia* decision of 1793. And all this was in addition to the 101 South Carolina appeals court cases that were sufficiently important to appear in printed reports that he argued in the 1830s and the 88 that he argued in the 1840s.[25]

Thus dogged, Petigru grumbled irritably at the stratagems by which the South Carolina legislature tried to stretch the state's too few judges to meet a steadily increasing caseload. In 1833 the legislature had abolished uniform times for trial sessions in each district so that judges could move more efficiently from one court seat to the next as soon as the business in the first was finished. For those lawyers not consistently riding circuit with the judges, this change made for wildly unpredictable schedules. Then, in 1835, when the legislature eliminated the single separate appeals bench and ordered all judges and chancellors to hear cases in both the lower and appellate courts, the time and resources allocated to each level were further curtailed. The "worst court" that "the confounded intermeddling of the Legislature" had produced, so Petigru complained, had thrown "everything into confusion"; it was a confusion that lasted until 1859.[26] There were also less enduring experiments, which created shorter-lived but equally intense inconvenience. In January 1842, for example, the city court and the state general sessions, common pleas, and equity courts for the Charleston District sat simultaneously. That same year the legislature mandated that all appeals court proceedings be held in Columbia. By removing all appeals court trials from Charleston the new arrangement placed a heavy burden on those attorneys who, for instance, in the 1843 May term had to represent clients in the more than 150 Charleston cases heard in a court 120 miles distant. Twenty-four of those cases were handled by the firm of Petigru and Lesesne.[27]

However much Petigru fumed at such "clumsy project[s]" adopted in the name of judicial reform, he coped in ways that built his reputation for skill and probity, and so attracted still more clients. At the same time, his desire to do more than practice law, which had led him into politics, made him undertake a variety of community activities. His enthusiastic support for education and his unfulfilled wish to teach led to his becoming a lay officer of several schools. During most of his lifetime the state supported public schools only for the very poorest white children, leaving all other primary and secondary education either to proprietary schools or those supported by private clubs and civic organizations. In Charleston, one of the most active among the latter was the Fellowship Society, whose $50,000 endowment was dedicated almost wholly to the primary schools it supported. Petigru served on the society's education committee for much of the 1830s. In 1831 he was also elected to the Board of Trustees of the College of Charleston, which was, at the time, being revived as an institution of higher education following years of operation as a grammar school. Although Petigru, who continued to serve the college until he died thirty-one years later, often missed board meetings and never became a major officer, he was active whenever his professional expertise or peacemaking mediation was needed. He oversaw the revision of its charter when the college simultaneously dropped its high school program and became, in 1838, the country's first municipal college. He participated in the selection of professors and presidents. And when students rebelled against college discipline, protesting faculty prerogatives or contesting presidential authority, Petigru proposed resolutions which, while upholding the honor of young southern gentlemen, also maintained the rights their seniors claimed.[28]

Petigru was appointed as well to serve on the board of his alma mater shortly after Thomas Cooper resigned his presidency. At the time, South Carolina College was in desperate straits, reduced to a student body of twenty-five and a tiny, scarcely more viable faculty. Yet here, where his personal ties were greater, Petigru played a far less active role than he did at the College of Charleston. Minutes from 1835 to 1841 record his attendance at only six of the board's thirty-four meetings; and the legislature's failure to reappoint him in 1841 suggests that he had made no mark at the few meetings he did attend.[29] This apparent negligence is difficult to explain except by his extremely busy professional life and the length and discomfort of the stagecoach trip from Charleston to Columbia. There is no reason to believe that Petigru ever lost his fondness for his old school or his sense of its importance to his own life. Nonetheless, he showed his zeal for higher education more in his addresses to various college audiences than in his record as a trustee.

Education was, Petigru believed, an essential bulwark of civilization. In a republic, where society's survival as well as the fate of the individual depended on its widespread accessibility, it was a special concern. But there were, he told the graduating class at Oglethorpe College in 1841, two kinds of education. One taught the "arts which conduce to the comforts of life and the increase of material wealth," those which were "deservedly and fitly called useful." The classical curriculum, however, though less demonstrably useful, stimulated "the investigation of truth, the observation of moral and physical phenomena, the study of the causes of things, and the exercise of the powers of the imagination." It was the latter that Petigru valued more, and he was almost autobiographical in spelling it out. Any young man who has learned through a liberal education to "know himself, and to understand the principles by which the moral and material world are governed," has, "even if he finds himself alone in the world without friends or fortune, . . . the key which will enable him to explore the mysteries of nature or of power." Such men, he told the students, become the intellectual leaders and explorers whose efforts ultimately maintain civilization. And that was why, in a republic, which depends on the voices of the many rather than the few, education is "the most important subject for society; not to the individual only, but to the community." [30]

That Petigru continued his own explorations of the moral and material universe beyond his college years is reflected in the cultural institutions he supported. In the 1830s he was an active participant in the efforts that revived both Charleston's Literary and Philosophical Society and the *Southern Review*, and he was a founder of the South Carolina Society for the Advancement of Learning. Still more of his effort went to professional organizations. By 1830 he was on the standing committee of the Charleston Bar Association, and it was he who was asked to deliver the association's eulogy for Chief Justice John Marshall in 1835. He served also on a court-appointed legal education committee asked to investigate a "course . . . of study . . . for law students," and was subsequently made an examiner of those applying for admission to practice in the state's courts. In 1837, Harvard awarded him an honorary doctorate, though that was probably more in recognition of his Unionist politics than of his legal preeminence.[31]

Paradoxically, his Unionism may account for some of Petigru's growing social preeminence at home in the years after nullification, years during which Charlestonians strove to reunite their divided city. Men on both sides of the controversy had been saddened by the personal hostilities that the crisis had generated. Petigru had grieved especially when politics had made him "almost a stranger" to municipal judge Samuel Prioleau, a friend of long standing, with whom he had formerly been "so intimate." Sensing that political divisions would leave Unionists ostracized forever, he warned the absent Hugh Legaré in 1834 against the social isolation he would face should he return to Charleston when his diplomatic service ended. He would, Petigru feared, "in all probability" be "excluded effectually from everything else except the Bible Society." Yet even at the height of partisan violence, Petigru's endeavors to maintain civility had shielded him from such ostracism. Within days after the brick-throwing encounter that marked the worst of the 1832 electoral mayhem, he had invited James Hamilton to join him and some Unionist friends at his Broad Street home for a late supper—and Hamilton had come. When, a few months later, a military confrontation between federal troops and state militia was a real possibility, he had responded jestingly to a Nullifier lady's warning that he might be hanged if he went to Columbia by asking whether she would then come to his aid and cut him down. She, quite seriously, had allowed that she would.[32]

Throughout this period Petigru strove constantly to separate political enmity from private friendship, a skill he maintained for the rest of his life. Indeed, in a letter to his Nullifier classmate William Grayson he had played down their differences. "You and I will never dispute much on politics and not at all on anything else." But had that spirit of reconciliation been only on one side, the postnullification process in which many Charleston clubs and societies reached out to expand their membership to ensure the inclusion of men of both factions would not have occurred. Even so, given his political visibility, Petigru's social acceptance was unusual. He continued to serve on the vestry of St. Michael's, one of the city's two most politically powerful and socially prestigious Episcopal churches. He was elected vice president in 1836 and president the next year of the equally prestigious Society for the

Relief of Orphans and Widows of the Clergy of the Protestant Episcopal Church. And in 1837 Charleston's most exclusive club, the St. Cecelia Society, made him vice president.[33] But all this is less surprising than the fact that he also regained a measure of political acceptance for himself—though not for his Unionism.

In 1836 Petigru was asked to join half a dozen other civic leaders in drafting a plan for reorganizing Charleston's government. They hoped to stimulate the city's lagging economy by providing an infrastructure that would encourage new commercial facilities and enhance public safety. Key to their plan was replacing the unpaid and part-time intendant with a full-time and amply salaried mayor and providing him with the resources to initiate changes to make city government more efficient. Once the citizens had endorsed the plan and the legislature had amended the city charter to encompass it, elections for the new mayor and city council were called. In the election campaign, Petigru backed James Hamilton for mayor.[34]

While that support was not a rejection of his former political connections, it and Petigru's direction of Hugh Legaré's campaign for Charleston's congressional seat in 1836 illustrate the murkiness of his state's newly realigned politics. Legaré, just back from four years as United States chargé d'affaires in Belgium, was challenging the incumbent, Henry L. Pinckney, a highly visible Nullifier and onetime Charleston intendant, in an election in which Pinckney's softness on abolition was the chief issue. When earlier that year the U.S. House of Representatives had adopted Pinckney's "gag resolution" to refer all antislavery petitions to a select committee charged with rejecting them, without a hearing, as outside Congress's constitutional power, Massachusetts Congressman John Quincy Adams attacked the gag rule as an infringement on citizens' First Amendment right to petition the Congress. But to Pinckney's fellow South Carolina representatives, who believed that even receiving such petitions was an unconstitutional assertion of congressional power to legislate on slavery, the gag resolution came close to treason—so close that John Calhoun intervened to prevent his reelection. Because Pinckney now appealed to old Unionist voters as a moderate and because the Nullifiers' initial candidate was admittedly weak, Calhoun promised the old Unionist leadership that he would back any candidate they nominated so long as he opposed the "gag rule."

Petigru saw this as an opportunity for his close friend Hugh Legaré to reenter politics. So, despite his own preference for Pinckney's "gag rule" over Calhoun's demand for outright rejection of the petitions—which, he thought, would "put the debate on the footing most advantageous to the abolitionists"—he took the proffered bait.[35] First, however, he had to convince other Unionists who, like him, scented victory but also had their own favorite candidates. Some backed Joel Poinsett; others, Daniel Huger. Only when these men refused to run did Legaré's candidacy become feasible. The process of finding a willing and acceptable nominee, however, generated lasting friction among the seven Unionist stalwarts who made the choice. Only four of them actually supported Legaré, who was understood by all to be Petigru's candidate. In the end, therefore, it was Petigru's management of the subsequent campaign—aided by the last-minute withdrawal of the original Nullifier candidate—that gave Legaré the two-hundred-vote margin by which he unseated Pinckney. Petigru could also take personal satisfaction in this election, for he attracted enough votes to win his own reelection to the South Carolina House of Representatives and an even larger vote within the city limits of his constituency than did Legaré. In good spirits, therefore, each set out for his new post in late November, Legaré to Washington, Petigru to Columbia.[36]

As he had not in his first term in the legislature, Petigru now addressed a wide variety of issues. Reflecting the humane concerns that had marked his years as attorney general, he introduced pension bills for powerless persons not even resident in his district—the widow of his first schoolteacher in Long Canes among them. He assisted voteless free blacks, seeking legislative permission for one to "emancipate his wife and children." He defended the traditional right of free blacks to trade in wood. More broadly he pressed for an act to punish any abductor of a free person of color with a minimum fine of $1000 and at least a year's imprisonment, to which a further sentence of thirty-nine lashes was added should the kidnapped free Negro have been sold as a slave. As a member of the Judiciary Committee, an assignment doubtless promoted by his service as attorney general, he proposed pensions for superannuated judges and sought improvements in the equity court system. And, almost in a populist vein, he challenged South Carolina's uniquely antidemocratic practices by introducing a bill to turn over the election of president and vice president to the voters in congressional districts—and thus to terminate the legislature's casting the state's vote in presidential elections.[37]

The larger part of his legislative activity, however, clearly identified Petigru as a nascent Whig. He favored state support for internal improvements. He voted to increase the salary of the superintendent of public works as a measure "absolutely necessary to prevent the entire abandonment of the whole system of internal improvements and public works." He backed the expansion of private transportation enterprises, presenting petitions to charter both the Charleston and New York and the Charleston and Savannah steam packet companies. When the House debated a bill authorizing limited partnerships, Petigru opposed amendments that would prohibit "assignments and liens in favor of preferred creditors" and thus restrict the new business form. Although he voted to close the state land office, he cosponsored a bill "to confer on aliens the [otherwise illegal] privilege of holding real estate" in the privately developed town of Hamburg, across the Savannah River from Augusta, Georgia. While he furthered Whig economics in his own state, he also supported the Whigs' national program, opposing a resolution to support the admission of Texas as a state because the "spirit of disunion" was rampant there.[38]

Petigru's Whiggish proclivities, however, were the final blow to his remaining hopes for political distinction, because just as a national two-party system was emerging in the late 1830s, South Carolina became a determinedly one-party state. And if that party was not wholly Jacksonian Democratic, it assuredly was not Whig. The specific crisis that sealed Petigru's fate arose through the Whigs' opposition to the Van Buren administration's plan for a federal "subtreasury" banking system, which was designed to serve as the government's bank and thus to provide a centralized replacement for the privately managed Second Bank of the United States, whose recharter Jackson had vetoed. Jackson had already destroyed the monopoly the bank had enjoyed as the sole depository of federal funds and the financial power it had had, as the country's central bank, to control other banks' issue of banknotes. But in placing federal accounts withdrawn from the Second Bank in state-chartered private banks (the so-called pet banks), Jackson had, quite unintentionally, destroyed all banking controls and unleashed a proliferation of credit, which fed speculation in government lands. And when the president had finally capped the wild emission of bank paper with his 1836 "specie circular," which mandated that all debts owed the United States be paid in gold and silver, the Panic of 1837 had followed.[39]

All along, Petigru had been a persistent critic of Jackson's economic policies. Clearly a remedy was needed. But in his eyes it was not Van Buren's subtreasury plan, which he denounced almost as soon as it became public. During the extra session of Congress that met in September 1837 to consider the new president's proposal, Petigru, who was in Washington at the time, went up to the Capitol to hear the debate. He was astounded by Calhoun's support of this "monstrous . . . scheme for doing away with bank paper and of course with credit, and ruining all who are in debt." Three months later, when the South Carolina legislature considered a resolution favoring a government bank that would collect and disburse federal monies in specie only, Petigru opposed it as forcefully as he could. Southern trade and commerce, he argued in his "Speech Against the Banking Resolution," depended on a credit system made possible only by banknotes and the private banks that issued them. Conceding that the present panic did indeed reveal significant problems in that system, he nevertheless maintained that a retrogression to a specie-based monetary system would be disastrous. "Paper money," he told the representatives, "is the child of civilization." Replacing "the bulky and cumbersome notation of metals" with "the more comprehensive and diffusive medium of paper" provided not just a flexible currency supply but the resources for economic expansion that, in turn, had made possible the "improvement of the social condition of mankind" and was itself the outgrowth of the "diffusion of intelligence, and the natural progress of commerce."[40]

He spoke in vain. The legislature adhered to "the new scheme that Mr. Calhoun patronize[d]" and backed the resolutions supporting it by votes of nine or ten to one. This left Petigru—once again—"in a dead minority." And Legaré, who opposed Van Buren's subtreasury bill in Congress, fared no better. His Whiggish course only deepened the split among Charleston Unionists that the struggle over his nomination in 1836 had begun. For Petigru as for Legaré, the nadir came when Joel Poinsett, now President Van Buren's secretary of war, opposed the nomination of any congressional candidate who failed to back the administration's measure. Both Legaré and Petigru stood firm. And both watched their Charleston constituency diminish until only the "commercial classes" remained. Finally, in the 1838 fall elections, Legaré lost his seat in Congress, and Petigru lost his in the state legislature.[41]

As South Carolina Unionists increasingly drifted into the Democratic ranks, where their former Nullifier opponents had already entrenched

Caroline Carson's copy (1881) of Thomas Sully's
romanticized portrait of James L. Petigru painted in 1842.
(South Carolina Historical Society)

themselves, Petigru was ever more conspicuous as a Whig. Already acknowledged in 1838 as the behind-the-scenes wheelhorse of the newly visible faction, he identified publicly with them in 1840, openly supporting the Whig ticket. Actually, Petigru would much have preferred Henry Clay to William Henry Harrison, whose nomination, he wryly observed, was one more proof of "the folly of mankind." And when Harrison died after only a month in office, Petigru scorned John Tyler as a "prig of a President." Even though Tyler appointed Legaré attorney general, the fruits of the 1840 election were bitter indeed. "His accidency," Petigru feared, was not just an "oddity" but an "imbecillity." The best Tyler could do would be either to "resign [the presidency] or go over to the Democrats."[42]

Long before this culmination of his political frustrations, Petigru had turned his yearning for something more toward economic ventures. He had determined to pursue that "taste for gain, the *sacra fames auri*," which he had convinced himself might be "the most innocent kind of excitement . . . [for] 'the middle ages.' " But the gains he anticipated were social as well as economic. In a society that associated high status with plantation ownership, it was common for men who had accumulated capital from commercial or professional careers to invest it in land and slaves to validate their success. Petigru was pressed to do likewise by his friends, among them William Grayson, who believed that however one had begun his career, he ended it, "if prosperous, as a proprietor of a rice or cotton plantation." Even before he had entered into active electoral politics Petigru had, in fact, acquired a plantation on the Savannah River. In 1830 he paid $15,000 for its six hundred acres and a workforce of forty-one slaves, both of which he intended to enlarge until they should provide an ample income and a future of leisurely retirement.

For nine years Petigru planted rice, added adjacent tracts of land, and bought additional slaves until his workforce numbered 125. To do so, however, he had constantly to borrow money, for which the newly purchased land and laborers were collateral. Moreover, despite its expansion, the plantation remained, in his eyes, "no great thing." In an area where multiple plantation ownership was common, it was, if not the "sorry undertaking" Petigru called it, still not a vast enterprise.[43] Like all farmers, Petigru faced good and bad years: an unexpectedly good crop in 1832 was canceled out by an almost total loss in 1834, when frost and fall storms pummeled his crops and a cholera epidemic threatened his slaves. In 1835, his peak crop year, he realized between $8000 and $9000; but his expenses ate up so much of his profits that his greatest satisfaction came from the "striking improvement in the moral and physical condition of the negroes" on his estate. "When I took them," he wrote Jane North, "they were naked and destitute, now, there is hardly one that has not a pig at least, and with few exceptions, they can kill their own poultry whenever they please."[44]

If his plantation represented traditional values, Petigru's other investments displayed his support for economic growth and innovation. A moderately heavy purchaser of shares in his state's first railroad in 1830, he actively promoted stock sales in Robert Hayne's visionary scheme for a Charleston to Cincinnati line in 1836. Although it seemed at the time a risky investment, Petigru went ahead anyway in the hope that the shares would "one day be worth more than they are now." And to ensure that his other investments gave a better return, he actively engaged in corporate oversight. For several years he served on the board of directors of the Santee Canal Company, which provided a water route to Charleston from an area that produced especially high quality cotton. A shareholder in the New Charleston Theater, perhaps more for cultural than economic reasons, he at least cut his losses by acting also as its solicitor through the years when the theater, which burned to the ground in 1838, was rebuilt and whose owners then defaulted on its loans.[45]

Most revealing of Petigru's economic outlook, however, was his involvement in banking. The Bank of Charleston, chartered in 1834 to provide the capital resources and commercial service that the Charleston branch of the Bank of the United States had formerly provided, was central to civic boosters' plans for the city's economic growth. Capitalized initially at $2 million, the new bank was launched amid intense speculative competition for its twenty thousand shares of stock. Established banks extended credit far beyond their reserves to speculators who readily acknowledged that they were subscribing far beyond their capacity to pay. When the subscription lists closed, avarice had generated pledges to buy forty times the number of available shares, for which, theoretically, subscribers were prepared to pay some $81 million.[46]

To Petigru all this resembled nothing quite so much as a "real Mississippi Scheme"—a bubble just waiting to burst. Yet he too was caught up in the speculation mania, even though he proved to be, "simple man" that he was, greatly undersubscribed—for he had signed on for only four times the number of shares that he actually wanted. Despite his association of this exuberant speculation with the extremism of nullification exponents, who now were dedicating themselves to "the riches of stock jobbing," he seemed as unable as they to resist the lure.[47] So, when James Hamilton, who had stoked the speculative fires to ensure his election as the bank's first president, asked Petigru to be its solicitor, the former law partner jumped at the chance.

In his new post Petigru fostered private banking as he could not in the legislature. After only two years of operation, the Bank of Charleston had so prospered that it reported deposits of $6 million and regularly paid 5 percent semiannual dividends on its stock. Accordingly, in February 1837, the shareholders voted to double its capitalization to take advantage of the full potential its charter permitted. But with a sharp eye to their own profits, they also resolved to limit the sale of the new stock, which presumably would be as much in demand as the original issue, to current stockholders. Petigru, defending this procedure, pointed out that the charter required that only the original stock offering be open to all would-be subscribers throughout the state.[48]

Many of those who owned no stock did not see it that way. So strident was their response, so reflective of Jacksonian antimonopoly sentiment, that in June a public protest meeting called by Theophilus Fisk nearly turned into a riot. Fisk, a peripatetic Yankee cleric who united, or so Petigru thought, "the character of a demagogue to that of a Universalist," touched raw nerves among those excluded from the bank's financial rewards as well as those who scorned its "sordid money getting disposition" altogether. In response, the bank's defenders, Petigru among them, fired back: "Before I knew what I was about," he wrote vividly to Jane North, "I was speaking or screaming with passion," drawing so much support that "poor Fisk was routed on every side."[49]

Routed poor Fisk may have been, but the bank soon held back for its own reasons. By June, Charlestonians, like other Americans, had already been caught short by the Panic of 1837. Crop prices plummeted; money became tight; merchants and land speculators were pinioned between government requirements that customs duties, land purchases, even postage be paid for in specie and all local banks' refusal to redeem their notes in hard money. It was only prudent that in such circumstances the Bank of Charleston postpone its second stock issue. Prudence, however, resembled blatant self-interest in the eyes of the bank's enemies, an impression reinforced two years later when the bank, better prepared for financial crisis than it had been in 1837, not only redeemed its own bank notes in specie but refused the notes of all other Charleston banks that, bowing to national pressures, were forced to suspend specie payments. Angered by its cavalier independence, the rest of the banking community joined the popular hostility by condemning what they perceived as the Bank of Charleston's unprincipled ploy to drive its competitors to the wall.

During the long depression that followed the panic, their collective ire sparked public actions to rein in the aggressive young bank. In 1838 the state sought a court order to compel the bank to sell its new stock issue, just as it had the old, on the open market. In presenting the state's case, Attorney General Henry Bailey reversed the opinion he had earlier given that the bank's plan was perfectly legal. Any embarrassment that reversal produced was only temporary, for both the lower and appeals courts ruled that Bailey had been right in the first place, that the Bank of Charleston could indeed limit sales of its new stock to its stockholders. Only Judge John Richardson dissented, and that in language more political than legal. At the very heart of his minority opinion was Richardson's blunt comparison of the Charleston bank with Nicholas Biddle's monopolistic Bank of the United States.[50]

Many shared Richardson's views, and popular anger persisted. Indeed, as the depression deepened, businesses failed, and unemployment soared, public hostility spread to all banks, until in 1840 the state legislature forbade any bank's suspending specie redemption of its notes and required all banks to amend their charters accordingly. Though it faced the loss of its charter if it did not comply, the Bank of Charleston defiantly refused to modify the terms of its incorporation. By May 1841, therefore, it was back in court fighting for its very existence. When, in an address to a Charleston bankers' convention the previous February, Petigru had outlined a bold challenge to the new law, he had been opposed by his former political colleague Christopher Memminger, solicitor for the Planters and Mechanics Bank. Memminger, who had as a legislator supported the independent treasury resolutions, made a Jacksonian defense of the legislature's action, denouncing both monopolies and unredeemable paper money and asserting that whenever a corporation "cease[d] to perform the trust for which it was created, or abuse[d] any of the power or privileges conferred," it automatically forfeited its charter. In response, Petigru attacked both the new law and Memminger's defense of it. Relying once again on the federal Constitution and following John Marshall's opinion in the 1819 *Dartmouth College* case, just as Judge O'Neall had done in the *Medical College* case nine years earlier, he contended that a state could not unilaterally alter or revoke a corporation's charter, "because a charter is a contract, which cannot be changed, without the consent of both parties."[51]

Of Charleston's seven banks, three followed Petigru's reasoning and refused to amend their charters. When the state moved to enforce the law, lawyers for both the State Bank and the Bank of South Carolina let Petigru take the lead, aware, as was Attorney General Bailey, that the case against the Bank of Charleston was the state's weakest. Petigru, with his partner, Henry Lesesne, fought back on far narrower grounds than Petigru had argued at the bank convention. Instead, they convinced the court that because the legislature had allowed the charter to stand unchallenged after the Bank of Charleston had suspended specie payments in 1837 and had, by implication, reaffirmed that charter when, in 1839, it passed an act permitting the bank to modify its schedule of installment payments for the new stock issue, the state was barred by its own actions from forcing a charter amendment in 1840. The argument was convincing and the bank won its case.[52]

After the state lost its case in the Court of Appeals at Law, it made a final appeal to the Court of Errors. But in February 1842 it lost there also. Chancellor William Harper, writing for a unanimous bench, concluded that the passage of the 1839 act that permitted the delay in paying new stock installments had indeed reconfirmed the bank's charter. Unfortunately, the other two banks that had refused to amend their charters had to rely for their defense on the interpretation of a state charter as a contract protected by the federal Constitution that Petigru had earlier espoused at the bank convention. In 1843 the South Carolina appeals court rejected that argument and the Bank of South Carolina was forced to revise its charter. The legal outcome suggests that Petigru's wide-ranging rejection of the law at the convention had been largely political in its intent; for in court, where his lawyer's obligation to protect his client's interests was paramount, he confined himself to a narrower and, as it turned out, much surer defense.[53]

A comprehensive view of Petigru's various roles in the financial crises of the late 1830s and the depression years that followed portrays the uncertain ground on which this urban, Whiggish, ambitious South Carolina lawyer stood. In a society where successful merchants and professional men looked to planting as the most socially desirable long-term investment, Petigru had, before he entered politics, bought the Savannah River rice plantation to secure his future. Yet he went on to advocate economic developments designed primarily to benefit urban Charleston, and he put his professional expertise at the service of a profit-driven private banking system that was minimally responsive to planters' credit needs. Moreover, with James Hamilton, Robert Y. Hayne, and other erstwhile nullification leaders, he was prominent in efforts to modernize city government and develop the transportation networks and commercial services they believed were essential to the city's prosperity. Theirs was a program in which the state's agricultural majority had little interest and which, when times were hard, that majority came to oppose vociferously. In the end, Petigru's drive toward riches, though shared with merchants and planters alike, produced the same result as had his Unionist politics, leaving him isolated amid a shrinking minority.

Nor did his own finances prosper. If in the state's war against the Bank of Charleston Petigru had proved a resourceful attorney and a shrewd tactician, he was considerably less astute in managing his own business affairs. While the rash speculation associated with its organization never tainted the bank's subsequent standing, other financial ventures into which James Hamilton drew Petigru embraced a wild extravagance that eventually brought financial ruin to both men. To understand Petigru's extraordinary involvement in Hamilton's tangled schemes demands more, however, than a simple acquaintance with nineteenth-century economic history. The extremely close friendship between two men apparently so different and the sense of obligation it imposed on Petigru reveal much about his personality. Hamilton, only three years his friend's senior, had attained with ease the advantages Petigru had gained only by hard personal effort. Hamilton came from a wealthy and well-connected family. He had a public persona that attracted the patronage of elite men and the votes of the populace. In economics as in politics he displayed an imaginative derring-do that knew no limits. In the mid-1830s Hamilton had grand plans for direct packet service between Charleston and Liverpool, but he managed to charter just two coastal lines and operate only one. After the panic drove cotton prices down, he tried, with a momentary success that preceded disaster, to corner the southern cotton market. Left virtually penniless, he then secured commission contracts to float a European loan for the newly independent Republic of Texas and to sell South Carolina state bonds in France and England. Hamilton's almost visionary style entranced Petigru and drew him irresistibly into utterly fantastic schemes. It was, in fact, a style Petigru knew well from his own father, from whose gambling and financial follies the young Petigru had struggled to escape. Yet, even as he approached fifty, he found the thrill of unrestrained adventure tempting, exciting, alluring.

Hamilton may have represented a part of Petigru's personality that the younger man had long kept at bay. Surely he had few defenses against Hamilton's enticing friendship and resisted none of the claims that it imposed. Petigru's openhandedness had long alarmed friends like Grayson, who saw in it a generosity "so profuse as to call for restraint." Indeed, Grayson had hoped that after he bought his plantation Petigru's hitherto unbridled proclivity to spend and lend would be curbed by the demands of his investment. Instead, being a planter seemed only to encourage Petigru's sense of noblesse oblige. Throughout the 1830s he lent money to friends on a grand scale. Often it was money he could ill afford to lose. When his own security was imperiled by the Panic of 1837, he responded to young R. Barnwell Rhett's confession that he faced ruin by saying, "You know I cannot keep money; but my credit is yours, in any manner you choose to use it, to the last dollar of the property I possess."[54]

In this way Petigru charted his own ruin. He could have covered his own speculations, but his obligations incurred with and for friends, mostly for the irresistible James Hamilton, far exceeded his worth. Together the two had formed the Ossawichee Company, through which they bought and operated a vast Alabama cotton plantation that, by the spring of 1842, had driven them $65,000 into debt. Together they had speculated in large chunks of the eight million acres of Choctaw lands in northern Mississippi that the federal government sold between 1833 and 1836 and were caught short when the Specie Circular ordered immediate payment in hard money. Huge though those debts were, they were overshadowed by Petigru's persistent willingness to sign Hamilton's notes as security for money the latter borrowed and spent on ventures in which his friend had no part and over which he exercised no control. In 1838 the Bank of Charleston alone held notes, cosigned by Petigru, for at least $25,000 owed by Hamilton, its former president and still one of its directors. Then, as the economic crisis worsened, other banks tallied Hamilton's indebtedness, which careened far beyond his—or Petigru's—ability to pay.[55]

Petigru realized his desperate position only gradually. As early as 1837 he knew that his western land speculations were "a great hindrance and clog." During the next five years his disillusionment came to include all his speculations. He had backed the Ossawichee Company obligations with mortgages on his Savannah River plantation, which he was therefore obliged to sell at a loss in 1839. Lacking specie, he, like many others, lost everything he had invested in Mississippi land.

By June 1842 his resources were virtually exhausted. But he was still responsible as security for at least $105,000 of Hamilton's debts (well over $1 million in 1990 dollars).[56]

Thus the road to riches on which Petigru had embarked ten years earlier ended in disaster. Demands for payment in specie, financial panic, drawn-out depression years, and, most of all, his naïveté in accommodating friends and his ineptitude in matters economic combined to kill his dreams for achieving something more than success as a lawyer. When he turned fifty in May 1839, he realized that his life was out of control. He had recently undergone another bout of severe illness and was "very much hampered [by] . . . symptoms of breaking down." Even though he soon bounced back and believed that he was finally on his "feet again strong," that illness cast its shadow. Tight finances fanned the growing tensions at home as tokens of social status slipped away with declining material resources. When he sold the plantation, he could only hope that Jane Amelia would in time become "reconciled to it, though she and Caroline dislike[d] it both very much." To add to their sense of decline as well as their discomfort, the family had, "for the first time in 14 years . . . no carriage, and at no time in 20 years," Petigru added, "has our house been so gloomy as at the very time when other people brush up and look as smart as they can to bring out a daughter." The very circumstances that curtailed Caroline's partying intensified her mother's insistence that her daughter marry money, while the loss of their carriage provided an irritant to rub raw Petigru's sense of responsibility for their misery. Jane Amelia's refusal to leave the house because "the humble footing on which our equipage now is, viz, the plan of borrowing" shamed her was both a private and a public rebuke. "Ruin," her husband concluded in 1842, is "a thing that has various modes of torment"—not least of which was his wife, "who like Rachel would not [be] comforted."[57]

In his darkest moments Petigru almost wished to end it all. He envied Robert Hayne, who was almost his exact contemporary, when he died suddenly in 1839, for it seemed "another instance of his good fortune" that he died "before his fortune had deserted him." Lamenting his own fate, he wrote Adele in 1841 asking, "What is there that Debt will not do? It is the next greatest destroyer to the grave." But it was not only debt. Dan was already deep in the trouble that led to his suspension from Princeton the next year; Caroline had just embarked on a marriage difficult from its start; Sue was in open rebellion against both parents; his wife was "very poor in health"; and he himself was "poor in every thing else." His only hope lay in the unlikely possibility that Hamilton would somehow collect the funds necessary to rescue them both. But when that consummate speculator returned late in 1841 with no commissions from his European missions, having failed to generate interest in either Texas or South Carolina investments, Petigru realized that his own fate was sealed. There was "scarcely a hope," he wrote to Legaré in January 1842, that he could avoid either accepting failure by assigning all his remaining assets to his creditors or arranging a somewhat less demeaning agreement to pay what he could and then be released.[58]

Yet, when he finally came to grips with that reality, he was surprised by the tranquility it brought. In June, when the several banks that held his own notes for $20,000 as well as those he had cosigned for others agreed to settle for ten cents on the dollar and to allow him to keep his Charleston home and office, he was almost joyful. He had at least escaped the stigma of bankruptcy under the new federal law, which in 1842 in South Carolina alone had produced four hundred bankruptcy actions. But to pay off even the 10 percent of his indebtedness that the settlement required, he had somehow to raise $13,000. Once again he borrowed, tapping his brother Tom, who had married well, and friends whose circumstances were better than his own. So he was still in debt. But most demanding of all, his sense of honor compelled him to devote a major portion of his future earnings to paying the banks the 90 percent from which they had just released him.[59]

Scarred in his mid-thirties by wrenching personal disaster, humbled in his mid-forties by thorough political defeat, Petigru at fifty-three looked back Janus-like on the loss of the material security he thought he had won and forward to the seemingly endless labor that redeeming his honor would demand.

FIVE

—•—◄⦂◉⦂►—•—

Practicing Law

For eleven years his debts of honor haunted James Petigru. By 1854, however, he had paid off every penny of the major indebtedness he had composed with the banks in 1842. But that was not all. As other Hamilton obligations came to light, he assumed all those for which he felt any responsibility. Few were as potentially catastrophic as those that were dragged through the courts in *Hamilton v. Hamilton* until it reached the Court of Errors in 1845.[1] The main thrust of the case was to separate Mrs. Hamilton's property from that of her husband so that it would be shielded from his creditors. The immediate issue that involved Petigru personally was the collaboration between James Adger, a powerful local businessman, and the Bank of Charleston, on whose board Adger sat, to rig the bidding on the court-ordered sale of Hamilton's Savannah River plantation, Rice Hope. Their plan was to guarantee that their own claims would be met—but at the expense of several smaller creditors whose notes were backed by the second and third mortgages on Rice Hope.

Petigru had arranged two of these smaller loans, assuring the lenders that their funds were adequately protected by that collateral. Consequently, as a matter of professional ethics he felt responsible for the debts. But he was otherwise uninvolved in the legal contest until, at the last minute, the attorney who had been handling it suddenly had to leave town. With less than a day to prepare a convincing argument in what already seemed a desperate case, he nonetheless did so and addressed the nine judges and chancellors on the bench for four hours "with great acceptation." Skillfully laying bare the fraudulent nature of the prearranged bidding, he won the case. His victory was doubly welcome. First, he secured the interests of all the creditors and thereby "escaped from the dreadful responsibility" of the $13,000 due to those

James L. Petigru, painted by George Flagg in 1854. (All rights reserved.
McKissick Museum, University of South Carolina)

he had put at risk; second, he saved Mrs. Hamilton's sizable interest in
Rice Hope.[2]

Such narrow escapes from the burden of redeeming still more obligations and, more important, his assiduous labor to earn enough to
pay off the huge sums he had composed in 1842, produced a joyous

Petigru family Christmas celebration in 1853. At last Petigru was free from debt—a freedom gained without disrupting his friendship with James Hamilton, the man largely responsible for it. When the family gathered that December at Dean Hall, J. Johnston Pettigrew observed that his cousin acted "like a young man entering the world afresh."[3] But James Petigru was no longer young; and he was barely more financially secure than he had been a decade earlier. Though he had long since been cured of his mania for speculation, he still lent unhesitatingly to friends, family members, even hard-pressed clients. Except for the Sullivan's Island house that Hamilton signed over to him in 1844, the eleven intervening years had added no property to his holdings. Even in succeeding years he added little beyond some railroad bonds and perhaps as many as 2500 acres of uncultivated land. As he confessed to his sister Adele in 1850, he simply lacked the self-discipline to put by for the future. His "wandering desultory mode of thinking" always left him paying for "things that are past & gone." What he once said of a friend he could as well have said of himself: he was a "spirited and generous" person but not the sort "that made money so easily, or so much of it."[4]

Yet Petigru did make money from his law practice. It brought in steady fees from clients who came to his office and others who corresponded with him from distant places. Somewhat more sporadically he earned large fees in court, and all in all he garnered an income considerably greater than that of most contemporary lawyers. An R. G. Dun rating in 1855 guessed that his law partnership grossed between $20,000 and $30,000 a year and warned businessmen that only "cases of great importance sh[oul]d be placed in their hands, when they will warrant the payment of a *big* fee." The largest of those big fees was the $10,000 Petigru received for appearing in the United States Supreme Court in 1854 to defend the will of Mrs. Eliza Kohne and its bequests of property that almost thirty years earlier her husband had left her to use for charitable purposes. More customary were the $1000 to $1500 fees he regularly received for arguing cases before one of the state appeals courts. At the other extreme were the individual charges, ranging from $2 to $10, for routine office business: drawing legal documents, collecting debts, writing letters, verifying deeds, and the like. That most clients paid the charges, large and small, willingly is borne out by a family story about one who did not. When a Charleston cotton factor returned a bill he thought extravagant, Petigru scribbled

across its face "Cheap as dirt," sent it back, and received full payment
at once.[5]

From the time he had become attorney general in 1822, moreover,
Petigru never lacked for private clients in a city that had boasted an
unusually talented bar since late colonial days, when a large proportion of its attorneys had studied in the English Inns of Court. During
the 1840s and 1850s, either alone or in conjunction with a partner, he
averaged ten appeals court cases a year that were of sufficient importance to be officially recorded in printed court reports. More than a
third of them in the 1840s and half in the 1850s were probate cases
involving wills, trusts, or other aspects of inheritance. Another fifth of
them were creditors' suits against debtors, in which, ironically, Petigru
was distinctly more likely to represent creditors suing to collect funds
or competing with other creditors for a debtor's assets than to represent
the debtor.[6]

In addition to handling appeals cases, Petigru remained active in
the lower courts as well. Although after 1842 he rarely took criminal
cases, he appeared in roughly one-fourth of all the cases that came before the Charleston County Court of Equity during the 1840s and in
almost one-fifth during the next decade. In the equity court alone he
or a partner in his firm handled an average of forty-six cases in each
court session during the 1840s, forty during the 1850s.[7] And while no
dockets for the Charleston County Court of Common Pleas survive, it
is probable that Petigru was involved with almost equal frequency in
the civil cases that came before it.

As the years went by, the pace and volume of Petigru's practice reflected few concessions to advancing age. As late as 1858, when he was
nearly seventy, he admitted that he was always ready to join a colleague
in a case that promised a good fee, for he was still, he said, among those
"practitioners . . . that have need of all they can do." At the same time,
the nature of his practice did change. Increasingly Petigru, despite his
role in debt cases, represented defendants more often than plaintiffs.
And in the 1850s he so often advised compromise that he frequently
represented all parties to a dispute. This was most common in the cases
he took to the equity court expressly to formalize a compromise already
worked out by the contending parties (see appendixes A, B, and C for
compilations).[8]

The same spirit of compromise and conciliation marked his outgoing
office correspondence as time and again he advised clients to compro-

mise differences if they could, to seek arbitration rather than confrontation if they could not. Whether it was a dispute between the Haynes and the Middletons over allocation of space in a family burial vault or a disagreement between neighbors over boundary lines or a conflict between former partners over business assets, Petigru's advice was the same.[9] At least once he even pressed it on angry young men eager for a duel. When Dr. DeSaussure impugned the quality of William Heyward's bridge, and Heyward the soundness of DeSaussure's horse; and when the resulting suit for the value of the horse, which had been injured when it had shied at the bridge, drove Heyward to post DeSaussure as "mean"; and when, in consequence, DeSaussure challenged Heyward to a meeting at dawn, Petigru intervened. He arranged for a mutual friend to lead the doctor back from the brink while he himself induced Heyward, a "live specimen of the genus Planter," to accept the "interposition of friends." The friends, including the old lawyer himself, then drafted a retraction that both parties could accept without either losing honor. His success under such circumstances only added to Petigru's distinction as a peacemaker. His reputation for arranging acceptable compromises spread so far that in 1853 he was called to New York to arbitrate a dispute whose resolution cost telegraph inventor Samuel F. B. Morse a penalty of $40,000.[10]

Part of Petigru's increasing preference for mediation and arbitration may reflect changing attitudes associated with aging. But undergirding all his legal practice was his persistent preoccupation with justice. From his days as attorney general, his legal career was a testament to the law's obligation to balance public and private interests. But to do so justly the law must secure individual rights against public intrusion and vest society with the institutions and authority to protect those rights. "Liberty," he said in an 1844 Fourth of July oration, "is but a name, where the weak are not protected against the strong, nor justice armed with the power of defending the innocent, and punishing the guilty." Law was "the very bond of society," he told an audience of students two years later in Athens, Georgia. "It has its origin in the moral relations of man, and its spirit and essence consist of the principles of natural equity and justice."[11]

Because societies change over time, however, a stagnant system of law cannot serve justice. In the 1853 case of *Irving* v. *Robertson*, which involved imprisonment for debt, Petigru made this point explicit. "The common law is constantly altering to suit the circumstances of the times and place," he said, and law that might have suited England in the eighteenth century might not serve any legitimate purpose in nineteenth-century South Carolina. Specifically, he argued, to use the law to incarcerate a poor eccentric merely to satisfy a desire for revenge on the part of a wealthy but stingy merchant was so obviously unjust that modern laws implicitly, if not explicitly, precluded that ancient practice. Having won this case, Petigru elaborated the process of legal change still further in his 1858 presidential address to the South Carolina Historical Society. Defending the necessity of an iconoclastic process to make law consonant with new social realities, he asserted that "the jurists say, with justice, that nothing is certain which has not been questioned." [12]

Such a process, however, creates dilemmas for the practicing attorney, whose primary concern must be protecting his clients' interests rather than upholding abstract theories of justice or reshaping the law to suit new conditions. On the other hand, the greater possibility of serving justice by making the law fit new circumstances may have been the very magnet that drew Petigru so insistently toward equity practice. But in equity as in law courts, successful pleading must accord with previous judicial rulings and decisions. So, as a practical matter, Petigru fretted at the unpredictability of chancellor-made equity law. On the one hand, he was troubled by rulings "inconsistent with [his] ideas of justice"; on the other, he realized that a lawyer could serve few clients if he was limited to serving his own ideal justice. He once commented that a young colleague, despite his genius in unraveling intricate evidence and sorting out overlapping precedents, would "never make an advocate" so long as "he must have equity, justice, law and morality all on his side before he will take a case." [13]

Pitting the pursuit of ideal justice against an attorney's obligation to advise his clients knowledgeably and defend their interests effectively made Petigru open to change only as long as it was gradual rather than abrupt, evolutionary rather than revolutionary. Indeed, he seldom confronted directly the questions that shaped antebellum legal innovation in northern states, especially in New England, where large corporate textile factories, burgeoning railroad networks, and extensive entrepreneurial development challenged the traditional legal landscape, a slightly modified American version of English common law and pre-Revolutionary legislation. If the hypothesis that in reality law largely reflects its social, political, and economic environment is true, then

Petigru's conservative reliance on that background is hardly surprising. After all, from 1844 until 1850 South Carolina added only 38 miles of track to the 260 miles laid between 1830 and 1843. And in 1850, except for Charleston with its 40,000 inhabitants, towns of 2500 or more accounted for less than 3 percent of the state's white population; and even the new textile mills built near them could not stem the overall 40 percent decline in cotton goods production during the decade. Indeed, even in 1850, its antebellum manufacturing heyday, South Carolina reported less than a million dollars invested in cotton manufacture.[14] Moreover, the state legislature, which chartered relatively few entrepreneurial ventures during the antebellum decades, was slow to modify traditional corporate forms designed for corporations whose primary purpose was to provide public service rather than private gain. Given its constituents' preference for investing in land and slaves rather than corporate stock, there was little pressure to do otherwise.

Yet, however much South Carolina law lacked the stimulus of rapid economic development and the legal controversies it spawned elsewhere over redefining the reasonable use of power-generating streams, corporate responsibility for injuries to persons and the property of others, and investors' responsibility for corporate debts, Petigru did face situations that demanded change. Such was the case in *Pell* v. *Ball,* whose complexity produced a series of contests and decisions that over a six-year period did indeed reshape old ways to accommodate modern needs.[15] The initial trial addressed evidentiary problems created by technological innovation. How should one interpret very scant circumstantial evidence to determine which heirs should inherit the property of Rhode Island–born Anna Channing Ball and her South Carolina husband, Hugh Swinton Ball, after both had died when the steamship *Pulaski* exploded and quickly sank just outside Charleston harbor on June 13, 1838?

At first glance the matter seemed simple enough to resolve, although the property involved was extensive and reflected the different sectional economies whence it derived. Hugh's will bequeathed to his wife all the stocks, bonds, and other intangible property, totalling nearly $71,000, that Anna had owned before her marriage but which became his by the common law governing femes covert (married women). He also left her one quarter of his own $175,000 estate, comprising mostly the land, slaves, buildings, and other appurtenances of a large plantation. The remainder of that plantation he left to his mother and brother.

But settling the question of who had died first when the *Pulaski* sank was essential, for that would determine how the will was administered. If Hugh had died before Anna, her sisters, Mary Channing Pell and Catharine Channing Sumner, would inherit all that Hugh had willed to his wife. But if Anna had died first, even if only by minutes, not only would any Yankee claim to Hugh's plantation be removed, but the part of Anna's wealth that her sisters and their husbands could claim would be notably diminished. It was that issue alone that was settled in the initial trial. Hugh Legaré, Petigru's associate in representing Anna's heirs, won the jury with a melodramatic rendition of one witness's rec-ollection of the *Pulaski*'s last minutes. Summoning her husband's aid as the ship slid beneath the waves, Anna "called, but he never answered. He was dead! dead! dead!" [16] It was a stunning performance. The jury concluded that Hugh had died before Anna and therefore that Anna's heirs could claim her full inheritance.

The Ball family's subsequent attempts to limit the size and nature of that claim played itself out in the equity courts and generated at least three appeals court decisions. In the first, Petigru persuaded the chancellors to include as Anna's property more than the specific stocks and bonds that she had inherited from Yankee kin and that Hugh still owned at his death. The court ruled that her estate included current holdings that Hugh's accounts showed he had bought with proceeds gained by selling some of the investments that Anna had owned on their wedding day. That decision not only favored the Pells and Sum-ners but substituted the monetary value her dowry represented for the continued ownership of specific stocks as the test to determine the ex-tent of the property that Hugh intended to return to Anna as her own. Subsequent decrees pushed this legal recognition of the cash nexus still further. The claims of Anna's heirs to one quarter of the money value of the Ball plantation was recognized, as was the inutility of passing part of a South Carolina plantation to residents of Rhode Island. On these grounds the court ordered its sale, with the proceeds to be divided as the will specified. In so doing, a South Carolina equity court refuted the contention of the Ball heirs that the plantation was a sociocultural as well as an economic unit that could not be sold without destroying the value of the three quarters that was their inheritance.

It is impossible to determine Petigru's underlying arguments in de-feating the final appeal, for the ostensible issue before the Court of Errors was the Balls' attempt to move the case from the equity courts to the law courts. But whatever the technicalities, there is little question that Petigru's argument in a lower court, whose ruling the Court of Errors left standing, had effectively demolished the Balls' insistence that the plantation was a special category of property and that selling it to convert its worth into more readily negotiable assets equally useful to Rhode Island and South Carolina heirs was inequitable. Whatever his logic, Petigru, by securing the interests of his clients in the *Pell* case, also promoted changes in judicial treatment of property in South Carolina that resembled changes that were rapidly altering contemporary northern practice.

Most of Petigru's probate work, however, did not have the far-reaching implications of the *Pell* case. Indeed, most of it never involved court appearances at all but was confined to counseling clients from his office. Those clients were almost always southerners, even when they were not Carolinians. As time wore on, and especially in the 1850s, his probate practice increasingly involved the wills and estates of old friends and colleagues whose adult children looked to their fathers' friend for legal guidance. Because their ties were personal as well as professional, they often got more than strictly legal advice. This was especially true when they engaged in family feuds over the distribution of property, the value of which and even the basic nature of which was agreed upon by all parties, as it was not in the *Pell* case.

Such was the controversy following the death of Langdon Cheves in 1857.[17] Cheves's will, written before his final illness and the mental confusion it produced, had not been altered when his youngest son, Hayne, died in Italy unmarried and without progeny. The elder Cheves, himself near death, was not informed of Hayne's death and therefore never contemplated how he might wish to handle the plantation his will set aside for that son. This circumstance threw Cheves's careful distribution of property among his children and their heirs into disarray. The will contained explicit bequests to each child and then directed that the residue of his estate should be equally divided among his three daughters as an equitable balance to the plantations he had long before his death given to each of his three older sons. How, then, should the plantation destined for Hayne be handled? Was it part of the residue to be divided among his sisters, which would give them an unintended advantage over their brothers? Or should all of Hayne's siblings receive an equal share of their dead brother's portion, since they were equally heirs at law to whatever the will did not bequeath specifically? Any adjudication would have to resolve whether the plantation earmarked for Hayne was or was not part of the residue. It was not the legal technicality but rather emotional assessments of greed and fairness, jealousy and justice that set family members against each other.

Langdon, Jr., his father's executor, turned to Petigru for legal advice; and Petigru, after a careful examination of the will to determine both its specific provisions and the elder Cheves's intent, advised Langdon that the bequest to Hayne should be divided among all the heirs at law. To avoid a dispute over conflicting interpretations, he urged Langdon to compromise within the family and stay away from a destructive court battle. But family members had other agendas. One Cheves son-in-law insisted on pressing his wife's claim as a residuary legatee to one-third rather than one-sixth of Hayne's share. Another equivocated. And Louisa Cheves McCord, a widowed sister, agonized over her desire for more property and her fear of the scandal a family squabble would produce. The two surviving brothers and the widow of a third adopted Petigru's advice. But even they were not in full agreement, for Langdon badly misunderstood his brother John's commitment to the slaves who, at Langdon, Sr.,'s death, were on the plantation meant for Hayne. John insisted on fulfilling the promise his father had made to them that they would be allowed, at some future time, to join their families on other Cheves holdings.

All these differences might have been negotiated amicably within the family circle had not Charles Haskell determined to go to court to secure his wife's claim to one-third of those slaves, whom he planned to take to his new plantation in Arkansas. In 1858 that decision led to *Haskell v. Cheves*, and all the restraints that had previously tempered the family dispute gave way. Petigru confronted an emotional and legal maelstrom as the heirs he represented—Langdon, John, Louisa, and the other brother-in-law—pressed their individual interests. Previously muted anticipations became angry demands. It was hard enough to juggle their incongruent expectations, but stress increased when, in 1859, the equity appeals court found that Hayne's share should be divided only among the sisters as residual heirs. With Haskell triumphant and eager to move his coffle to Arkansas, family acrimony reached a peak. Brother John was outraged that Petigru had not represented his claims more vigorously. Langdon, in defeat, sided with John in blaming Petigru. In defiance of the court order they tried to block the sale of the disputed plantation. Thoroughly exasperated, Petigru chided Langdon that going to court was not child's play; nor was obeying the court's orders "a matter of discretion." "The order of the court is the law, and the law must be obeyed."[18] Only the force of that external compulsion propelled the warring family members to the mutual concessions that Petigru had advised in the first place. Haskell let the Cheves brothers and the other brother-in-law buy his wife's share of the slaves. McCord similarly turned her share into cash. Family honor, however strained, was at last redeemed by an arrangement accommodating the promises old Langdon had made to his slaves. And Petigru at last "rejoice[d] in the general pacification of all interests in the family politics."[19]

It was not only the Cheves family politics that enmeshed him at this time, for Petigru had to deal simultaneously with the feuds set off by the death of his old mentor, Daniel Elliott Huger. The Huger estate was large but not easily divisible. Nonetheless, Petigru hoped to keep disputes about its distribution out of court. Once again, however, he ended up in the equity courts, as attorney this time for the four sons whom the will named as executors. Again the fate of family slaves was made the nub of a much broader competition. The executors allowed Jackey, the steward and key keeper on Huger's extremely profitable Savannah River plantation, to designate which of the nine heirs should inherit him and his family. Seemingly this was a small matter to the heirs, though of great moment to a favorite servant. But so critical was Jackey to the successful operation of the plantation that his failure to choose one son-in-law as his new owner allegedly put that son-in-law at an impossible disadvantage in family negotiations that otherwise would have permitted him to buy that plantation. In the end, the court upheld the executors' right to recognize Jackey's choice of owners and settled a number of lesser disputes in a way that seemed to Petigru "likely to please all parties."[20] It did not, and Daniel, Jr., in a "public exhibition of impotent resentment," sought to appeal the decision. At that point, more as his father's friend than as a lawyer, Petigru told him bluntly that he could no longer represent a man "bent on running a muck" against so fair and decent an outcome.[21]

While his long friendships with the testators made the *Cheves* and *Huger* cases somewhat atypical of his extensive probate practice, Petigru's role as counselor in them was reasonably representative. All told, settling estates demanded that he expend emotional as well as intellectual energy and exposed him to endless examples of individual greed and family squabbling. Moreover, it bred an impatience with long-drawn-out procedures that he expressed most forcefully when, late in his career, while representing American heirs of an English will, he discovered that the British courts he had formerly revered could move at such a glacier-like pace as to deny justice altogether. His task, when he first undertook it, seemed simple enough. Working through the English firm that claimed to represent the estate's executors, he tried to arrange a simple distribution. After two years of negotiations, the London solicitors insisted that the settlement they had arranged must pass through a court of chancery. After another two years, still without a distribution, Petigru became suspicious: "The case wears very much the appearance of a suit got up for the sake of the costs, for the Master of the Rolls had decided no question, nor is there as far as I can see any question at all for his deliberation." Nor did changing his English correspondents resolve the matter. After eight years the case still languished in the same court, and Petigru was compelled to reflect on his lost idealism. "I used to suppose that everything English was best and carried this prepossession into professional affairs. . . . I am somewhat disabused of my credulity," he concluded wryly, "and like one that has been cured of a pleasing delusion, am sorry for it." [22] Nonetheless, if his probate practice bred a certain cynicism about human behavior, it also gave him many opportunities to guide clients away from litigation and toward the conciliation and compromise he much preferred.

Comparatively sparse though it was in his state, technological and corporate innovation did confront Petigru when his clients' problems forced him to address at a practical level what William Nelson has called the Americanization of the law, and Morton Horwitz, the transformation of American law. This became clear in a series of cases centered on the extent and limits of liability for fire damage caused when sparks thrown off by steam engines ignited cargoes they were transporting. In South Carolina both railroad and steamboat shipments overwhelmingly comprised baled cotton, a highly flammable substance and the state's primary cash crop. Before the introduction of steam power, custom and common law had held the carrier responsible for goods damaged under transport. But the decisions in some six appeals court cases between 1838 and 1847 forced South Carolina to follow the national pattern, which allowed steamboat and railroad operators to disclaim liability for both fire and water damage if they so forewarned shippers as part of a written contract.

Because Petigru represented railroad and steamboat operators in some cases, planters shipping cotton in others, and insurance companies in still another, he necessarily argued all sides of the issue and consequently developed neither a consistent theory of liability nor any uniform rationale for the shift. Nonetheless, though his role was far less clear-cut than that of the judges who rendered the decisions, he was part of the process that shifted the risks of steam-powered transportation from the entrepreneurs who profited from the new technology to the agricultural shippers who paid for it.[23]

In a similarly indirect way Petigru helped redefine the legal status of corporations. In 1842 he argued one of the two cases in which his appearance before the United States Supreme Court was reported. The case determined whether and under what circumstances a corporation—in this instance the Louisville, Cincinnati, and Charleston Rail Road—could be sued in federal courts.[24] Thomas W. Letson, a contractor, had sued the railroad for $18,140 owed him on a completed construction contract. The Federal Circuit Court for South Carolina, which heard the case, gave Letson the verdict, and the railroad responded with an action to remove the claim from federal jurisdiction. Nobody questioned that Letson was a New Yorker or that he was suing a corporation chartered by the South Carolina legislature and headquartered in Charleston. If that corporation was held to be a resident of South Carolina, the suit would fall under the provision of Article III of the United States Constitution, which permits a citizen of one state to sue a citizen of another in federal court. But the railroad maintained that it was not a citizen of South Carolina because some of its stockholders lived in other states. Therefore it could not be sued in a federal court.

Petigru, defending Letson's right to sue in federal court, answered the railroad's argument on relatively narrow and traditional grounds. If he were barred from the federal courts, Letson would have no appropriate recourse for the wrong done him. The railroad's assets were all in South Carolina and therefore beyond the reach of the state courts of New York, where Letson resided. And if the railroad's claim that its stockholders' varied residences made it a technical resident of no state, it would be beyond the reach of any state court. Surely, then, it would be erroneous "to hold that the plaintiff cannot proceed in the federal court against the corporation, because A. is a defendant; and yet that A. cannot be sued . . . anywhere or in any court."[25] At the next

level, Petigru sought to establish that the railroad was, in fact, a "resident" of South Carolina because it took action and assumed corporate
responsibility not through its stockholders but through its board of directors, all of whom did reside in the state. Likening a corporation to
a trust, he argued by analogy that a corporate board of directors was,
in essence, a trustee for all the stockholders. Thus the corporate headquarters and the residence of its directors determined its location, just
as a trustee's residence and place of business determined the location
of a trust. Stretching the analogy still further, he concluded that "a
corporation is but a state in miniature . . . the persons in whom the
powers of government are vested, are everywhere considered trustees
for the rest of the community."[26]

It was, however, not Petigru but Hugh Legaré, entering the *Letson*
case in his official capacity as United States attorney general, who argued for a new definition that reshaped legal doctrine. A corporation,
he asserted, was a legal person with all the rights the federal Constitution guaranteed other citizens, including access to the federal courts. In
formulating their strategy, as these two old friends and colleagues undoubtedly did, Petigru and Legaré developed alternative rationales for
subjecting a state-chartered corporation to the jurisdiction of federal
courts. Their goals, however, differed. Legaré, representing the public
interest, acted consciously to modify the law in response to the rapid
growth of the corporation as a business form. For him, Letson's consequent victory was incidental. He not only could but must stake out
broad grounds.

Petigru, on the other hand, was a private attorney responsible to his
client. Settling Letson's claim was his goal, and any legal redefinition
of a corporation was secondary. It was therefore appropriate for him to
be prudent, to argue his case in traditional terms and apply the long-
established legal definition of a trust to the business corporation. It is
ironic that Legaré's radical departure rather than Petigru's conservative premises secured Letson's access to federal courts. And though
the two lawyers had doubtless collaborated, it is significant of Petigru's preference for gradual change that he accepted the new definition
slowly and only partially. Subsequently he referred to corporations as
partnerships. But at least once, in 1844, the year of the *Letson* decision, he did call a corporation an "*individual*" with but "one will."[27]
In short, he accommodated his own arguments to change rather than
pioneering new legal theory.

A major obstacle to analyzing Petigru's legal response to nineteenth-century economic growth is that he handled so few relevant cases. One case, however, was so unusual that it drew the marked attention of his contemporaries. From 1856 until the Civil War intervened, in circumstances almost the exact reverse of *Letson*, Petigru represented without fee a railroad caught in the toils of an apparently corrupt builder.[28] The Blue Ridge Rail Road had contracted in 1853 with Anson Bangs and Company to construct its road through difficult mountainous terrain in the northwestern corner of South Carolina. Bangs, though he was an experienced contractor, was so debt-ridden that within two years he reorganized his company and turned over the Blue Ridge project to A. Birdsall and Company. Birdsall had absolutely no experience in building railroads. The Blue Ridge therefore pronounced its contract with Bangs forfeited, and Birdsall immediately sued the railroad for damages.[29] From 1856 on, Petigru defended the Blue Ridge from the suits Birdsall pressed in federal district courts sitting variously at Marietta and Athens. Traveling to these Georgia towns not only exposed him to long and tiring journeys but fostered a series of mishaps, of which opposing counsel, resident in Marietta, near Georgia's western border, took every advantage. At times this pursuit of justice from a distance created a muddle fully as bad as Petigru's concurrent dealings with the English chancery courts. His letter seeking postponement of the first date set for the trial was lost in the mail, and, unknown to him, the trial proceeded as scheduled. In the absence of defense counsel the judge ruled that by failing to contest Birdsall's claim for compensation equal to the full amount of the original Bangs contract, the railroad had, in fact, agreed to pay.[30]

Then began a long series of moves and countermoves in which Birdsall's lawyers conceded not an inch to professional courtesy. Their readiness to press every advantage that their location gave them convinced Petigru that opposing counsel was every bit as dishonorable as Bangs and Birdsall. From pursuing the claims of another client, he was already familiar with Bangs's devious maneuvers to dodge his debts by constantly changing his company's form and location. Given the collusion between the two companies, he suspected that Birdsall was equally shifty. When his investigation of the latter's standing in his native New York turned up nothing incriminating, however, Petigru chose to believe that Birdsall's behavior only confirmed the old truism that "when folks go abroad to acquire a fortune" they often neglect "the rules of right and wrong between equals" that they may have followed at home.[31]

However unprincipled he believed the contractors were, Petigru focused his immediate ire on Birdsall's Georgia law firm, Cobb and Hull. He was infuriated, for example, by their frequent use of technical objections, like their refusal to agree to any exception or delay without demanding a quid pro quo. So when he caught Thomas R. R. Cobb, brother of Secretary of the Treasury Howell Cobb and codifier of Georgia law, in a series of technical errors, things rather looked up. With his characteristic humor Petigru described to his friends the "wonderful change" that made the Georgia lawyers "so tame instead of roaring"; and he joked with his colleagues about their legal crudities.[32] But while he wrote stern letters to Cobb and Hull exhorting them to more ethical behavior, he also extended to them the consideration and courtesy they had denied to him. When the case finally came to trial, the verdict in favor of the Blue Ridge Rail Road seemed to justify the considerable efforts he had made for the corporation.

The sense of relief that swept over him was, however, only momentary. Birdsall decided at once to appeal to the Supreme Court. Exhausted by the lengthy proceedings and disgusted by the tactics of opposing counsel, Petigru tried to defuse further litigation. Already testimony had involved close to one hundred witnesses scattered from New York to Georgia and had generated verbiage enough to fill 2500 printed pages. By 1858 court costs had already climbed to $10,000. And five years of repeated journeys to remote Georgia towns as the case "dragg[ed] its slow length along" had taken its physical toll on the chief defense counsel.[33]

So when Birdsall threatened to drag it out still further, Petigru was wholly dismayed. "I would," he wrote Thomas Cobb in 1860, "ten times rather settle without argument than undertake to show by argument what I believe." Although he regarded Birdsall and Company's claims as no better than a "ticket which they hold in the Lottery of opinion," he offered to buy out the firm's claim for $10,000 if they would take the jury verdict he had just won in the federal district court "as a positive thing; a decision, a finality."[34] They did not, and Petigru resigned himself to continue fighting. Ordinarily such arduous work over so long a period would have brought in a substantial fee. And in these last years of his life, when his health and practice had already begun to decline, such a fee would have been most welcome. But once again Petigru's idealism intervened. Because he believed that the railroad, funded in large part by public monies, had been wronged, he refused any compensation in this most unusual instance of pro bono representation.

Petigru's professional style, developed during his career to serve a wide variety of clients and causes, distinguished him among his contemporaries at least as much as did his legal knowledge and mastery of jurisprudence. But while many praised it, few recorded it. Yet there are enough contemporary reports and allusions to provide a glimpse of his ways with clients in his office and with jurors, witnesses, lawyers, and judges in the courtroom.

When in February 1849 J. Johnston Pettigrew first visited James Petigru, he waited his turn in one of several chairs placed in the back of the office to accommodate callers. Only a screen separated him from the attorney, who, though invisible, was not inaudible as he counseled the clients then with him. Listening unobserved, young Pettigrew caught the essence of his cousin's style. The older man questioned his clients closely and systematically to elicit all the information that might bear on their case. But apparently suspecting some "unfair dealing" on their part, he also "prob[ed] them to discover the truth." At no point did he offend them, for as Johnston wrote to another kinsman, "the reception [his clients] gave to his remarks was proof of his unbounded popularity, and was, at the same time, very amusing."[35]

Less amusing was Petigru's temper, which, though he customarily controlled it, sometimes flared unrestrained before students, clerks, and partners. On occasion he would, so Johnston reported, "distort his face, tear his hair, and look a picture of woe on account of a lost paper"— losses that increased with his age. On the other hand, observers agreed, his "want of controul over his passion" never broke out in court, though his familiars were well aware that a raised vein in his forehead signaled the anger that his "perfect mastery over himself upon what he considers a great occasion" hid from others.[36]

So too Petigru hid from all but friends and family members his boredom with long-drawn-out courtroom presentations. He once confessed to his brother-in-law Robert Allston that he was writing his letter "during a long speech" by opposing counsel, who probably thought he was "taking notes of his speech, but God knows," he added with a twinkle, "I am much better employed." His scorn for prolixity in others extended to himself. The brevity of his summations and the tightness of his arguments were famous "in an age when length and diffusiveness of speech [were] considered . . . a fundamental part of oratory." After studying with him and working in his office, Johnston Pettigrew was impressed by his cousin's "faculty of condensation" both in and out of court, his ability to say "all that he has to say in as short a time as possible."[37]

While published court records give the same impression, they are too dry to convey a stage presence that even actors might envy. One colleague recalled the wide range of Petigru's voice in a romantic metaphor. At its highest it resembled the shrillness of a bagpipe; at its softest, the breath of a flute; at its loudest, the blast of a bugle; at its deepest, the thunder of organ swells.[38] Petigru, however, was better remembered for the cultivated comic relief, the folksy humor he used to relieve courtroom tensions. A former juryman many years later recounted one such instance. Petigru, he recalled, began his case for the defense by bowing "to the jury an' ever'body very perlite. He didn't bring no books. He started easy like, an' said that his friend Lowyer Noble talked very nice, but all that he had read out of the books had nothin' to do with this case; an' before he had talked five minits he had Lowyer Noble's argyment busted wide open. He then begin to talk better'n any preacher I ever hear."[39] In such performances Petigru was fully conscious of the effect he wanted. He once instructed his colleague Benjamin Perry, who was to fill in at a trial that Petigru could not attend, in the techniques of courtroom theatrics. Perry should start the final summary of the case "humble and submissive as becomes a debtor, for in scripture there is little difference between a Debtor and Sinner. Try to get a postponement; which they will probably refuse. But when you have drained the cup of penitence, turn upon them like a tyger & my word for it you will scatter them."[40]

But if Petigru consciously cultivated the jurors and taught opposing counsel by example, he was brusque with colleagues who failed in their commitments to him and his clients. A fellow attorney who reneged on his expressed willingness to serve as a trustee with an excuse of last-minute reservations engaged, so Petigru fumed, in "nothing more nor less than prevarication." When a North Carolina lawyer failed to institute proceedings he had agreed to undertake, Petigru reprimanded him sharply for his failure to act as "a faithful agent." But just as he was ready to damn the shoddy and unethical, Petigru was also ready with praise for those whose legal acumen and personal integrity lived up to his professional standards. Eulogizing Henry Bailey, South Carolina's attorney general from 1836 to 1849, Petigru lauded his values as much as his career. Bailey's practice had been "aloof from the contagion of any sordid art. His mind had no sympathy with evasion or deceit; and his ideas of the law were elevated by the purest conceptions of justice and equity."[41]

It was these values and ideals as much as Petigru's expertise and courtroom successes that inspired the admiration of fledgling attorneys. In 1845 a group of young Charleston lawyers commissioned Clarke Mills to sculpt a bust of Petigru, which they wanted to put on public display. When Harvard law students elected Petigru president of their Story Association in 1852, they reflected a similar admiration from aspiring northern lawyers, who had only read about him or heard him mentioned in lectures. But admiration was not confined to novices. S. W. Trotti, an officer of the Barnwell Bar Association, noted in 1854, almost as a truism, that Petigru was the "head of the profession in South Carolina." And John Belton O'Neall, who in 1859 became his state's chief justice, that same year recognized Petigru's standing as "the most experienced practicing lawyer of the state," distinguished for his "virtues, talents, learning and benevolence."[42]

Yet Petigru was no purist. He knew all the tricks of legal warfare and used them. When a client's interests demanded it, Petigru deserted the office and courtroom to lobby in cloakrooms and to monitor more formal legislative proceedings. In his prolonged efforts to extract from Georgia the sizable claims awarded the Trezevant family by the 1793 United States Supreme Court decision in *Chisholm v. Georgia*, he spent as much time socializing with individual legislators and cultivating a series of Georgia governors as he did in formal presentations of the Trezevants' claims. He expounded legal and moral arguments against legislative assertions that a debt dating back half a century could not possibly be valid. But he also plied undecided and wavering members of the legislature with the "contents of a small Dutch liquor case" and urged his daughter Sue to pay flattering attention to the ladies of their families.[43] From 1838 until 1847 he argued and refuted, flattered and cajoled until the legislature finally voted a bond issue to pay the principal—though not the accumulated fifty-five years of interest—on the claim, and, when the governor vetoed the bill, overrode him. By this performance Petigru not only earned his commission, which amounted to half the claim, he also demonstrated unusual skill as a lobbyist.[44]

It was a skill he honed frequently at the annual December sessions of the South Carolina legislature, where he regularly shepherded a variety of projects through committees and on to the floor. So effective as a lobbyist was this failed politician that when Franklin H. Elmore, president of the Bank of the State of South Carolina, was the subject of an official investigation, more for political than fiduciary reasons, he engaged Petigru to defend him.[45] Conducting the case before a legis-lative committee rather than a court of law required a sophisticated combination of talents. Petigru had to still politically inspired charges of corruption without offending strong antibank sentiment and to de-fend individual bank officers against charges of illegal conduct in an atmosphere where a challenge to veracity could lead to a duel. His effectiveness in this instance demonstrated why he was so successful a lobbyist in others. His legal expertise inspired a respect that tran-scended political differences; his sociability enabled him to maintain contacts and cultivate friendships with men in power.

Between 1842 and 1853, Petigru had earned the money to pay his old debts and support his family, and he had earned it in ways that in-creased his professional reputation. Had his politics been confined to lobbying or his practice solely to making the money he so needed, his life would illuminate little more than a prominent lawyer's experience in nineteenth-century America. The years after 1853 would have been denouement, the story of a man growing old, unlikely to undertake new ventures, incapable of playing a significant role on the public stage. Such, however, was not Petigru's fate.

SIX

Pursuing Justice

In May 1849 Petigru turned sixty. To mark the occasion and to celebrate his move into his elegant new Italianate office building at 8 St. Michael's Alley, a party of family and friends gathered there. His daughters, Sue and Caroline, "in their usual high spirits" and aided by two aunts and two cousins, presided over a midday feast of cold meats, strawberries and cream, ice cream, and an "abundance of champagne & punch," which they shared with eight men—young and middle-aged—seven of whom had studied law with Petigru. But the guest of honor never got to the party, for he was in federal court arguing a patent case and facing as opposing counsel William Henry Seward, the newly elected senator from New York.[1]

The party and his absence from it symbolize Petigru's life as he began his seventh decade. All those at the party were younger than he—most by a generation—yet it was he who was kept away by work. Work and family remained the central foci of his life as they had been almost from its start. As a southerner Petigru lived in a society whose ideology and reality stressed the extended family ties to which he was dedicated. Though head of his clan he still surely was, the aging of his generation and the maturation of the next allowed, and sometimes imposed, marked changes in the satisfactions and obligations those ties imposed. Like his own advancing years, the experiences of younger kin reshaped some of his professional perspectives as his freedom from heavy debts allowed him to pursue more fully the idealism that had survived some forty years of legal practice.

For all his sixty years, his was still a commanding physical presence. Seeming taller than his actual five feet ten inches, he would stride down the street and into court with an "elastic" step, brandishing his gold-headed walking stick and swinging his green baize bookbag. His full,

Law office of James L. Petigru at 8 St. Michael's Alley, Charleston, built in 1849. (South Carolina Historical Society)

still dark hair nearly swept his shoulders. His gray eyes never lost their luster. And with the flourish of his gold snuffbox and his resounding sneeze he remained as ever the consummate courtroom actor.[2]

But there were signs of advancing age. Petigru had gained weight, indeed had become portly. He was increasingly short of breath. He suffered more frequently from colds, coughs, and bilious attacks.[3] Slips of memory led to errors and confusion for which he had ever more often to apologize to clients. His forgetfulness, he admitted, was the "vice of age"; but the procrastination that contributed to it was an ongoing "fault of my nature," which only self-discipline had controlled in the past. Now fretful letters from clients reminded him of correspondence "of which till now we had lost sight." He was especially embarrassed to have to explain one oversight that delayed a trial for half a year. And at least once he lost a case because, as he confessed to the appeals bench, he "had actually ceased almost entirely to read the current decisions of the highest court of his own state."[4]

But most devastating of all, perhaps, was his growing sense of loss as old friends died. Long ago, in 1833, Petigru had been shocked when his contemporary and close friend from Coosawhatchie days, Judge William Martin, had died suddenly and quite alone in a Charleston hotel room. Ten years later he was deeply disturbed by Hugh Legaré's equally unexpected death in far-off Boston. It was "the greatest loss that [he] could sustain by the death of friends." Legaré had been an alter ego with whom he could talk "without reserve" on any topic, and on "many of which [he] could speak only to him."[5] But after 1850 the ever more frequent deaths of friends no longer surprised him. He was almost equally saddened by the deaths of Daniel Huger, his old mentor, and James Hamilton, his personal friend as well as his political and financial nemesis. He felt the loss of intellectual companionship when Harvard-educated Unitarian clergyman Samuel Gilman and College of Charleston trustee Charles Fraser went to their graves. But when his brother Thomas died in 1857, a sense of his own mortality overpowered him. "When one loses a brother he feels that his turn ought to be near[.] For why tarry when friends are gone."[6]

Petigru could still, of course, take pride when his pleading promised to reverse a judgment against the South Carolina Rail Road Company and win an appeals court decision worth "$30,000 to the railroad and a great deal to me in credit." Yet, "at three-score years and ten," such a triumph was "not as joyful as it was fifty years ago." More and more his sisters sensed their brother's diminished joy in his work and in life generally. After he had spent a day in 1856 at the Allstons' Chicora Wood plantation, Adele reported to her son, "I believe he has a great weight of care at his heart." Even at Badwell, where he was most at ease, Petigru seemed dispirited. Three years after Adele's observation, Mary praised her brother's efforts to keep up a good appearance but lamented how frequently he looked "very sad."[7]

These periods of depression, which marked the 1850s, were sharpened by volatile interactions between family and work. Just a year after Petigru and Lesesne had moved into their wonderful new offices, the decade-long partnership came to an end. That it was Lesesne who initiated the break made the whole affair "extremely embarrassing" to Petigru. As a practical matter he did not know how he could handle the workload alone. And emotionally the breakup seemed the "next thing in my feelings to a dissolution of the Union." Although Lesesne couched his leavetaking in the polite language of ill health and his consequent inability to fulfill the heavy demands that the joint practice made on him, family members sensed that, at thirty-nine, he rather resented the "subordinate position" that he occupied in the firm. And it was a resentment intensified, so Louise wrote Adele, by the fact that "Brother . . . never treated him in the frank & friendly manner which he would have desired." She sensed, she said, "some peculiar idiosyncrasy" that made Petigru unable to appreciate Lesesne's contributions. There was, she concluded, never "sympathy enough between them to make them *friends.*"[8]

Petigru's subsequent arrangements made it quite clear that he did indeed expect a partner to be a subordinate. Henry King, daughter Sue's husband, had always been a rather lethargic young man who, his father-in-law thought, would probably never work very hard. Nonetheless, Petigru opted for this family member as his next partner. Almost at once he came to believe that "before a year is over [King will] be completely broken from his childish and idle ways."[9] By year's end his son-in-law had delighted him by taking over the office management and the immediate supervision of student clerks, both of which Petigru found burdensome but which King far preferred to courtroom pleading. With no expectation on either side that it would be a partnership of equals, Petigru and King worked well together and seemed satisfied with the arrangement.

Just as Henry King resolved many problems in the office, vacations at Badwell became an ever more important safety valve for Petigru's personal tensions. The debts that forced him to sell his Savannah River plantation had long ago destroyed his early dream of gentlemanly retirement as a low country planter. But Badwell, although it was little more than an upcountry farm, allowed him to play country squire during his annual August vacations. Even in his youth a place of solace, it became in his older years a haven from disappointed hopes and foiled ambitions. At Badwell Petigru recaptured the sense of physical wellbeing that labor in the fields and work on the roads gave him. He mulled over plans to enrich poor soil, avoid erosion, and combat the ill effects of quirky weather. Grandly dreaming, he bought up surrounding land, planted and replanted oaks along the avenue, and hired an assortment of well diggers and engineers in a vain attempt to develop

a reliable supply of good water. Badwell let Petigru throw "off the rec-
ollections of the bar and the world almost and [revert] to the Adamic
State, carrying out the old song of 'When Adam delved and Eve span /
Who was then the Gentleman?' "[10]

However Edenic, Badwell was haunted by the specter of his father's
alcoholism, for it was there that Petigru encountered his intemperate
brothers. James himself was no abstainer, though he drank less as he
grew older. Teetotaling Baptist minister Basil Manly observed when he
met him in 1857, after a twenty-year interval, that "Petigru's habits
are scarcely so temperate as his friends could wish," though, he admitted, "less objectionable than formerly." All told, Petigru probably
drank no more at any point in his life than did most of his colleagues
and friends; and there is nothing in surviving records to suggest that
his drinking exceeded accepted patterns of sociability at a time when
adult Americans consumed five to seven gallons of alcohol each year.[11]

His worried references to the excesses of others in letters to family
members indicate, however, that drinking was an ongoing if largely
subliminal concern. Most grievous was brother Jack, who in January
1855 arrived at Badwell to live out the remnant of his shattered life.
Enfeebled and impoverished by his dissipation, Jack was, as his sister
Jane wrote Adele, "in his character, Father over again." Thirty years
earlier his older brother had turned his back on Jack, sending him west
and refusing him any help until he reformed. Yet on his return, James
assumed one more family responsibility. Jack's wife was as "helpless
and infirm" as Jack, and the couple needed not just food and housing
but personal care. So when brother Tom, who had both an unoccupied
house and several servants on a farm adjacent to Badwell, refused Jack
their use, James built him a house and bought him a slave.[12]

Thomas Petigru not only failed to help, he contributed positively to
the family's problems. He was not, it is true, a financial burden, for he
had married well, held a commission in the United States Navy, and
owned two plantations. But he too had a drinking problem—severe
enough to blight his naval career. Although he enlisted as a midship-
man during the War of 1812, he had advanced very slowly through the
ranks, getting his first command only in 1849, when he was ordered to
take the sloop-of-war *Falmouth* around the Horn to California.[13] James
was gratified. In the interest of manly independence, he had pressed his
younger brother to continue in the navy after his marriage to wealthy
Mary Anne LaBruce had made his service career financially unneces-

sary. That his Pacific tour of duty turned out as it did was, therefore, a severe blow to family pride.

Commander of a lumbering old vessel, reputed to be the "dullest sailer in the navy," Tom was hard put to keep his crew intact while the *Falmouth* was berthed in gold-rush San Francisco.[14] But Tom managed the external challenges of command far better than he did the internal stress they imposed. His subordinates alleged that he was often drunk on duty. But it was the charge that he had used his ship for private gain that led, two years later, to a court-martial. He had been ordered to sail the *Falmouth* down the California coast to Mexico to bring home supplies left there by the United States Army after the Mexican War. This he did. But he also, while on this mission, undertook to capture and return to California a man wanted for murder in San Francisco for whom an enticing $3000 reward was posted. From all this Tom escaped fairly lightly. The charges made at his court-martial that he had not been "in such possession of his faculties as falls to the lot of sober men only" were not proved,[15] and he was not assessed the cost of using his command for a privately rewarding mission. But the whole proceeding was very disagreeable, especially to his brother James.

Strangely, the implicit scandal after so mediocre a career did not block Tom's appointment in 1855 as superintendent of the Washington Navy Yard. But when, the next year, the navy dropped Tom altogether during a general retrenchment, the old allegations resurfaced. And once again James detected a slur on family honor. "The more I think of it," he wrote, "the more bitter is the sense of wrong that I have suffered in my name and feelings."[16] So rather than shrug it off as another of Tom's pecadillos, Petigru undertook a public campaign for his brother's reinstatement. He encouraged family members to defend the captain in the press, and he exploited his own connections in Washington in a vain effort to exonerate Tom, humble the Naval Board that had dismissed him, and remove the implicit dishonor that he felt so personally.[17]

He and his sisters knew that Tom was not blameless. Worse still, they associated his indiscretions with a fatal hereditary flaw. Jane North, for one, wondered openly why it was "that those descended of pious ancestors but a short way back should be so utterly destitute of high moral character." Her doubts about Tom's morals were only reinforced when he insisted on returning to Washington in 1857 to seek an inquiry into the actions that had led to his dismissal. Then, suddenly and without any warning, Tom died. The unexpectedness of that death and the circumstances in which it took place took a double toll. For James, his brother's death left "a blank in my existence."[18] Moreover, because Tom died before the Naval Board could be forced to reverse his arbitrary dismissal, an ineradicable stain remained on the family name, a name James himself had made unique to his branch of the family.

Moreover, Tom's death could scarcely have come at a worse time in his brother's life. Already aware that his own professional prowess was declining, Petigru at exactly this same time experienced the most searing defeat of his legal career. He had expected the *Croom* case to be a repeat of his triumph in *Pell* v. *Ball*, for, like that earlier case, *Smith* v. *Croom* hinged on the order of family deaths in a shipwreck and thus on whether the wife's or the husband's heirs at law would inherit the Croom property in Florida.[19] Because he argued the case in the Florida courts, where one of the contending heirs lived, and because the appeals process dragged it out, Petigru spent prolonged periods as a guest in the home of his client, Bryan Croom, who became a good friend. Whether because he thus was too personally involved or because he had succumbed to hubris, Petigru was absolutely sure he would win the case and so advised Croom not to accept a sizable compromise settlement out of court. It was surprising advice, singularly at odds with his customary practice. And it proved also to be bad advice, for the Florida Supreme Court found for the opposing party, and Croom lost all his anticipated inheritance.

Petigru was mortified. He had harmed his client. He had been struck down professionally. And news of the final decision arrived just when he was suffering "the depression of grief for poor Tom." For him the two losses merged into one indistinguishable torment. "I would rather have lost my life," he wrote Adele, than to have lost this case. In the ensuing days it was his own failure that tortured him. He doubted that "Mr Croom has been out of my thoughts 5 minutes at a time since I heard the fatal news, unless when asleep & even then, this horrid case continually intrudes upon my dreams." His only escape from this incessant brooding lay in restoring his professional pride. He finally came to terms with the *Croom* case by attributing his loss to the "ignorance of Judges" and defining his failure as that of a responsible lawyer who had not succeeded in teaching them to "do right even if they did so unwillingly."[20]

There may have been some self-delusion in that self-exculpation.

Still, its acerbic pith reflects Petigru's growing irritation with the judges of his own state. His impatience with their ill-considered rulings surfaced frequently in his personal and professional correspondence throughout the 1850s. The incompetence of the bench was probably not the only factor causing his disaffection. Until his partnership with Lesesne dissolved, Petigru had consistently won more appeals cases than he lost—close to two victories for every defeat. But during the 1850s his record declined to an almost even split. Part of that decline doubtless reflects the fact that he attracted clients whose cases, especially in equity court, were complex, difficult, and occasionally downright desperate. Moreover, even in the 1840s he had been notably more likely to lose equity appeals cases than law court appeals.[21] But despite these mitigating factors, there is little doubt that judicial incompetence played some role. South Carolina's minimal remuneration for its judges, its failure to increase the number of judges as the caseload grew, and its retention from 1835 to 1859 of appeals courts staffed with the same judges who presided over the lower courts did indeed produce ill-considered and often erratic final judgments.[22]

Still more frequent than his complaints about South Carolina's flawed judicial structure were Petigru's unflattering assessments of individual judges. In his eyes, John Richardson epitomized the partisan judge who played favorites among contending lawyers. By 1847, in fact, Richardson's long delays in handing down opinions had irritated so many people that the legislature resolved that year to remove him on grounds of "bodily and mental infirmity."[23] Tellingly, his defense, which he grounded in personal honor, not only defeated the efforts to impeach him but curtailed all efforts to remove any other sitting judges. Moreover, or at least so Petigru thought, political partisanship had much to do with the appointment and retention of judges. Chancellor William Harper's vehement support of nullification on and off the bench may have helped him retain his post despite his frequent bouts of inebriation.[24] On the other hand, few would dispute that Harper was learned in the law and thoughtful in his opinions. So much could not be said of several of his colleagues. All South Carolina judges were, after all, appointed by legislative vote; and judgeships were understood by many to be just another step on the ladder of political preferment. Given also the constraints of time and the proliferation of cases under which it labored, the system essentially precluded assembling a bench of high-caliber jurists. The legislature appointed few judges who were "eminent for wisdom and learning, commanding by . . . reason, and indefatigable in the despatch of business."[25] And even when it did, it overtaxed them with a caseload they could not reasonably handle.

Most trying to Petigru during the 1850s was a marked increase in the practice of chancellors' fashioning their own law, ungoverned by either legal tradition or logic. The judicial inconsistencies they created made equity proceedings so unpredictable that Petigru more and more warned clients that he could not advise them with any confidence whether or not to pursue their claims in court.[26] Such uncertainties doubtless contributed also to his growing preference for mediation and arbitration outside the courts.

Yet many clients, guided by preference or driven by circumstances, did proceed to litigation. When this took him into the equity courts, Petigru more often than not confronted one of two chancellors whom he believed to be downright incompetent: Job Johnston and Francis H. Wardlaw. "I dont believe," he wrote a colleague, "that any weight of wisdom or authority would move a court where such a man as Job Johnston presides. . . . In fact, he never seems to think himself in the right way except when he is taking the side of some body that is taking some pitiful advantage of the truth." And Wardlaw was no better. His "awkward and bungling acknowledgment . . . that his decision is wrong, while he don't correct it, . . . like his halfway repentence about condemning you in costs for bringing a righteous claim before the Court" infuriated Petigru in more than one case. He well recognized that he could never educate such chancellors. As he quipped after one particularly trying session, he had "a mind to take to lecturing" because he would rather teach receptive boys than judges deaf to reason.[27]

That was not mere fantasizing, for teaching gave Petigru pleasure throughout his life. He took pride in the many young men who had, following the custom of the day, read law under his supervision and learned its routines as his clerks. As much as his professional prestige, his method and his enthusiasm made his office a particularly popular law school. There the liberal arts were valued as much as the technical ability to draft writs, wills, and deeds. There students divided their time equally between "the cultivation of literature and science," on the one hand, and the study of legal treatises and court reports, on the other.

Accordingly, Petigru attracted as students a tenth of all those admitted to practice in the South Carolina Court of Appeals in Law between 1825 and 1860.[28]

None of these young men gave him more pleasure, none generated more pride, and none won his admiration more than his North Carolina cousin James Johnston Pettigrew. Around him, Petigru rekindled the dreams stifled since little Albert's death. In him he found an object for the hopes that had been dashed when his talented younger brother Charles died before he could resign his commission to study law.[29] And to Johnston, as he was known, the older man gave the attention and counseling he would have given his own son Dan—had only Dan not been Dan.

In the years since he had been suspended from Princeton, Dan had, to be sure, read law and been admitted to practice. But he had done little more. Jane North believed that he was hobbled by having inherited the worst attributes of both parents' families. "A compound of Jim Postell and our poor brother Jack," Dan was erratic and too devoid of ambition to excel at anything. He had volunteered to raise a company for the Mexican War but had found only a dozen men willing to follow him into battle. He had managed, with his father's help, to land a patronage job at the Savannah Customs House, only to be fired shortly thereafter. On returning to Charleston he was listed in city directories as a lawyer, but, except for the years he acted as his father's assistant in the United States district attorney's office, his only address was his parents' home. Even at the family dining table father and son found little to talk about. Always his "idleness and immorality" and the family's "mortification and . . . disgrace" lay between them.[30]

So when J. Johnston Pettigrew arrived in Petigru's law office in 1849 he was triply welcome. Almost at once he came to personify all the older man's hopes for the next generation. Johnston symbolized the best of the Pettigrew family heritage, for the North Carolina branch comprised prosperous planters who were respected as churchmen and well connected politically. Highly intelligent, he had, after graduating with honors from the college at Chapel Hill, been employed as Mathew Maury's assistant at the National Observatory in Washington, where his extraordinary mathematical skills won much attention. And when he turned his attention to the law, he promised to become "one of the most considerable men of his age," with intellectual ability and personal bearing capable, so his cousin believed, of taking him into the ranks of "the greatest lawyers in America."[31]

Teaching him was a joy limited only by its brevity, for within a year Johnston was fully prepared to practice law in South Carolina. In fact, his formal admission to the bar had to be delayed for several months after he qualified because he was not yet twenty-one. Then Petigru, preferring always to balance legal with liberal education, urged Johnston to study abroad for a year or two; and he convinced Johnston's older brother and his equally generous godfather to fund the young lawyer's study of civil law in Germany and pay for an additional year of travel throughout Europe.[32]

Johnston returned to Charleston full of enthusiasm but unsure about his future. Petigru outlined the pros and cons of leaving the Carolinas for New Orleans, an option he had once considered for himself. But he pressed hardest an opportunity he had never had in urging his talented young cousin to consider practicing law in North Carolina, where his family's prominence promised a distinguished political career. After much hesitation Johnston finally chose to remain in Charleston and accepted Petigru's invitation to join him and Henry King as a partner. Despite having advised him to do otherwise, Petigru could not have been more delighted.[33]

If Petigru's familial satisfactions increased with Johnston's arrival, his strained relationship with Jane Amelia and the alarming state of both daughters' marriages tugged hard in the opposite direction. "Happiness," he reflected sadly, was "a thing rare in our family."[34] In his immediate family there seemed to be a compelling dynamic that worked against it. Dan was, at least in part, cast in the role of mischievous youth and dissolute man by his father's abiding fear that he was fated to be such. And Dan must have sensed from adolescence, if not from the time of Albert's death, that his father anticipated just that. So too did Jane Amelia come increasingly to personify for her husband the weaknesses he so feared in himself as her increased consumption of drugs and alcohol supplemented her ill health as the means to gain attention, establish personal autonomy, and exert more power within her home. Although her health improved in the mid-1840s, during the two years after both daughters had married and the worst of Petigru's financial crisis had passed, that remission, associated most immediately with the self-hypnosis of mesmerism,[35] was only temporary. Like the other, briefer periods when social diversions had lured her back to an active life, this too ended when familiar pressures reduced her again to semi-invalidism and frequent losses of emotional control.

Whether caused by Jane Amelia's ever more intense clashes with daughter Sue, her jealous demands for James's constant attention, her apparent attempted suicide by chloroform in 1850,[36] or simply the aging of both spouses, family politics changed markedly during the 1850s. Gradually Petigru distanced himself from his wife, although law, social convention, and his own compelling sense of family responsibility kept the outer shell of their marriage intact. His sister Louise reported as early as 1849 that while James still paid Jane Amelia "the full mead of attention which contents other women," he had "ceased to act the lover, or to suffer anguish under the cloud of her ill humour." He was probably most disturbed when that cloud descended on Johnston, a new competitor for her husband's attention, and almost drove him from Charleston. But the tedium of an inescapable marriage was grimmest during long, hot summer evenings on Sullivan's Island when Petigru could not escape by going back to the office or out to his club. Worst of all for claustrophobic boredom was the summer of 1852, when, grudgingly acceding to her importunities, James spent considerable sums and much time taking Jane Amelia to the Virginia springs for her health.[37]

Thereafter the summer tension lessened as Jane Amelia began to board for several weeks at a time in the pineland village of Summerville, well away from the Sullivan's Island family retreat. Once, she spent almost the whole summer in the North Carolina mountain resort of Flat Rock. Thus freed, Petigru extended his long vacations at Badwell, which already had become his customary August haven. Even at their home in Charleston, where they spent most of the year, the two gradually evolved new and somewhat different marital patterns. Jane Amelia made up secrets which she told to others while warning them emphatically not to tell James. James, for his part, frequently took tea with other women and enjoyed their lively, well-informed conversation. Their new independence from one another more clearly revealed the strain between them to others. James advised his daughters not to mention to their mother certain events about which he wrote them. Jane Amelia so unrestrainedly complained to family friends about James's deficiencies that in 1860 she rambled on to Congressman William Porcher Miles that her husband had "certainly had no business to get married, as no mule is more [obstinate] than he is, and he has no right to involve so many in misery, because he chooses to go his own way." Family happiness, in truth, was rare.[38]

In the Carson household as well happiness was scarce by 1850. Caroline later confessed that she had never been in love with William Carson and had married him with little apparent thought beyond the glitter of his material assets. She resented becoming pregnant after only three months. She announced to her aunt Louise that the very "idea of *a baby* [was] odious," and, at least until little William was born— almost exactly on his parents' first wedding anniversary—confessed to disliking children. By the time her second and last child, James Petigru Carson, was born three years later, his father's vaunted wealth was already fast diminishing. The east branch of the Cooper River, on which the Dean Hall rice crop depended for irrigation, was becoming salt. But William Carson refused to plant the cotton that his land could still produce and continued to plant the rice he preferred to grow but which languished without a lavish supply of fresh water. Year after year he lost his crop and went ever deeper into debt. Moreover, income from his Charleston wharf and other business properties in the city so declined during the prolonged depression of the 1840s that he was forced to sell them at prices too low even to cover the debts he had incurred to buy them.[39]

It was hardly surprising that when Caroline suffered a severe illness following young James's birth, the boy's father was reluctant to leave his crops. It was her father, therefore, who took Caroline first to the Virginia springs and then on to New York for medical treatment. Five years later, in 1850, it was again her father who took her north to be treated for a uterine tumor. It was only when Caroline stayed on in New York alone for several months and then refused to come home, even when her husband traveled north to get her, that others realized how deeply into disarray the Carson marriage had fallen.[40]

Thereafter Caroline's persistent ill health created transparent excuses for more frequent and prolonged separations from her husband. Though temporary reconciliations followed, their quick dissipation drove home the truth that personal and emotional as well as financial and physical problems were disrupting the Carsons' lives. Like so many of his Petigru and Postell in-laws, William Carson too had a drinking problem. For a long time he kept it within acceptable bounds. But as his financial problems grew, alcohol became his major consolation. Despite repeated promises to reform, he persisted and gave way to "brutal habits & low propensities" that soon disturbed the whole Petigru family. But their efforts to turn things around failed to change William or free Caroline. Louise Porcher, though she admitted that "things [had] gone too far ever to be accommodated between [Caroline] & her husband," nonetheless advised her niece that "in becoming [Carson's] wife her duties were plain, tho most unwelcome & arduous." The best that could be hoped was that "decencies will still be preserved." At least once James Petigru confronted his son-in-law in an unpleasant showdown about his behavior, but to little effect. Made "silent & abstracted" by the situation, Petigru welcomed Caroline when she sought refuge for herself and her two sons in her parents' home but also advised her to return to Dean Hall when she could and rear her children in their father's home.[41]

By 1854, if not before, William Carson realized that he was killing himself, but still he could not control his "habitual indulgence in strong drink."[42] Finally, in 1856, it did kill him. Although his death ended Caroline's marital anguish and his will left her the customary widow's third of the income his property produced, Caroline still depended on her father for support. She had to cope with an estate so encumbered with debt that it produced no usable income until Dean Hall was sold. Moreover, during the three years it took to settle the estate, Caroline was almost as much an invalid as her mother. And so she continued to drain her father's emotional and financial resources.[43]

By comparison with Caroline's, her younger sister Sue's marital problems were minimal. It was her feistiness and unpredictable behavior rather than any spousal aberrancies about which the family fretted. Henry King, whom she had married in 1843, was the son of Mitchell King, a very wealthy Charleston lawyer and a good friend of her father. Henry, however, had been slow to take on adult responsibilities. His law practice throughout the 1840s was insignificant. Even after the birth of their first and only child, Adele, in 1844, he had balked at moving out of his parents' home into a house of his own. These arrangements kept Sue from the independence she craved and probably encouraged her to continue flirting with other men and to tease short, stout Henry about his less than glamorous attributes. Yet even after 1846, when they moved into a house Henry had purchased, their marriage did not improve. Nor did things get better when four years later he became Petigru's partner and at last began actively to pursue his own occupation.[44] So Sue began to vent her disillusionment with marriage in her novels, which, from 1854 until 1860, were published in New York, and her short stories, which appeared in the *Knickerbocker Magazine* as well as in Charleston's *Russell's Magazine.*

During all those years Sue's behavior alarmed her close kin. At least twice she went north for prolonged stays, leaving Henry and Adele behind. At home she set tongues wagging with intimate little parties, outrageous public appearances, and provocative friendships with handsome young bachelors. Her fiction, with its only slightly veiled references to well-known Charlestonians, further alienated the society whose leaders she both despised and yearned to join. She never stopped feuding with her mother. And over the years she and Henry grew farther and farther apart. Altogether there was good reason for her father, who admitted some pride in her literary accomplishments, to be deeply troubled by his youngest child. "If you could see how much misery you cause to me," he wrote her in 1858, "you would relent I am sure, for tho' you have argued yourself into opposition to everything that I approve of or recommend, I hope that your affections are not perverted into downright hatred." Torn and hurt by this wayward daughter, whose estimate of "what is right and what is prudent" so differed from his, yet who was of all his children perhaps most like him, Petigru reached out to her forlornly. "If you will only allow me to love you according to my own nature, and to serve you according to the only measure of service that I am capable of," he implored, "I would soon . . . feel that you were still one of the main stays and comforts in life, as well as an object of the just pride of your father." But Sue was no more able to change than was her father.[45]

That the growing turmoil and sadness within his own and his children's households shaped some of Petigru's law practice during the 1850s seems more than likely. He had, it is true, long represented women clients whose property rights were at risk in maladministered trusts and wills. But now, for the first time, he dealt with issues involving the plight of women caught in the toils of miserable marriages. In so doing, albeit less by sophisticated arguments to modify legal doctrine than by astute appeals to the customary usage by which South Carolina courts extended paternalistic protection to the weaker sex, Petigru promoted a redistribution of legal benefits, however slight, from men to women. Most often at stake was property and alimony, but women's autonomy and personal safety and the fate of their children were often unmentioned subtexts. On the one hand, this new practice doubtless reflected the growing number of separation, divorce, and child custody cases that were fought out in American courts. Possibly the increased attention to married women's property rights in various state legislatures also influenced Petigru's responses. But his admission that he had largely stopped reading South Carolina law reports during the 1850s makes it more likely that circumstances closer to home played the critical role. That in 1852 he gained for one woman the custody of her three children after having represented her husband in arranging their separation six years earlier signaled his altered perspective. That in 1856 he refused even "to be the organ of any communication emanating" from a man who had brutalized his wife, then Petigru's client, suggests lessons learned from his own family.[46]

In at least two other instances during the 1850s Petigru handled, as he had not before, cases involving violent wife abuse. The first case concerned a wealthy widow who had in 1849 married the propertyless pastor of her parish's Episcopal church. After the wedding, this second husband had demanded a postnuptial settlement giving him full control of the plantation his wife had inherited from her first husband as well as joint use of the income it generated. Marion Singleton DeVeaux Converse had agreed, preferring to transfer its control rather than abandon her comfortable home for a ramshackle country parsonage. But Mr. Converse had his eye on more than the manly self-respect inherent in governing his household. When Mrs. Converse's father died, he demanded for his own use one quarter of the income from the much larger plantation that his wife then inherited. To that she also agreed. Still Converse was not content, and he grew steadily more morose. Then, in March 1854, reports of the Converses' domestic irregularities spread from Sumter District to set tongues wagging as far away as Georgetown. "I heard today," Adele Allston wrote her brother, "that there has been a great disturbance between Mr & Mrs Converse" in which she and her daughter "were obliged to leave the house in the night, and in the rain and seek protection from a neighbour."[47]

Shortly after that event Marion Converse called on Petigru, whom she already knew as her father's and her first husband's attorney. At first he tried to arrange a compromise, offering Mr. Converse $10,000 in exchange for any claim on the True Blue Singleton plantation. For surrendering joint use of the whole income generated by the Ruins, as the DeVeaux plantation was aptly named, he proffered half the annual income. Or, if Converse would surrender all his claims on the Ruins, Petigru would negotiate a sizable lump sum settlement. But "His Reverence," as Petigru disdainfully called him, refused to surrender any claims contained in the two postnuptial marriage contracts. So off to court they went.[48]

The initial equity hearings before Chancellor George Dargan involved testimony so scandalous that much of it was stricken from the published record. Even so, Dargan summarized the minister's cruelty as an "annoyance, insult and personal outrage . . . what is meant by the term saevitia in the civil law."[49] Although the worst had been expunged, the acknowledged events behind the rumors that circulated in Georgetown were lurid enough. On the night of January 18, 1854, A. L. Converse had quarreled violently with his wife about what clothes one of her daughters should take to boarding school. The parson emphasized his views by pinning his wife to the piazza floor and holding her there by her hair. When Annie Moore, a visiting daughter, tried to cut her mother loose, her stepfather snatched the scissors. When she tried to protect her mother from the cold night air, Mr. Converse grabbed the shawl she had brought and put it around himself. Finally, Marion Converse gave in and accompanied her husband to their bedroom. There loud talk and then sounds of more physical violence could be heard. Annie Moore again came to her mother's aid, helping her, bruised and bleeding, to escape through a back door. The two women hid in a shed, where they were soon discovered by Mr. Converse, who, a servant warned them, intended to nail them in. Again the women made a run for it, disappearing into a cornfield, from which they were finally rescued by a neighbor.

For all the tawdry drama, the issues with which *V. M. Converse by Next Friend* v. *A. L. Converse* confronted the court, first in a hearing before Chancellor Dargan, then in the Court of Appeals in Equity, the Court of Errors, and once again the equity appeals court, were not charges of assault and battery but only the wife's petition to change her name back to DeVeaux and to cancel the postnuptial settlements, to which, she said, she had agreed under duress. The first request Chancellor Dargan denied outright. "How do I know," he asked with unbelievable insensitivity, "that these parties may not become reconciled? . . . It would be wrong in the Court to throw any impediment in the way of such reconciliation."[50] His response to the second issue was of the same tenor, although he did end the joint-use provision so that income from the Ruins could be divided evenly between the spouses. Petigru's largely technical challenges to both settlements and his references to earlier chancery proceedings establishing the terms under which Marion Converse had come into possession of True Blue and the slaves later employed at the Ruins, terms that were quite at odds with those of the settlements, had no effect on Dargan's decision. When the case went to appeal, the results were no more favorable. As to Mrs. Converse changing her name, Chancellor Francis Wardlaw, writing for the equity appeals bench in the final disposition of the case, observed that "wives have surnames by courtesy only, adopted from their husbands."[51]

The Court of Errors decision was equally revealing of the social assumptions underlying its interpretation of the law. The court upheld both postnuptial marriage settlements and rejected Mrs. Converse's appeal largely because her whole bearing in the "unhappy domestic dissentions" gave no evidence that her "character and disposition were of that soft and yielding material, over which coercion of any kind, could have been successfully exerted." Rather, she had revealed "an uncommon strength and tenacity of will, and an indomitable courage, and firmness in resisting requirements, that were not agreeable to her." Consequently she had no claim to the special protection that courts customarily provided weak females. As for the poor husband of a rich wife, "Whatever may have been his misconduct in conjugal relations we do not perceive the propriety of unnecessarily impoverishing him."[52]

Petigru, who had little respect anyhow for Wardlaw's judicial opinions, believed the chancellor had proved his total incompetence by this decision, in which he not only denied justice but deserted honor. "If I were to give way to indignation I never would set my foot again within the limits of that hall where Converse v. Converse to the shame of Manhood and disgrace of reason was confirmed." Yet as a lawyer he must continue to represent his client and salvage what he could despite "the mortification of a failure which implies disgrace of the heaviest kind viz: the disgrace of being beaten by an imbecile and worthless enemy."[53]

Once again, therefore, but now on a playing field tilted against his client by equity decrees and appeals court decisions, Petigru sought an acceptable out-of-court settlement. The galling negotiations with Franklin J. Moses, Mr. Converse's attorney, dragged on for a year; but finally Petigru arranged for John Moore, son-in-law of Mrs. DeVeaux (thus did she defy the chancellors), to buy out Converse's claims on both plantations. That settlement, whose financial provisions cost his clients dearly, also at least partially satisfied honor. It forced "Diabolus," as Petigru now called "His Reverence," to return to his wife her clothing, her jewelry, and her personal correspondence, all of which she had been forced to leave behind when she fled the Ruins.[54] But although Mrs. DeVeaux gained the satisfaction that nothing that had ever belonged to her remained with the man who had abused her, she was still married to him, could never divorce him in a state where neither courts nor legislature provided that option, and understood that the law would never punish him for his assaults upon her.

However burdensome the law's restrictions, Mrs. DeVeaux had the resources to arrange a reasonably satisfactory separation and still live comfortably thereafter. In a word, she had the dual advantages of extensive property and family position. She could afford to pay Petigru's fees; and his long association with her father made him the more willing to represent her in courts sitting in Sumter and Columbia. Julia Winberg, however, had no such resources. Yet when she came to Petigru, a badly battered pregnant woman already the mother of two small children, he responded to her needs as forcefully and for fully as long as he later did to Mrs. DeVeaux's. John Winberg, a none-too-successful storekeeper, had beaten his wife so viciously that she had fled, taking her children with her, and sought refuge with friends in Charleston. When Mr. Winberg found her there in December 1851, he swore out a warrant to keep the peace against those who had sheltered her and, going to their house with a constable, seized the children. Only then, desperate to regain them, had Mrs. Winberg turned to Petigru.[55]

He at once sought a writ of habeas corpus for the children. With only a few lawyers and law students present in Judge J. N. Whitner's chambers, Petigru pulled out all the stops to argue decency and justice rather than points of law. "When he rose," one of the students recalled forty years later, "it was evident from the convulsive movement of his lips how intensely he felt; and [t]hen, after enumerating simply and evidently with suppressed emotion, the various acts of brutality to which his client had been subjected, he pointed to her as she sat beside him, soon to become again a mother, and asked whether the child unborn should be seized by such a father?"[56]

Whether or not the judge was, as reported, reduced to tears, he did grant the writ. Mrs. Winberg did retrieve her children, and shortly thereafter she and the children took the boat from Charleston to Philadelphia. Her departure, however, did not end Petigru's services to her. In 1854 he arranged the Winbergs' legal separation, including a division of their assets, after convincing John, a debtor with minimal access to legal services, that it was better to concede so much voluntarily than to face a bruising court battle. Petigru's actions enabled Julia to shelter from her husband's creditors the small property she had gained in the North and, shortly thereafter, to become self-sufficient by opening her own retail business as a feme sole trader in Georgia.[57]

Just as insights gained from his private life pressed Petigru to represent abused wives, so public controversy over slavery, which after the Mexican War increasingly defined both national and South Carolina politics, extended his defense of civil liberties. Yet even here personal circumstances are relevant. Petigru had been a slaveholder ever since his marriage, when their prenuptial marriage settlement had given him joint use and control of Jane Amelia's 10 slaves. In addition, his Savannah River rice plantation had at its peak about 125 slaves, which Petigru had owned outright. And even after he had sold them, the 1840 federal census recorded 22 slaves living in the yard of his Charleston home. Not even the 1842 composition with his creditors stripped his Charleston household of slaves, for the 1850 census still reported 8 adult slaves, who lived with their children in his Broad Street household, and 2 other adults who lived elsewhere, perhaps in his office. There was thus no overt irony in William Grayson's dedicating his proslavery poem, "The Hireling and the Slave," to Petigru.[58]

Grayson sensed, if he did not know, the ambiguities in his friend's responses to the peculiar institution. Certainly Petigru did not openly condemn slavery. In the 1850s he still purchased slaves to meet his family's convenience. Furthermore, he displayed both the virtues and the limitations of the "good master." He was willing to make extensive detours so that Sammy, his coachman, could visit his wife, but unwilling, because he already owned more household slaves than he needed, to buy that wife so the couple could live together. And when his or the Badwell slaves were recalcitrant or disobedient, he sanctioned flogging as an appropriate punishment.[59] Yet he also emancipated an elderly slave who had long served the Gibert and Petigru families and arranged emancipation for the slaves of others, legally when possible and illegally when that was the only option. With a single recorded exception, however, even political opponents in the heat of debate never implied that he was an abolitionist. In fact, he had, in his professional capacity, blocked a bequest to a Pennsylvania antislavery society in an 1854 case argued before the United States Supreme Court. All told, his response to slavery, with the exception of his support for manumission, accorded reasonably well with the majority of appellate decisions in cases involving injury to slaves. He challenged neither the system of separate Magistrates and Freeholders Courts, which tried blacks without benefit of jury, nor South Carolina's still broader legal premise stated by Judge David Wardlaw in 1847 that a slave could "invoke neither *magna charta* nor common law" to establish legal rights. But Petigru's professional, like his personal, stance was akin to the paternalism by which appellate courts fairly consistently provided "due protection and ordered process" in cases where slaves had been killed or injured by whites.[60]

Unsheltered from public ire by a tenured seat on the bench, however, his ambiguity about race, like his dissent from proslavery exuberance, sometimes attracted heated attention that judicial decisions escaped. The competing threads of his racial attitudes are evident in an 1841 oration to an Oglethorpe University audience that contrasted the conditions of savage and civilized races. Asserting, on the one hand, that the differences between races were greater than those between individuals within each race and that the uncivilized were inferior to the civilized, Petigru nonetheless insisted, on the other hand, that the inferior were "neither contemptible nor weak." What set them apart from their betters was their lack of knowledge; and that, he believed, could be remedied by education, which would "humanize" them. Though the terms grate on modern ears, his message was far different from the widely accepted theories of the Carolina-born ethnologist and physician Josiah Nott, who argued that Africans and Caucasians were, as races, unalterably different, distinct, and separate.[61]

Even so modest a deviation from popular views as Petigru's might seem subversive to those who lived in a city whose population was almost evenly balanced between whites and blacks but where all whites were free citizens and 85 percent of the blacks were slaves. Generally the potential for open hostility between the races was smothered, but an occasional incident sparked fears and unleashed resentments that threatened violent confrontation. Committed to the law as an instrument of justice, Petigru nonetheless understood that "even the lowest people may be raised by despair to the commission of great crimes."[62] Those crimes he could not condone, but neither would he sanction revenge as punishment or unreasonable restraint as prevention.

In July 1849, crime, punishment, and prevention became an explosive reality in Charleston. Nicholas, a slave who had been sentenced to death for assaulting a police officer with a deadly weapon, was awaiting execution in the workhouse, which served as a jail and correctional institution for blacks both slave and free. On July 13, maddened by his suspicion that a kinswoman was being taken from the workhouse to be sold, Nicholas attacked the keeper with an ax—or perhaps only an ax handle—and then led a jailbreak of thirty-six fellow inmates armed with sledgehammers. Most were recaptured within hours, but a few remained at large the following day. Angered by the escape and fearing worse to come, a white crowd gathered that Saturday night to destroy a newly built Episcopal church specifically intended for the religious instruction of slaves. To its sponsors, the church was a means to instill Christian self-discipline, but to the mob it symbolized a fatal leniency that threatened their safety. That the city guard successfully defended Calvary Church from the torch only fed the rage of the infuriated mob that reassembled in front of city hall on Monday morning to demand that the church be demolished.[63]

Despite the legend that it was Petigru who calmed the crowd and saved Calvary Church from the torch on Saturday night, he was apparently out of town at that time. But he was back home by Monday morning and went as usual to his office, which was little more than a block from city hall. Clearly he had learned beforehand of the weekend's events. Hearing the crowd as it called out the mayor, he rushed to the scene and mounted the high steps of city hall. Looking across the street to his own St. Michael's Church and then down at the angry men, he urged them to let a meeting of Charleston citizens decide the fate of Calvary Church. If they would permit that, he would pledge himself to abide by the results, whatever they might be. And he further pledged that if they were right, if those who had built the new church were indeed creating the preconditions for revolt, "I will go with you. If you are wrong, you will carry out your purpose over my dead body."[64]

Perhaps because public meetings of citizens were a familiar way of addressing urban problems, Petigru's strategem worked. The crowd pulled back. Then the mayor called a meeting for the following Monday. When it assembled, on July 23, Petigru was ready with a resolution that proposed a thorough investigation of the "organization of 'Calvary Church,' and . . . the management of the slave population of our city." In a move that was doubtless choreographed ahead of time, the mayor in response appointed an investigating committee of fifty, headed by Petigru. Its conclusions, however, were not predetermined except that they must preserve the public peace. Petigru, in a private letter to his brother-in-law Robert Allston, confirmed that the principal purpose of these moves was to "suppress" the "lawless spirit" of the mob. But if those backing the church were also fomenting social unrest, the committee would "concur in the policy of suppressing" Calvary.[65]

Nearly four months later, on November 13, the committee's three subcommittees presented their reports at yet another public gathering. They exonerated Calvary and its backers, who had arranged from the beginning for white supervision of all activities to be held at the new church. After the three subcommittees' reports were read, Petigru, as chairman of the full committee, successfully urged their acceptance in a speech that focused on religious freedom rather than on racial hostility or social peace. It was a shrewd tack, for it united public opinion positively around the "liberty of teaching" and left little room for public expression of fears that could never be fully quelled.[66]

But other incursions against civil liberties bred by a racially divided slave society could not be countered so easily. As he had before 1850, Petigru continued aiding white clients who wished to free favorite slaves and defending the de facto freedom of African Americans for whom deceased owners had stretched South Carolina law to its limits. Always, however, the would-be benefactors were hamstrung by their state's 1820 prohibition against any private emancipation, and, after 1841, its positive ban on any manumission, even secret arrangements for de facto slaves to live as free persons. Thus the liberty chipped out by circumvention was always tenuous. Petigru's most extensive efforts were made in this context, on behalf of the slaves for whom George Broad's will had provided. Broad, an English-born farmer who had settled in St. John's Berkeley, had in 1836 placed his eleven children, their mother, and her two grandchildren, all of whom were in fact his slaves as well, in a trust to be administered by John Dangerfield, who was to let them work on the Broad farm and consume whatever it produced.

Almost at once Broad's intent came under challenge. Between 1839 and 1842 Petigru had already conducted a series of appeals cases that defended the legitimacy of the trust and defeated efforts by the white relatives of Broad's deceased wife to gain control of the slaves.[67] In 1854, however, the Broad slaves—for slaves they still were in the eyes of the law—again came to Petigru for help. This time it was the trustee's heirs who, after Dangerfield's death, claimed ownership. Determined now to forestall forever the Broad slaves' return to de facto slavery, Petigru arranged with the American Colonization Society for their emigration to Liberia and raised the funds to cover their passage and settlement there. Before they could leave, however, all claims of the Dangerfield heirs had to be extinguished. To achieve this resolution required the cooperation of South Carolina's attorney general and the support of numerous prosperous residents of St. John's Berkeley, who petitioned the legislature on behalf of the black Broad family. Moreover, Petigru himself had to perform an abrupt legal about-face. In a triumph of pragmatism over theoretical consistency, he now argued, in *F. A. Ford, Escheator ex rel. J. Ferguson* v. *Starling J. Dangerfield*, that because the Broad will did indeed violate state law the Dangerfield trust had never been valid. Therefore any claims by the Dangerfield heirs must be without substance. Moreover, because the will was void, George Broad had in fact died intestate. Finally, therefore, in the absence of legal heirs, the law required that the state confiscate Broad's estate for its own use.[68]

In January 1856 the Court of Appeals in Equity so decided. As soon as it did, Petigru was ready with petitions in which so many "gentlemen" urged the state legislature to emancipate the Broad slaves and to dedicate the proceeds of the Broad estate to their support that the legislature did just that. In the last act of this extended drama, Petigru located the man to whom Dangerfield had, before his death, sold Sammy and Simon Broad in violation of the trust. Purchasing them with the funds escheated from the Broad estate and appropriated by the legislature, he sent them, along with the rest of their family, to Liberia.[69]

Although resolution of the *Broad* case required unusual legislative action in addition to judicial consideration, and although at least one other similar case, involving botched maneuvers to free the slave-born children of a Mr. Wigg,[70] reached trial court, neither case made the mark that Petigru's efforts to protect the liberty of black British seamen did. In his sharpest confrontation with state law since the test oath case two decades earlier, Petigru represented the British consul in Charleston from 1850 until 1856 in that official's campaign to eliminate the arbitrary imprisonment of black sailors mandated by South Carolina's Negro Seamen's Acts.

Consul William Mathew had arrived in the city fully determined to force legislative revisions of the laws, as other British consuls had done with similar statutes in North Carolina, Alabama, and Louisiana. His acerbic personality and undiplomatic style, however, doomed his lobbying efforts. His impatience when he failed to achieve his purpose in his first year as consul led him to publish a lengthy attack against the governor and the legislature as well as against the offensive laws. The Charleston newspapers that carried Mathew's extended commentary on South Carolina law and politics included Petigru's logically developed and meticulously prepared brief, which had been intended for the consul's private use.[71] That memorandum elaborated Petigru's conviction that the Negro Seamen's Acts violated the federal Constitution. To make that point he drew heavily on Judge William Johnson's 1823 opinion in the *Elkison* case, which asserted that the Constitution made treaties with foreign nations superior to state laws. But even if it did not, Petigru continued, the 1815 commercial treaty between Great Britain and the United States was a contract guaranteeing all "inhabitants of the two countries . . . liberty freely and securely to come with their ships and cargoes to all such places . . . to which other foreigners are permitted to come" as part of the "reciprocal liberty of commerce" the treaty embodied. The treaty was, he argued, a contract between the two countries and, like any other contract, was sheltered by the constitutional provision that states may pass no laws impairing the obligations of contracts. Furthermore, since the Constitution denies states the power to make treaties with foreign nations, South Carolina most certainly was prohibited from altering or breaking a treaty. Petigru capped his argument by quoting South Carolina's own John C. Calhoun, who as secretary of state had asserted that it "cannot be pretended that the rights guarantied, by Treaty between two independent Powers, may be abridged or modified by the municipal regulations of one of the parties, without and against the consent of the other." [72]

His analysis was rock-solid. But Petigru the lawyer was above all a realist, and, in a private letter that Mathew chose not to publish, he questioned whether the British government could win its point in any South Carolina court, federal or state. On the one hand, he asserted, federal courts lacked jurisdiction to render judgments in suits for damages less than $500, a sum that far exceeded both customary costs for maintaining black seamen in Charleston's jail for the time their ships were in port and the amount any South Carolina jury would award for vindictive damages. Perversely, then, an action in a state court would be more likely to create a viable test case, since any South Carolina judge would rule that the Negro Seamen's Acts were constitutional and would thereby give good grounds for an appeal to the federal Supreme Court. But then what? Even if the Supreme Court found the acts unconstitutional the decision would be a "barren victory," for the initial case would necessarily be remanded to a state court for a verdict on the evidence. No South Carolina jury would award damages of more than a few pennies. Nor would the state cease locking up free black seamen. "In the present temper of the people here, the unconstitutionality of the law would not stagger them at all. They would continue to enforce it, even after the Supreme Court had declared it void, & if it produced a collision [with the federal government] the result would only [be] so much the more to their taste." [73]

Given that reality, Petigru urged Mathew to treat "with Governor [John] Means as puissance a puissance" and gain his support for legislative amendment. Unfortunately, however, Mathew's tactless style had already blocked that route. [74] So, against his own better judgment, Petigru undertook two actions in whose outcome he had little faith. On April 5, 1852, following the consul's instructions, he went to a state judge seeking a writ of habeas corpus for Manuel Pereira, a British merchant seaman who had just been jailed under provisions of the Negro Seamen's Acts. The steward of a storm-damaged vessel forced into Charleston harbor for repairs, Pereira, a "Portuguese mestizo" though a British subject, was caught in an 1835 revision of the law that had removed the previous exemption for sailors driven into a South Carolina harbor by shipwreck. Treating Pereira's case as routine, Judge Thomas Withers summarily dismissed his petition, and Petigru immediately appealed. But the law appeals court would not sit in Charleston until the following January, long after Pereira's captain and Consul Mathew had agreed to pay his jail fees so that he could sail with his ship. As a result, when the case did come before the appeals court, Judge John Belton O'Neall, ruling for a unanimous bench, struck it from the docket because, with Pereira already released, the court "should do a vain act to hear this appeal." [75] Certainly if O'Neall, known for his sympathetic codification of all South Carolina laws dealing with blacks, avoided the issue, it was unlikely that any other challenge to the Negro Seamen's Acts could succeed in any state court.

So, in the next case, Mathew ordered Petigru to seek damages of $4,000 in federal circuit court on behalf of Reuben Roberts, a Nassau-born cook aboard the British ship *Clyde*. Barely six weeks after Judge Withers had rejected the *Pereira* petition, Roberts had been imprisoned for the eight days his vessel was in port. But it was nearly a year before United States District Court judge Robert Gilchrist, presiding alone in the circuit court in the unexpected absence of Supreme Court justice James Wayne, heard the case. Roberts's absence, however, was not an impediment to this case, since this was a suit against Sheriff Jeremiah D. Yates for "assault, battery, and false imprisonment" rather than an action to free the sailor.[76] The legal talent assembled to defend Yates included Isaac Hayne, South Carolina's attorney general, Senator and former state judge Andrew P. Butler, and two leading Charleston lawyers, Christopher Memminger and Edward McCready. All were fully aware that Petigru's strategy was to move the case as swiftly as possible to the Supreme Court. His argument at the circuit court level thus avoided constitutional argument beyond the simple assertion "that the laws and statutes of South Carolina" on which the defense relied contravened "the treaty of 1815, and the reciprocity [act] and proclamation of 1830," and were therefore "unconstitutional . . . invalid and of no force." Just as Petigru had predicted, Judge Gilchrist instructed the jury that the South Carolina laws were constitutional, and the jury accordingly found for Yates.[77]

The year that elapsed between Roberts's incarceration and the circuit court verdict in April 1853 sabotaged the planned appeal to the Supreme Court. Mathew, whose confrontational style had accomplished nothing, was called home. His government replaced him with Robert Bunch, who, as British consul in Philadelphia, had already demonstrated a suave alternative to Mathew's abrasive manner. His transfer to Charleston signaled a deliberate change in British policy. The Foreign Office had decided to put aside judicial challenges for another try at legislative modification of the offensive laws. That approach, however, became feasible only after Secretary of State Daniel Webster died in October 1852, for Webster had protested official British efforts to lobby state governments on issues involving American foreign policy. Moreover, had there been any tacit collaboration with the Fillmore administration, for whom Petigru acted as United States district attorney for South Carolina during the very period when he pressed the *Pereira* and *Roberts* cases, it ended in March 1853 when Franklin Pierce assumed the presidency.

In light of all this, Bunch dropped the *Roberts* appeal and lobbied the state legislature instead. It was a wise decision, for within three years the law was modified. The changes were minimal. But they did eliminate the arbitrary jailing of British subjects. After 1856 a ship captain could opt to post bond for a black seaman in his employ, who would then be allowed to remain aboard ship while it was docked in a South Carolina harbor. Although this did not give black seamen the liberty guaranteed to all other British sailors, it did spare them the indignity of jail and their captains the maintenance fees charged by the sheriff. Just what role Petigru may have played in this outcome is unclear. The new law was, however, passed in December 1856, immediately after his brother-in-law Robert Allston had been elected governor. Furthermore, Consul Bunch gave credit for the modification of the law to two key legislators, one of whom was Petigru's close friend Alfred Huger.[78]

Whether Petigru's role in *Pereira* and *Roberts* was more a matter of politics than of law cannot be determined from the surviving documents. But that he acted as an attorney for the British government while he served as a federal district attorney and that he had accepted the latter post only when President Fillmore could find no other Carolinian willing to take it hint strongly that if there was not active collaboration with Washington, there was at least knowledgeable assent to his course. It may also be significant that Petigru's legal career was otherwise devoid of cases undertaken to alter the laws affecting either slaves or free African Americans. Even his representation in the ambiguous cases of quasi-free blacks involved no challenges to public law. Yet in undertaking such cases and in his rationale for doing so there was an implicit political statement of which he surely was well aware.

At bottom, however, Petigru understood the trial process not as a way to legislate but as a tool to protect the interests of specific individuals. It was that perception that shaped the most dramatic of all the civil liberties cases he handled in the 1850s, the case of Reuben Smalle, a cantankerous and allegedly abolitionist Yankee whose life and liberty were endangered by lynch law. In 1851 Smalle had come from Massachusetts to the Beaufort area to pursue his trade as an independent woodcutter. He quickly irritated local landowners, with whom he haggled over fees for stumpage rights, and storekeepers, with whom he bargained sharply for supplies. Shunned accordingly by most whites and all planters, Smalle further aroused suspicions by associating with slaves. The animosity he generated was so widespread that at one point he and his adolescent son were set adrift in a canoe on the Edisto River and refused permission to land at any of the abutting plantations.

When even that kind of treatment failed to drive him out, Smalle was arrested on trumped-up charges of having stolen some used rope. While he was jailed awaiting trial, Smalle, perhaps with Petigru's assistance, sought and obtained a writ of habeas corpus. Once freed, he launched a vituperative counteroffensive, charging his accusers with malicious prosecution, assault, and trespass. Rearrested for the same larceny, he was speedily tried, convicted, and sentenced to receive five lashes—a punishment usually reserved to blacks. But then tempers cooled. Smalle's persecutors delayed the flogging. Smalle sought a pardon. And the five men who had instigated the whole proceeding offered to lend him the money to pay court and jail costs, on which they said his release depended. But then Smalle balked. He refused the proffered sum. And so he was whipped.[79]

At this point, if not before, Petigru took up Smalle's case and advised him to sue the five "gentry of St Bartholomew's [Parish who] had abused and treated [him] like a dog."[80] In late November 1854 the suit came before the federal district court in Columbia. Carolina Hall, where the court regularly sat, was packed that day with citizens who thought that Smalle had got what he deserved. Petigru, anticipating as much, had spent much of the previous two months collecting evidence from character witnesses in Smalle's native Massachusetts and from observers of events in South Carolina. He well knew that pressing the claims of a self-proclaimed Yankee and alleged abolitionist would generate hostility. He was familiar, too, with planter, politician, and Beaufort attorney Richard De Treville, but he had not expected him to play so much on prevailing prejudice. De Treville's "clear, concise, and eminently caustic" summation for the defense praised his clients for resorting to lynch law to control a person widely suspected of "efforts to subvert the institutions of the State." De Treville's argument was, so a sympathetic reporter concluded, both intellectually convincing and emotionally moving.[81]

When De Treville finished, Petigru rose to make the closing argument for his client. He began at the emotional pitch on which De Treville had ended and built from there. Flashing evidence of his anger to those who recognized the meaning of the raised flame-red vein on his forehead, he was nonetheless fully in control, sweeping, even in such hostile circumstances, both jury and spectators to his side. He translated Smalle's otherwise offensive resort to a federal rather than a state court into an appeal to the only "unprejudiced tribunal" available. The man previously labeled an "abolition emissary" emerged as only a "hardy and honest woodcutter." And Petigru's unseemly association with an "abolitionist" became an effort to "shield a victim from oppression." Having deflected De Treville's implications of his own guilt by association, Petigru turned at last to the peril that Smalle's treatment posed for the civil liberties of all. Only by giving a favorable verdict to this insignificant woodcutter could the jury "save the State from an enunciation of the monstrous doctrine that odium is guilt, and that it is worse than crime to incur the charge of an unpopular offence."[82]

Petigru later admitted that he had not planned that speech. Indeed, his patience had been sorely tried by his "low Yankee" client, whose case he had taken without fee only to be bargained with over minor court costs and offended by the constant support that Smalle needed to make him "act like a man." It was, rather, De Treville's "downright appeal to party and prejudice" and his confounding the attorney with the client that inspired Petigru's passion in defense of fair trial, due process, and the freedom to differ from majority opinion.[83] He made those the issues, and he won a stunning victory. One reporter could scarcely believe the early rumor that the jury would award Smalle damages of $500. Yet the final verdict gave him five times that sum—and that in December 1854, the same month in which the state legislature elected one of the five defendants a master-in-chancery and made De Treville lieutenant governor of South Carolina.[84]

Unfortunately, however, Smalle's troubles had not ended. He did not collect his award for more than a year and a half; and even then Petigru had to seek the help of the United States marshal to force payment. Six months later, Smalle was committed to the state insane asylum. Once again Petigru came to his aid, although he could salvage only $500 from the "rogue" to whom the confused Yankee had handed over his entire award before he had been institutionalized. In the end, when Petigru arranged for Smalle's return to Massachusetts, their smashing victory seemed something less than total, for "the noble Chivalry of St Barts" was left only a little poorer and not a whit chastened.[85]

In May 1859 Petigru turned seventy. The following December the South Carolina legislature appointed him to codify the state's statute law at a salary greater than that paid any other state official. It was a tribute to the man and a recognition of his preeminent legal expertise, all the more stunning after his recent defense of unpopular causes and his willingness to confront popular prejudice. It also illuminates his place in legal history. He had pled cases in each of the four general areas in which scholars have posited regional distinctions in the interpretation and application of American law. If indeed southern laws and courts generally gave preference to rural and agricultural interests and consequently inhibited the transformation of American law to favor commercial values, Petigru differed from his region's style. He was an attorney for banks, railroads, and other corporations. In debt cases he more frequently represented creditors than debtors. This practice doubtless diverged from that of the majority of lawyers in the South, where there were few cities, limited banking facilities, and minimal railroad construction. Yet it did not set Petigru altogether apart from his colleagues, for his practice was varied. In probate, trust, and real estate cases, which constituted his most extensive practice and in which planters were his most likely clients, law changed slowly and Petigru leaned heavily on his expertise in pre-Revolutionary English precedent. Indeed, in one case he surprised even a South Carolina court by executing and defending a medieval-style deed of "feoffment, with livery of seizin" symbolized by the exchange of turf and twig between the contracting parties.

Like all southern lawyers and unlike all northern ones after 1825, Petigru functioned in a society whose laws defined most African Americans as property and extended even to free blacks little of the protection assumed to be the natural and constitutional right of whites. He did not challenge those legal constraints even when he attempted to circumvent them. Where he deviated most clearly from southern legal convention was in his direct confutation of incursions on the individual rights of white persons, which were generally tolerated as a necessary concession to social stability. Those cases he undertook in the 1850s to challenge unlimited male domination within marriage and to champion a pauper imprisoned for debt and a Yankee who fraternized with slaves marked a commitment to civil liberty unusual anywhere in the United States. Finally, his loyalty to the federal Constitution, which he believed was an essential bulwark against his fellow citizens' proclivity to infringe on individual rights, had long set him apart from the prevailing sentiment of his professional associates in South Carolina.[86]

While his position on constitutional law was inextricably linked with his politics, and his handling of clients' economic interest was determined primarily by practical realities, Petigru's circumvention of the laws governing slavery, like his rejection of the unlimited power of one individual over another, had deep personal roots. Throughout the 1850s he had held fast to principle while he developed new sympathies for the emotional needs and dilemmas of others. As a lawyer he increasingly advocated the peaceful resolution of disputes, yet in seeking reasonable compromise he never conceded the priority of justice. Now three score years and ten, in declining health, and more aware than ever of his own mortality, James Petigru faced the most trying years of his life, years of civil war, personal loss, and intellectual isolation.

SEVEN

Enduring War

When, on December 20, 1860, South Carolina seceded from the Union, James Petigru declared that he had seen "the last happy day of my life."[1] He had, in fact, little more than two years left to live. But they were long and unhappy years, years whose colossal conflicts dwarfed all earlier internal contradictions between the political conservatism in which he believed and the southern culture of which he was a part. Remaining in the Civil War South but still convinced that the United States Constitution best protected public order and individual freedom, he was intellectually isolated, a dissenter in a world his friends and kin had shaped. For Petigru, the Civil War was fought not only on the battlefield but within his mind, his household, and his family. And his sympathies lay with both sides.

Petigru's loyalty to the Union was an inherent part of his essential conservatism, which, like all conservatism, was necessarily rooted in the past. Not surprisingly, he valued the study of history. He was a founding member and the first president of the South Carolina Historical Society and an honorary member of the Massachusetts Historical Society. Like most well-educated Americans of his time, he had studied the history of ancient Greece and Rome in school. Like many more of his contemporaries, he was fascinated by the past of his own country, so fascinated that from 1855 to 1860 he actively oversaw the collection and publication of many South Carolina colonial documents.[2]

His was, however, no antiquarian quest, for Petigru believed that the record of the past held essential lessons for the present. Examining the evidence produced by practical experience was a necessary test of abstract reasoning that, no matter how logical, might otherwise lead even wise persons to grievous error. As is true with most historians, Petigru's

James L. Petigru, carte de visite, 1861.
(South Caroliniana Library, University of South Carolina)

conception of the past was shaped both by the questions he asked of it and by the values against which he measured its evidence. Nowhere was this more true than in his understanding of the American Revolution. To him, the Revolution was an example of amazing restraint in which a victorious but minimally rewarded army ceded power to a government of elected civilians to create a republic whose nature was as commendably different from that of revolutionary France as it was from the experience of Greece and Rome. Yet his praise of a distinctive American event did not lead him to the blind patriotism that made heroes of all who fought for independence and villains of all their opponents. Indeed, in 1858 he rather identified with the Tories, whom he understood not as "a horde of ruffians" but rather as conservatives whose error had lain "in carrying to excess the sentiment of loyalty, which is founded in virtue."[3]

More praiseworthy even than post-revolutionary restraint was the creation of the federal government. As Petigru understood it, the United States Constitution confirmed what the Revolution had aimed to achieve. Reversing the Confederation's dispersal of power was but a minor part of its accomplishment, for it had by its division of legitimate governmental power between the individual states and the federal union ensured the Revolution's goals of restricting centralized public authority in the interests of individual liberty. But individual freedom, as Petigru said in his 1844 Fourth of July oration, required positive government as well as restraints on legitimate power. This too the Constitution had accomplished with its system of checks and balances. Without both the powers allotted and the restraints imposed, "there could be no barrier between a dominant majority and the object which they mean to effect."[4] Thus, by creating a constitutional union that divided sovereignty between state and nation and checked the evil of concentrated power in any one branch of government, the American people had fulfilled the promise of their revolution.

But the problem of abuse of power was not obviated by the broadly democratic underpinning of the American experiment. Nowhere did Petigru more clearly address that dilemma than in the question he asked that Independence Day audience: "For who shall control where all are equal, or how shall the people restrain the will of the people?" The best means to control the popular passions implied in his question was education. If a republic was to survive, he thought, its government must provide the schools necessary to cultivate in all its citizens the

intellectual independence that was "the bright side of Democracy."
Without access to knowledge, citizens would lack the ability to challenge their government, and individuals the means to protect their
freedom. Only access to learning guaranteed the diversity that could
withstand the force of majority opinion. And given Petigru's opinion
that "the Majority are wicked is a truth that passed long since into a
proverb," republican government could not long survive unless it sponsored that learning, for "what hope is there for the human race when
there is no minority."[5]

And yet the same Petigru who argued so forcefully for individual
freedom, who so opposed governmental and majority tyranny, and who
could see no difference between a political and a religious test oath,
himself subverted religious liberty in an extended defense of municipal blue laws requiring the observance of the Christian Sabbath. The
1847 case of *City Council of Charleston* v. *S. A. Benjamin* reveals an
extraordinary inconsistency in his theorizing. The case was first tried
in municipal court in 1846, and in that trial Petigru played no role.
Solomon A. Benjamin, an orthodox Jewish retailer, had, in defiance
of a Charleston ordinance, sold a pair of gloves on a Sunday. But the
city's right to assure all citizens a day of rest was not the issue in the
municipal court trial, for no one questioned that Benjamin observed
the Sabbath of his own faith. Rather, the issue was the city's right to
make the Sabbath of the Christian majority the day on which no commerce could be transacted. Following the judge's instructions that in a
"community where there is a complete severance between Church and
State" no government could impose a religious observance, the jury
found for Benjamin.[6]

The city attorney pressed an appeal in which Petigru joined, although
whether he did so as a public service or for a fee is not clear. In either
case, his defense of the restrictive ordinance was so unlike his usual
presentations, so repetitious and drawn-out, so full of citations to statutes and precedents, that it hints at his uneasiness with his own argument. Asserting and reasserting that Christianity was "a part of the
law," he contended that the South Carolina Constitution's prohibition
of a religious qualification for civil office did not alter the fundamental
proposition that "Christianity is part and parcel of the common law."
And it was explicitly Christianity—neither a single denomination nor
all religions—that Petigru maintained was essential to legitimate social
control. "Christianity," he expounded, "has reference to the principles

of right and wrong; to the obligations of natural justice; it is the foundation of those morals and manners upon which our society is formed; it is their basis. Remove this and they would fall, there would be no harmony, the law would be one of force." In this case as in no other, Petigru argued the right of public authorities to limit individual civil liberties in the interest of social order. "To speak against religion (the Christian) is breaking down the bond of good government."[7]

The Court of Errors largely agreed. Writing for the majority, Judge John Belton O'Neall echoed much of Petigru's argument. But he concluded that the power of civil authorities to appoint "a Sabbath, or day of rest from labor" was only "a municipal institution, conducive of civil expedience."[8] What Judge O'Neall, an Evangelical Baptist, had not said was what Petigru, a noncommunicant Episcopalian, had: that Christianity was part of the common law.

When Petigru considered the inherent conflict between a republic premised in egalitarianism and South Carolina's social stratification, he displayed similar inconsistencies. Remembering his humble rural beginnings but more accustomed to life in the upper reaches of a sophisticated urban center, his class loyalties tugged in two directions. Sure that social and economic differences were inevitable, he believed that it was the "will of God that the poor be always with us." Yet he believed that such differences should not disqualify citizens from political participation. As a legislator in the 1830s he had sought to give South Carolina voters the direct election of presidential electors, removing their selection from a legislature apportioned by wealth as much as it was by population. But he did not challenge the state's property qualification for officeholding. As a lawyer he trusted juries, not judges, to give the best evaluations of evidence and thus produce the fairest common law verdict. But he insisted also that it was essential for judges to instruct jurors on the law's meaning. If he mistrusted *demos* and said so repeatedly, he also mistrusted the arrogance and ambition of *aristoi*. He condemned the irrationality of the majority no more than he did the unpredictability of chancellors who manufactured equity law out of their own prejudices, and the delusions of low country planters who in legislating secession produced revolution. It is not surprising, then, that although he considered a republic the best form of government, he believed that republics must inevitably be short-lived. The ambivalence implicit in that anticipation became explicit in his observations to J. Johnston Pettigrew in 1853. He began with the observation that "the political power of the Country must fall eventually into the hands of certain great families as it always has done in other republics." He ended with the advice that his protégé should cultivate his standing in one of those great families to be ready to wield that power.[9]

Petigru himself had wielded precious little political power since the nullification years. Never again after he lost his bid for the state legislature in 1838 did he run for elective office. Despite the similarity of his views to John Calhoun's fear of an unrestrained majority, by 1850 there was probably no constituency in South Carolina that would elect a man of his principles. State politics were by then played out between Cooperationists—those who thought South Carolina should not secede unless accompanied by other southern states—and Secessionists, who favored a go-it-alone policy. Petigru was still, as he had been in 1830, an out-and-out Unionist. Yet, in 1833, when tariff compromise had ended the nullification crisis, he had believed that disunion was only postponed. He had predicted that a "devilish[ly] evil day" awaited the next generation, when slavery would have replaced the tariff as the divisive issue, for even then he felt certain that the "Nullifiers mean to pick a quarrel with the North about negroes." Succeeding events did nothing to diminish his belief that pitting a fire-eating, slaveholding culture against abolitionist fanaticism would ultimately foment disunion, wreck the federal Constitution, and produce at last "war between the States."[10]

   While he expressed no sympathy with abolitionists, Petigru's open support for the Union blocked any political future in his own state. And without a sound political base at home, he was unlikely to be appointed to any desirable federal post, even in those rare years when the Whigs were in power. Nevertheless, and in spite of the exclusion from power it caused, his unwavering political convictions made him a visible critic of his state's course. His friends thought him perverse in refusing to do the things that might have broadened his political options. If it was the substance of his Whiggery that offended the overwhelming majority of his agricultural state, the style of his politics agitated even those who shared many of his views. In 1849 Benjamin Perry, a Democrat but also a Unionist, who admired Petigru as "the ablest & most accomplished lawyer in the United States," disparaged him "as a statesman . . . below mediocrity [who] should never engage in politics again." Yet Petigru was not devoid of political skills, as his successful lobbying attested. Even his brother-in-law Robert Allston, an avowed Nullifier in the 1830s and a Secessionist through most of the 1850s, turned to him for "counsel & aid" when he faced legislative elections for the presidency of the state senate and the governorship of South Carolina.[11] Petigru's presumed mediocrity thus lay not in lack of know-how or unfamiliarity with the system but rather in his open expression of unpopular views, his acknowledged preference for Henry Clay over more electable Whig presidential candidates, his unhidden contempt for renegade Virginia Whig John Tyler, and his friendly association with Massachusetts Whigs Daniel Webster, Edward Everett, and Robert Winthrop.

It was therefore ironic that Petigru's political career showed signs, however brief, of reviving in 1850. The coincidence of Whig president Zachary Taylor's election in 1848, his death in office eighteen months later, and the sectional tumult over the issues of the Compromise of 1850 allowed President Millard Fillmore to consider appointing Petigru his attorney general. Petigru, however, despite his Washington connections, had no support from his state's congressional delegation and was therefore rapidly eclipsed by Kentucky Whig John Crittenden, who had solid backing from his home state. Unflustered, Petigru continued to advise the president on South Carolina appointments; and when no other respectable lawyer would serve there as United States district attorney, Petigru reluctantly accepted that office.[12]

Because the Fillmore administration wholeheartedly backed the Compromise of 1850, which South Carolinians almost unanimously opposed, Petigru found himself ever more a political outsider at home. He scorned the "middle ground" charted by the Cooperationists, for their sanction of secession sometime in the future threatened the Union no less than did the enthusiasm for immediate secession. Even as a tactical maneuver he would not budge from an unflinching commitment to the Union as it was. Consequently Petigru watched the minority of which he had long been part shrink until it was only a miniscule collection of impotent dissidents—excepting only Benjamin Perry, who continued to represent Greenville in the South Carolina House of Representatives until 1860. Of himself, Petigru wrote Daniel Webster, "If one has not influence to stem the torrent of popular delusion he is reduced to the melancholy part of a spectator in the midst of the ruin."[13]

Still, the Cooperationists did at least postpone the ruin. In December 1850 the state legislature voted to delay from October 1851 until April

1852 the convention scheduled to consider South Carolina's secession and then proposed that it be preceded by a southern regional convention, which Cooperationists hoped would steal the Secessionists' thunder. Such equivocations did not reassure Petigru. Although he agreed that they "would avert a catastrophe" in the immediate present, he feared that in the long run they would only give the Secessionists more time "to vapour about their narrow and provincial patriotism" and build support for it.[14]

Any remaining optimism Petigru might have cherished was further dampened by the election of Franklin Pierce in 1852. The Democrats' choice of this New Hampshire nonentity as their presidential candidate, "as obscure a man as any person in the United States that ever was a Senator or general," boded ill for the future. Eighteen months later, Petigru's forebodings were realized when Pierce endorsed the Kansas-Nebraska Bill with its explicit repeal of the Missouri Compromise. Destroying that long-uncontested balance of regional interests in the unsettled West was, Petigru lamented, "the worst thing that has been done in 20 years." Well might he lament, for, given the presidential candidates in 1856, he was forced to support James Buchanan. Although certainly more acceptable than radical Republican John C. Frémont, whose candidacy lit fires under the secessionist cauldron, the Pennsylvania Democrat was at best only a more realistic choice than Millard Fillmore, who was running on the Know-Nothing ticket. So Petigru's preference for Buchanan meant little. And once Buchanan was elected, Petigru dismissed his Kansas policy as a "paltry affair," albeit he did give limited approval to the proslavery Lecompton constitution, which was never, except for the single article guaranteeing slavery, referred to the voters.[15]

Thereafter Petigru had little to say about the frictions that chafed away at the Union. He was still a Unionist. He was also a slaveholder in a state whose population was more than half slave. In both law and politics he preferred compromise to confrontation. But again and again events slammed shut the doors to sectional compromise: bleeding Kansas, the *Dred Scott* decision, John Brown's raid. Long since, the doors leading to political power had been closed to Petigru. Now he simply watched and waited, never quite giving up hope.

On May 3, 1860, a week before his seventy-first birthday, Petigru attended a session of the national Democratic Nominating Convention, held that year in Charleston. The delegates were as clearly—and as murkily—split along sectional lines as the country for which they were to nominate a presidential candidate. In his address to the convention, Benjamin Perry was a lone South Carolina voice as he begged the delegates to "guard [the South] against evils which no one can foresee or foretell" by choosing a candidate who would sustain the Union. His speech fell on mostly hostile ears, including those of a "fellow [sitting] on the next bench" to Petigru, who hissed Perry. The old lawyer "longed to pull his nose. I really think I would have done it, or at least have told [him] he was a scoundrel; but I was with ladies and with friends I would not compromise and [therefore] let the miscreant alone." But more than southern chivalry restrained him. Continuing his letter to Perry he confessed, "I have contracted a disinclination to write or to speak, when truth is in question." [16]

Whatever the cause of Petigru's disinclination—old age, disillusionment, physical exhaustion, or the detachment that long experience in public affairs can give those who accept their own powerlessness—he still hoped for compromise. Consequently, against his averred disinclination, he openly backed the John Bell–Edward Everett Constitutional Union ticket rather than either the Northern Democrat Stephen Douglas or the Southern Democrat John Breckinridge. He did not, of course, consider supporting the Republican candidate. Yet even the election of Abraham Lincoln should not, he thought, make secession inevitable. In September Petigru wrote his old friend Alfred Huger that "no possible issue could be more untenable than to make [Lincoln's] bare election a casus belli, without any overt act against the Constitution or even, the Dred Scott decision." Several weeks later he wrote Everett, a personal friend who had been a guest in his Charleston home, that although a Republican victory would "give the Union a great strain," he did not think it would make South Carolina secede at once or alone.[17] He was, however, only whistling in the dark.

The South Carolina legislature met on November 5 to cast the state's ballots for presidential electors, and its members stayed on in Columbia long enough to learn the returns from the elections in all the other states. Finding that Lincoln's plurality of popular votes guaranteed his victory in the electoral college, the legislature quickly moved to call a state secession convention. When it met, Petigru faced the reality that he would probably outlive the federal Constitution, which was but two months older than he. With appeals to reason now seemingly fruitless, he began to churn out the humorous epigrams that have become a part of his legend. While the secession convention was meeting in Columbia, Petigru, who was there on other business, was asked by a stranger for directions to the state insane asylum. The "building, my friend," he replied, "stands upon the outskirts of the town, but," he added, pointing to the First Baptist Church, where the convention was in session, "I think you will find the inmates yonder." The same metaphor surfaced in his assessment that South Carolina was too small to be a nation and too large for an insane asylum. When he was informed that Louisiana had seceded, he exclaimed, "Good Lord . . . , I thought we bought Louisiana." And when the rector of St. Michael's failed to offer the customary prayer for the well-being of the president of the United States, Petigru rose from his pew and left the service. "Mr. Petigru has such a keen sense of the ridiculous," wrote Mary Boykin Chesnut, South Carolina's most famous Civil War diarist, "he must be laughing in his sleeve at the hubbub this untimely trait of independence has raised."[18]

His humor, however, veiled deep despair and failed to dull his worst anticipations. The fast pace of events leading to secession induced in Petigru an "awful foreboding of what is to come when the passions of the mob are let loose[;] and the truth is our gentlemen are little distinguished in a mob from the rabble." When "joy bells" rang out in Charleston to celebrate passage of the Ordinance of Secession, Petigru heard the alarm of firebells in the night. "They have this day set a blazing torch to the temple of constitutional liberty and, [if it] please God, we shall have no more peace forever." Bitter in spirit, he was astounded by the "apathy and carelessness that mark[ed] the behaviour of men otherwise respectable," former supporters of union who fell strangely silent now.[19]

Just as he had deluded himself with assurances that secession could be avoided, Petigru, in the early months of 1861, clung to the possibility that war was not inevitable. A man of peace, though not a pacifist, he entertained few romantic notions about battlefield glory. War was a "reign of violence," "the scourge of the human race." Hardly cheered by those long-held convictions, he watched the events that made real his worst fears. In Charleston harbor, on January 9, state forces fired on the federal ship *Star of the West*, which had been sent to supply Fort Sumter, the new island garrison to which federal troops had been moved from less defensible installations. The day before, and just as portentous of the bloody war to follow, a South Carolinian had been shot to death by a fellow militiaman while on sentry duty at Castle Pinckney, a fortified island even closer to the city than Sumter, where both were stationed. "He was the first victim of the war and died by mistake."[20]

Shaken by both events, Petigru was afraid that Governor Francis Pickens was preparing an open assault on Fort Sumter, in which young family members might be killed—especially Colonel Johnston Petti-grew, Commander of the First Regiment of Rifles of South Carolina, who was then stationed at Castle Pinckney. Thus fearful, Petigru wel-comed the formation of the Confederate States of America as a brake on the rash action contemplated by South Carolina fire-eaters. Indeed, he convinced himself that Jefferson Davis might undertake direct nego-tiations with Washington rather than begin a war at Fort Sumter. If both sides met in the interest of peace, then the leaders in Washing-ton might also pull back and compromise. Referring to constitutional limits on the use of force, Petigru went so far as to predict, in a wild burst of euphoria, that the whole "business will end in a treaty." On such improbabilities did his hopes for peace depend.[21]

Though it did not extinguish them completely, President Lincoln's inauguration on March 4 greatly dimmed those hopes. But Petigru, as he watched the growing tenseness over Fort Sumter, believed that Lincoln as yet had no fixed plan,[22] an idea reinforced by the visit of two White House emissaries to his home on Sunday, March 24. It was a strange visit under such circumstances and doubtless left all three men perplexed. Ward Lamon, a longtime Lincoln associate, Petigru knew not at all. He did, however, know Stephen Hurlbut, the son of his old friend Martin Hurlbut, with whom he had taught at Beaufort College. In the early 1840s, young Stephen had read law and clerked in Petigru's office. But he had been forced to leave Charleston under the cloud of an unusual financial manipulation and had settled in Illi-nois, where he had established ties with Lincoln. Lamon and Hurlbut talked with Petigru for a couple of hours to test the waters. Then, later that evening, Lamon returned alone to talk again. Hurlbut, though he poked around town for a few days, apparently made no further contact. Petigru concluded that their probing for information about the con-dition of federal forces at Fort Sumter, like their soundings of public opinion, signaled that the administration in Washington was still very much unsettled as to its proper course.[23]

He was wrong. Only two weeks later President Lincoln notified Governor Pickens that he had sent a naval expedition to resupply Sumter. That was on April 6. On April 12, 1861, at 4:30 A.M., after Major Robert Anderson had refused an ultimatum to surrender, General Pierre Gustave Toutant Beauregard ordered shore batteries to open fire on the island fort. Charlestonians rushed to the rooftops and third-story piazzas of the houses lining the high battery to watch the shells explode and to cheer on their troops. At last, something was happening. Everywhere there was excitement. When, after thirty-four hours of constant shelling, Anderson finally surrendered, a thrill of power possessed and military superiority proved rippled through the city. In the midst of it all, Petigru, his heart heavy, sat alone in his office "while all the world is gone to witness the bombardment of Fort Sumter by the collective forces of South Carolina." That day marked the end of peace. "Our politicians have succeeded in evoking the spirit of hostility on both sides."[24]

By June, Petigru had to confess that the Union had been destroyed and that all hope of reconstructing it as it had been was gone. What was he to do now? How should he face so bleak a future? How should he act? With which side should he cast his lot? For more than forty years he had practiced law and undertaken civic action within a polity defined by constitutional limitations on public authority and within a federal system that balanced the "semi sovereignty of the U.S." against the "quasi sovereignty of the State."[25] To be sure, it was not a perfect system. Its boundaries were neither sharp nor clear. Yet the restraints it imposed were the safest bulwark against the exercise of arbitrary power and the most effective guarantee of individual rights. Once again, Petigru confronted the dilemmas of unlimited democracy. What protection was there now for the minority when an impassioned, overwhelming, and unrestrained majority had embarked on war?

"I made a great mistake in 1832, when I might have quit the country . . . with the prospect of doing something," Petigru wrote ruefully even before war came. Yet however much he might "really wish" that he was "on the other side of the Potomac" in the summer of 1861, he acknowledged the bonds that precluded his doing in 1861 what "I heartily wish that I had done 40 years ago." His age, his health, and his obligations to family members all barred his way, as did his persistent inability to save money for his old age. And so, still needing a livelihood, he was dependent on his Charleston law practice. Looking at matters practically, he realized, though with some exaggeration, that as an émigré in the North "my best business would be beggary."[26]

In fact, however, emotional reasons pressed just as hard as financial ones. Except for his daughter Caroline, who left South Carolina for good in June 1861, all his family were in the South and would remain there. Moreover, although he differed from his friends and neighbors, he was neither ostracized by them nor harassed by those whose political folly he still openly criticized. At least one contemporary journalist and several modern historians have maintained that this was no more than the tolerance extended to an elderly eccentric who was no more to be taken seriously than the village idiot. Yet Petigru's many friends, most of whom had remained so despite long years of sharp political difference, saw it otherwise. Long ago planter Richard Singleton had defined the binding attraction to his friend that had survived even the fiercest battles of nullification: "Personally nothing can destroy that confidence, esteem, & (I may add) love which may properly be said *to nestle* in the hearts of those who know you well & who have cause to know you as *a friend.*" Neither secession nor civil war destroyed the charm that cemented such social relations. Until his Broad Street house burned to the ground in December 1861, Petigru's regular Sunday dinner parties transcended political divisions. At the same table at which William T. Sherman, Edward Everett, and William H. Seward had once sat, Governor Francis Pickens and former governors John Manning and Robert Allston dined in the spring of 1861. All supported secession and the new Confederacy. Other frequent guests were Congressman William Porcher Miles, who had vacated his seat in Washington to serve in the Confederate Congress, and General Beauregard, commander of Confederate forces in the Charleston area. Mary Chesnut was perplexed by Petigru's "astounding pluck," which "raised him in the estimation of the people he flouts and contradicts in their tenderest points." Plowden Weston, who in 1860 kept more than three hundred slaves on his Georgetown rice plantations, was one of them. Yet he observed in March 1863 that after two years of war and a lifetime of dissent, Petigru had "had almost every distinguished contemporary for a political opponent" and not one of them as a "personal enemy." And Robert Barnwell Rhett, who as editor of the fire-eating *Charleston Mercury* marked the extreme of political opposition, insisted that never once in the thirty years they had known each other had Petigru been "induced to say to me an unkind word or do an unkind deed." So it was not all sentiment when his political colleague Benjamin Perry observed that Petigru "drew every one to him, high or low, by his cordial heart."[27] However eulogistic, however nostalgic such observations doubtless were, they explain more about Petigru's ability to remain in wartime Charleston than do allegations of bees in an old man's bonnet.

Ironically, it was within his family circle that Petigru felt himself most isolated. Convinced that clergymen and women were the most fanatic proponents of war and the most resolute opponents of reasonable political compromise, Petigru found ample evidence right at home. Both Sue and Jane Amelia were ardent Secessionists—though his wife's ardor did not extend to contributing the household silver when Governor Pickens ordered all citizens to "bring their plate to be melted down." All Petigru's sisters, too, backed Secession, supported the Confederacy, and justified the War for Southern Independence in which the lives of their sons, husbands, nephews, and cousins were at stake. Even Jane North, who had shared her brother's political preferences until 1861, now opted for loyalty to state and section over union and nation. When he was with them, Petigru felt more alone than he did among friends or strangers, for although they remained close in other respects, the family unity he so valued was severely strained. Yet as the war progressed, he could not be "sorry that none of you share my opinions, for what would be the use of keener optics if they only served to bring to view painful sights?"[28]

Nor could Caroline Carson, who shared her father's opinions, help him. Only with great difficulty could she even communicate with him, for mail between North and South had to be either sent by way of Nassau or even England to circumvent the naval blockade or handcarried by those given military permission to cross the front lines under flags of truce. Additionally, her absence imposed still greater burdens on Petigru's resources, for she still needed his financial assistance. It was he who furnished funds for her to travel to Europe in 1861 for her health. It was he who had to oversee the arrangements she made for the Carson property before she went north. Most emotionally taxing, however, was his responsibility for his grandson. James Carson, who was barely sixteen when his mother left the South, wanted desperately to enlist in the Confederate Army. His mother absolutely forbade it. In 1862, when she was settled in New York City, she insisted that he join her. But young Jem refused. And his grandfather constantly mediated by shaping stratagems to keep him out of the army and in southern schools.[29]

Only once was there the slightest possibility that Unionist father and daughter would be reunited. In 1862 a group of politically powerful New Yorkers urged President Lincoln to appoint Petigru an associate justice of the Supreme Court to fill the vacancy created when Alabaman John Campbell had resigned to go home. But their petitions came to nothing.[30] And it is doubtful that Petigru knew much, if anything, of their efforts on his behalf.

By the time fighting began in earnest, in July 1861 at the battle of Manassas, or Bull Run, Petigru had already lost hope that the Union could be saved or even restored. Nonetheless, he responded bitterly to the South's first great victory. Manassas had been won, he wrote Jane North, by that "ferocity of our people" that had been "whetted by the practice of gouging first under the Colonial Government and of using the Bowie knife in later times." It was, in short, a return to the savagery that had scarred upcountry South Carolina for much of the eighteenth century, when uncontrolled violence had blotted out law and justice. Similarly, in the late fall, when the United States Navy attacked Port Royal, invaded the Sea Islands, and threatened the entire South Carolina coast, Petigru sarcastically condemned wartime depredations against civilians. In a letter to Robert Allston, whose Georgetown plantations seemed endangered, he wrote, "Let us hope for the best: But what is the best? Perhaps, that Beauregard may whip McClellen, and overrun the whole North, and make Jef[ferson] Davis Emperor. If he and McLellan [*sic*] stand face to face eating up the substance of the country, it will not be long before famine is added to Insolvency." The response of the Sea Island planters to Yankee invasion clearly demonstrated the economic irrationality to which war drove civilians. They had fled their plantations on short notice, leaving their slaves and other property behind. That was foolish enough. But more ominous were the subsequent threats of other planters to burn their plantations rather than let them fall under enemy or slave control. And positively horrifying were military plans for a scorched earth policy extending even to proposals that the entire city of Charleston be burned to the ground. With withering sarcasm Petigru told his sister Jane that he advised "all them that are blustering about their intentions to burn their houses to keep the Yankees out to resort to a more significant way of spiting the enemy by hanging themselves."[31]

As he reflected on the brutalities of war—the fatal brawls between soldiers, the mutinies within crack Confederate units, the battlefield slaughter, and the projected destruction of whole cities—Petigru conceded his impotence to impose the civilized restraint he so prized. Yet, one field of action was open to him. He could, as an attorney, try to block governmental intrusions on individual rights. Specifically, he struggled to counteract the Confederacy's new laws confiscating the property of Carolinians who had left the state before hostilities began. Where courts still functioned, he found his own way to combat war-induced injustice.

Issues of constitutionality had plagued him since the very formation of the Confederacy. At its initial session, when the capital was in Montgomery, Alabama, the Confederate Congress had adopted most of the United States Constitution as its own. But that legislative body had been neither elected nor given any authority to make or revise a constitution. In doing so, it had violated the critical distinction between a convention called to frame fundamental law and a legislature summoned to adopt statutes within the limits set by such a constitution. Thus there was, as Petigru wrote Benjamin Perry, no "line between the things that lie within their Legislative powers and those that do not." They assumed the authority to shape or reshape a constitution in order to legitimize their power to pass any law they wished. Even after the government was established in more permanent form in Richmond, Virginia, it continued to do "as it pleases, whether in public or private without anything for authority except the undisputed will of the people."[32] Once again Petigru confronted the dangers of a majority unrestrained by constitutional limits on its power.

It was within this context that Petigru reacted to the series of confiscation laws adopted by the Confederate Congress. The first, passed in May 1861, provided only for sequestering debts that southerners owed to residents of the United States. It required that such debts be paid not to the creditors but to the Confederate government. The second, passed the following August, made a sweeping extension of confiscation. In retaliation against a similar and recently adopted United States law, it provided for the seizure of all property belonging to "any alien enemy" and required every citizen "speedily to give information" about all such property within the Confederacy. Petigru, who believed that an individual's right to his property was fundamental to civil liberty, was appalled at the disdain for "the rules of civilized warfare" inherent in both northern and southern confiscation laws.[33]

About the nothern statute, of course, Petigru could do nothing. But when the Confederate district court first sat in Charleston in October 1861, he stood before former United States district judge Andrew G. Magrath, to whom he had taught the law, and refused absolutely to furnish the information required by the new enactment. Indeed, his initial response was confined to defying its intrusion not only upon attorney-client confidentiality but upon trust and honor among friends. No clause in the Confederate Constitution, he argued, empowered the government to "set up an inquisition" designed to extract accusations against another person from either lawyer or layman. The sole historical precedent for the writs of garnishment for information that this law authorized was the "odious usurpation of power" by the English monarchy's Star Chamber. Even the procedures of Torquemada, the Spanish grand inquisitor of Toledo, were less menacing, for he burned "Jews and Protestants without calling upon their best friends to inform against them and making it penal not to do so." How could a law be innocent that called "upon one to commit a breach of trust? To break faith with a friend" or compel an attorney "to do what will make him despised by all honorable men?"[34]

With searing irony, Petigru quietly sidestepped his customary disdain for extreme states' rights arguments. He allowed that he "might recognize" South Carolina's authority to enact such a law "because in a State like South Carolina a sufferer has no security or remedy against those in power, unless from some guarantee in the Constitution of the State." But District Attorney Richard Miles, taking his argument literally, missed the irony and charged the longtime Unionist with invoking "the strictest and sternest construction of States Rights that had ever been contended for even in South Carolina, in opposition to the power of the Confederate Government." Exuding near-reverent patriotism for that government, Miles then charged Petigru with hurling invectives at the bench and showing disrespect for the court.[35]

When Miles had finished, Petigru asked and received permission from Judge Magrath to file a demurrer. Meanwhile, Miles's colleagues, who shared the warmth of his loyalties, sat stunned by his vituperation. Then one of them, William Whaley, addressed the bench. Differenti-

ating legal principles from political beliefs, he joined Petigru's protest
against the law. For him, too, the writ of garnishment amounted to a
violation of professional confidence and an imputation against personal
honor. And over the course of the next week most other "respectable
Lawyers" joined in this assessment—much to Petigru's satisfaction.[36]

Reassured by their support, Petigru, eight days later, presented his
second defense of individual liberties against the government's un-
compensated confiscation of private property. Conscious that he was
speaking for others as well as for himself, he heeded the advice his
old friend Alfred Huger gave him to eliminate political allusions, stick
to the constitutional issues, and curb his sarcasm. Focusing now more
exclusively on the rights of clients rather than the obligations of attorneys, he argued that the writ of garnishment was a procedure unknown
to the common law. Moreover, the Confederate Congress lacked the
power to alter that law because there was no clause in the Confederate
Constitution that empowered it to do so. In passing the Confiscation
Acts, therefore, the Confederate government had infringed on the sovereignty expressly reserved to the states. Consequently the government
had "no right to order a private citizen to come forward and act as an
informer, even if the information sought was conducive to an object
within its legitimate sphere of action"—which it was not.[37]

His argument against the arbitrary confiscation of private property
was similar but expanded in scope. Because confiscation violated "the
common birth-right of a free man" to hold the property in his possession "till a better title is shown," it was not a legitimate sphere of action
for any government.[38] Addressing specifically the May sequestration
act, Petigru continued that an attempt by a government to collect debts
that its citizens owed to others betrayed simple ignorance of the law,
because it was the creditor, not the debtor, who owned the debt. These
arguments did have an effect. Petigru could take a modest pleasure in
the fact that he had indeed forced some changes in the law: the elimination of the writs of garnishment and a more limited definition of
alien enemy. But otherwise the laws remained in force.[39]

For the rest of his life, therefore, Petigru appeared regularly in court
to protect the funds of the Ladies Mount Vernon Association and the
South Carolina trust established for the Philadelphia beneficiaries of
the Kohne estate, or to defend the property of former clients now resident in the North—Rawlins and William Lowndes, Angelica Singleton
Van Buren, Amy Willis, Rosa Izard, and Dr. Samuel Dickson among

them. Perversely, he often had to beg these clients in absentia for affidavits and information that would exempt their property from seizure. Clearly, therefore, he was driven not by any promise of fees or the pressure for action from those he represented but rather by his sense of the law's injustice. Sequestration was, he wrote J. Johnston Pettigrew, "like the biting and gouging of men not ashamed of brutality," and in pursuing it, he told Jane North, the Confederate government had "like a desperate gamester . . . gone beyond anything in the annals of tyranny."[40]

Less publicly Petigru worked to free Martin Hurlbut's son, William Hurlbert, who had journeyed south in June 1861 ostensibly to visit his sister and report on the war. Because he had earlier published articles critical of slavery, he was suspected of spying and was arrested in Atlanta. From there he was sent to Richmond, where he was held without bail or formal charge or access to a trial.[41] Petigru came to his aid, even though he suspected that Hurlbert was a deserter and believed that he was a man who had "lost character." In part he acted out of friendship for the young man's father; in part he may have been pressed by some interest his daughter Sue had in Hurlbert. But mostly he simply deplored the "impropriety" of the Confederate government's holding Hurlbert "a sort of State's prisoner accused of nothing, but having a bad name." "The sneaking privilege of keeping a man in prison, merely because they can do so with impunity" defied Magna Carta.[42] Denied recourse either to a petition for habeas corpus or a prompt trial on a specified charge, Petigru could do little more than seek the intervention of Carolinians then serving in the Richmond government. Not surprisingly, therefore, it was intervention by the British minister in Washington that arranged the unusual circumstances by which Hurlbert was allowed to escape.[43]

With similar cases occurring in the North, Petigru concluded that the war was "likely to inflict on both North and South a heavy misfortune in the loss of their liberties." There was little anyone could do to improve the situation, for "the administration of Lincoln is arbitrary and the Richmond Congress is a revolutionary body." Yet the war also nourished the promise of freedom and civil liberties to slaves, who without it had neither. As their state slid toward secession, many white South Carolinians expressed fears that a servile war, threatening their own lives and property, might follow. Although at Badwell, Mary Petigru and Jane North lived with ominous rumors and slept uneasily,[44] their brother made light of their fears. Nonetheless, when, in the tension that preceded secession, a neighbor seized the gun that young James Carson had lent a slave to go hunting, Petigru advised his sisters to let matters rest. It was more prudent to keep peace with their neighbors than to try to reclaim their property. "In the distempered state of the public mind," he counseled, "we must expect to meet with some annoyance, and if our neighbors think fit to confiscate our guns, we must take it as one of the penalties of society." In short, he understood the neighbor's fear and the folly of denying it. But when he found that same fear in his immediate family, he deplored its irrationality. He was especially troubled when he discovered that Caroline, safe in the North, lived "in fear of insurrection," for he had had no idea that "she was the victim of such idle rumors. But," he concluded in a letter to Jane North—on whom the message would not have been lost—"every day discloses to us new proofs of human weakness." His assurance that the slaves posed no threat was at odds with Petigru's own admission that, even in peace-time, oppression might induce its victims to commit "great crimes." It was also contradicted by the thousands of contrabands who escaped behind federal lines and by the black Sea Islanders, who refused to flee with their owners when the Yankees invaded. Nonetheless, war seems to have made little change in how Petigru thought about slavery. He certainly was not converted to abolition. As late as 1863, he paid taxes on six slaves. Nor is there any evidence that he drew back from the position he had iterated in 1851 to a northern liberal that he had "never given the least encouragement to any doubts concerning the propriety and necessity of maintaining the relations that exist between the two races bond & free by whom the soil is inhabited." [45]

Petigru also continued his subtle subversion of racial distinctions. In 1860 he arranged for the daughter of a Charleston doctor and a slave woman to be reared as a free white child. In 1862 he defended a black mariner set free by Federal troops after they seized his sloop whom Confederate authorities "wanted to hang though guilty of nothing else but refusing to go with the Yankees to Hilton Head." [46] And in his codification of South Carolina statute law, he exercised the authority given him to rationalize conflicting statutes to benefit his state's African-American residents—both slave and free.

His appointment in 1859 to do so was, in truth, an amazing testament to the high esteem in which Petigru was held. Certainly he had never been an enthusiastic supporter of codification. When, in the 1820s, republican reformers had proposed codifying both statute and common law in order to simplify legal processes, eliminate most lawyers, and democratize the courts, Petigru had responded only with a limited plan for reorganizing the equity courts. Thereafter he said little more about codification, even though his criticism of equity court processes and personnel persisted.[47] As a practicing lawyer, however, Petigru had doubtless been frustrated more than once as he or his clerks had searched through Thomas Cooper's compilation of all the laws passed by colonial and state legislatures from 1680 to 1838—whether or not they were still in force or internally contradictory—and then consulted the year-by-year volumes of new statutes that David McCord and others had edited since 1838. So although he had turned down the legislature's first offer in 1858, he was again elected in 1859, this time by a thumping majority over his closest competitor, Judge David Wardlaw, and he undertook the daunting but financially rewarding task.[48] With never more than two junior assistants, he set to work scrutinizing every colonial and state law, systemizing those that had not been superceded and revising them to produce a consistent and compact compendium of South Carolina's civil statute law.

Whether out of personal pique, political indignation, or jurisprudential difference of opinion, Judge Wardlaw was harshly critical of the first section of the code when Petigru submitted it to the legislature in the fall of 1860. Writing sub rosa to state assemblyman Samuel McGowan, Wardlaw began his subterranean struggle to amend if not defeat the code. Although he protested that he had had time to give Petigru's work only a "hasty" examination, he penned a seven-page critique. In his minute, cramped hand, he laid out what he implied were only a small proportion of the code's and the codifier's general deficiencies: Petigru had, by organizing the code to accord with Blackstone's influential *Commentaries on the Law,* failed to make it easily accessible to laypeople; he had revised some statutes without proper cause; he had failed to include recent revisions of some older statutes; he had introduced new inconsistencies; his text was littered with poorly crafted sentences and marred by grammatical and stylistic obscurities. All in all, Wardlaw hinted, Petigru "was not sufficiently aware" that he was required to assemble what, with legislative approval, would be "the law of the land."[49]

When he got down to the substance with which he differed, Wardlaw went straight for the statutes dealing with African Americans. Petigru, he thought, had been too lenient in defining the status of free blacks and had undermined existing restrictions on slaves. He had lessened the punishment for permissive masters who failed to control their slaves and had set too low the maximum number of hours that slaves could be forced to work. Wardlaw's critique may have reflected the same fears that haunted the neighbor who had confiscated James Carson's gun from the Badwell slave to whom it had been lent, for his letter was written on December 10, 1860, when secession was imminent and the future unpredictable. Any modification of the customary restrictions and controls on blacks might have seemed particularly threatening to the half of South Carolina's population that was free and white. But the conspiratorial tenor of Wardlaw's letter, his assertion that Petigru had failed to do "what was expected," and his implicit message that the seventy-one-year-old commissioner was unfit for his work made it clear that he believed the draft code treated the law of race relations very cavalierly.[50]

Despite Wardlaw's misgivings, the legislature renewed Petigru's appointment in 1860 and again in 1861, although in the latter year it nearly defeated the appropriation for his salary.[51] But with his partners already in the army and the few potential codification assistants who were competent likely to enlist on short notice, the intensive labor of analyzing, organizing, and reconciling hundreds of statutes drained Petigru's energy. Mentally tormented by the war and physically ailing, he found the work a heavy burden. On the rare occasions when J. Johnston Pettigrew was home on leave, or when Henry Lesesne was in town and free of business, they did help him over particularly difficult spots. But mostly he struggled on alone. From fall to spring he worked, first at his otherwise empty office and later, after he had closed the office altogether, in Johnston's house, kept open by his cousin's two servants. In the summer of 1861 and for much of 1862, Petigru moved his work to dreary Summerville, where he and Jane Amelia endured the hot weather together after his Sullivan's Island house had been confiscated by the military. Yet, despite the impediments, he finished the code on schedule, oversaw its printing, and carried the full draft to Columbia to submit to the legislature in November 1862.[52]

After receiving the code, the legislature appointed a special commission to review it. Its members never discussed the code with Petigru, whose ill health made that impossible the one time they called on him in Charleston to do so. Given the exigencies of war, however, that failure probably had little to do with the delays that followed. In any event, the commission did not report on the code until the legislative session of December 1864. When it did, the majority report differed sharply from the spirit of near unanimity that had marked Petigru's selection for the job. Chairman Franklin Moses, whose conduct as opposing counsel in the *Converse* case had aroused Petigru's open scorn, had prepared a document similar in tone and content to Wardlaw's behind-the-scenes criticisms of 1861. In form the code was "too scientific for ordinary minds." In substance the majority of four found it flawed in at least ten different sections. The minority of three, made up of Petigru's brother-in-law Henry Lesesne, his old Unionist friend Benjamin Perry, and attorney William Whaley, who had been the first to back Petigru's opposition to the Confiscation Acts, defended the code's organization. They thought it was scientific in the best sense of that word and approved its substance as a fulfillment of the charge specifically given Petigru to reconcile inconsistent statutes and propose desirable modifications of laws already on the books.[53]

How Petigru would have responded to his code's mixed reception can only be guessed. He did not live to hear it. But it is clear that the making of it nearly crushed him. On the other hand, the salary it provided was a financial godsend in supplementing his much-reduced wartime income. By the fall of 1861 his private practice had virtually ceased. Because of the war, courts sat only sporadically, if at all. The legislature passed stay laws precluding suits for debts. And courts, when they were open, heard only those cases that both parties agreed should go to trial. In 1861 Petigru's professional fees, although they were already slipping sharply, still amounted to almost $14,000. In 1862 his practice returned less than $2000. It was this precipitate decline in business that late in 1861 made him close his elaborate office, where only a year earlier two partners and three clerks had worked with him.[54]

To cope with this drastic change, Petigru attempted unaccustomed economies. Yet in March 1862, when he still had his $5000 salary as codification commissioner, he complained that he would face "sheer want" if clients who owed him for past services refused to pay. Though that was, at the time, an exaggeration, it reflected his long-range situation reasonably well. He faced steadily increasing living expenses, for cut as he would the satisfactions of his own table, and control as he could Jane Amelia's preference for luxuries to ease her invalidism, soaring wartime inflation taxed their limited budget. In addition, Petigru had to eke out grandson James's boarding school and college fees, make sizable contributions to Caroline's expenses in New York and Europe, and assist Jane North as she provided for family members who sought refuge at Badwell from the dangers of war.[55]

More sharply traumatic than this steady drain was the devastating Charleston fire that, on the night of December 9, 1861, destroyed his Broad Street house. Petigru was in Columbia while the fire raged, and the news reached him only the next day when he was dining with the governor. With barely enough time to catch the late train, he arrived home to find total destruction. There was, of course, little that he could have done had he been there. The fire had swept across the peninsular city from east to west, burning a two-to-three-block-wide swath from the Cooper River to the Ashley. Friends and servants had thought the Petigru house would escape the devastation racing toward it because it was on the city's west side and in the lee of St. Finbar's high brick walls. But when the church tower caught fire, the wind blew sparks diagonally across the street onto Petigru's house. Last-minute efforts to save the building's contents while only the roof was yet burning saved little. Gone was the house, its elegant furnishings, its notable wine cellar, and almost all Petigru's personal possessions, including his papers and books. Indeed, virtually everything except the silver, which he had taken to Columbia just days before for safekeeping should the Yankees invade Charleston, and the paintings, which were rescued in the first minutes of the fire, was lost.[56]

When it was over, the Petigrus were homeless. Until the following June they accepted the kindness of friends and relatives, moving from one vacant house to another in the city. Then they settled in a rented cottage in Summerville, twenty-five miles from Charleston. Their finances were as disarrayed as their lives. The contents of the house had been uninsured. The $6000 the insurance did pay for the grossly underinsured house itself was soon spent on day-to-day expenses, which rose steadily.[57]

Petigru responded with his only remaining resources still in plentiful supply: stoicism and gritty humor. After two cataclysmic fires in the mid-1830s had destroyed more than a quarter of Charleston's buildings but not his property, he had taken an active role in the city's recovery program, collecting aid for the victims and pressing the legislature to guarantee private loans for rebuilding. Now, amid the disruptions of war, there was no special aid for the fire's victims; nor could Petigru, seventy-two and in poor health, have offered much help anyway. So he had no alternative but to resign himself to his personal loss as he had once done when fire had destroyed some critical legal evidence, leaving only a "heap of ashes scattered to the winds," which, he added, "is all that history will know about the burning." Writing to Caroline a week after the house burned, he said that he didn't "feel it as much as you suppose" because individual loss "shrinks into insignificance in comparison with" the extent of the community's suffering. In a letter to Sue three months later, he even made light of his predicament. He recounted his reply to a friend who had asked him how he was doing. " 'Growing richer every day,' " he said, "for as rich and poor are relative terms, when the rich are growing poor, it is pretty much the same as if the poor were growing rich. Nobody is poor when the distinction between rich and poor is destroyed." But just how poor he was becoming he admitted only to Caroline. "I am living now on my pay as the Redacter of the Statute law, for all law business is at a stand."[58] And that pay would end in seven months.

Petigru's own plight, however, was dwarfed by the fates of his young kinsmen. On June 3, 1862, word came that Brigadier General J. Johnston Pettigrew had been mortally wounded in the battle of Fair Oaks. Happily, that report proved to be wrong. Nonetheless, that Johnston had, in fact, been wounded and left for dead on the field of battle only to be taken prisoner by the Yankees, who nursed him back to health, was traumatic enough. Then, on June 16, two weeks after Fair Oaks, Captain Henry King, Sue's husband, died from a wound received in a small battle at Secessionville, just south of Charleston.[59] His death was the more bitter to his father-in-law because he believed that Henry had been "a martyr to a cause that was not his own." And in October his grief was rubbed raw when his nephew Captain Benjamin Allston, a West Point graduate, was wounded and taken prisoner at Vicksburg.[60]

Even Dan, a private in the Calhoun Guards, who never came under fire, fell victim to the war. While on duty he contracted a severe throat ulceration, which was probably exacerbated by the mercury with which the family's physician treated it. In September 1862 he was in such poor health that he joined his parents in Summerville. There he lived so quietly that once again, for the last time, he raised his father's hopes "that he might yet be a useful member of society." But when Dan was found dead in a Charleston boardinghouse on January 6, 1863, and then a letter arrived that revealed yet another irregular relationship, his death was one more blow struck by the specter that haunted the

Petigru men. And it was that specter that most alarmed the old lawyer as he faced the possibility that his grandson James Carson might
be drafted and, like so many other beardless youths, "fall, not by the
sword, but worse, by low company."[61]

Only stoicism allowed Petigru to control his grief for those already
lost and his fears for the rest. In a business letter to a Liverpool cor-
respondent, he disclosed more than he meant to. "I have lost Henry
King. . . . Johnston Pettigrew [is] a prisoner and wounded. . . . My house
is burnt . . . and Mrs Petigru suffers from nervous debility as much
as usual." Rarely did he reveal even that much of his anguish. But to
Jane North, after he had received the false report of Johnston's death,
he bared his inner torment. "When the dread blow came I have found
it too much for me. It seems to be the will of Heaven that our family
should never rise." Yet even then he reined in his emotions: "Let us be
resigned and make no parade of our grief."[62]

In the midst of his private suffering, Petigru struggled to sort out the
public circumstances that underlay it, as he remained throughout the
war torn between an unwavering intellectual commitment to the Union
and a deep emotional identification with the South. The interaction
of the two led him into highly complex and not always consistent assessments of the Confederacy and the War Between the States. During
1861 he came gradually to accept the fact that, having chosen to remain in Charleston, he could no longer function as a citizen of the
United States. Still, he clung tenaciously to his lifelong dedication to
the principles underlying the old Union: constitutional restraint, the
division of sovereignty, and the internal balances that checked governmental power. But with North and South at war, such principles
seemed increasingly irrelevant, and his lasting commitment to them
little more than loyalty to a past long gone. Sickened by the brutality
of the struggle and appalled at the abuses of constitutionally defined
power on both sides, he condemned the Washington and Richmond
governments alike. When events seemingly compelled allegiance to
one or the other, he refused to support the Confederate government.
Yet when the Sea Islands fell to federal forces and many believed that
Charleston too would soon be taken, he told his sister Mary that he
would never take an "oath of allegiance to Lincoln." On the other hand,
he wrote Caroline several months later that if a successful assault were
made on Charleston, he would "capitulate if allowed to go on parole."

His only voluntary act in support of the Confederacy, whose legitimacy he denied but whose reality he accepted, was to buy a single ticket to a concert at which a distant relative sang patriotic songs. It was, he boasted to Jane North, "the first dollar that I have given to the cause yet."[63] Unable to pledge loyalty to a Union that embraced only the North and unwilling to support a Confederacy that had destroyed the old Union, Petigru had, in essence, become a man without a country.

Of all the events he lamented, Petigru most condemned the political folly of the South and the madness to which it had led. He had long thought that *demos* was a fickle force; he had only recently realized that it was "fully as much addicted to" war as were the kings of old. And though he did not blame the masses for the misery that war inflicted, letting that guilt fall upon their leaders, he believed that only after a change in popular opinion could peace be achieved. And of that reversal he saw no sign. After the first year of fighting he concluded that "the pulse of the People is still so high as to call for more bleeding, before quinine can be administered with any hope of benefit." Yet it was the suffering visited on those people that made the situation almost more than he could bear with sanity. "Soldiers are badly clothed and often have to sleep on the bare ground, and their subsistence and pay [are] precarious." Flawed military strategy and plain bad planning exposed "innocent inhabitants to the rage of the conqueror, merely to stick a feather in the General's cap as a fighting man." When General John Pemberton determined to defend the city "to the last extremity," claiming that "it was better to make a ruin of Charleston than let the Yankees sleep in it," Petigru despaired of reason. But Pemberton's was only a threat; the murderous peninsular campaign in Virginia was real. Of it and its patriotic justification, Petigru wrote only that "it does not, surely, require such torrents of blood to satisfy any reasonable man that nothing can be a more impious presumption than for either side to think themselves entitled to count the Almighty as an ally in such a pitiful dispay of human passion."[64]

His indignation at the excesses of both armies, like his grief for killed and wounded family members, nourished the impression that South Carolina's last Unionist had gone soft. James Louis Petigru, it was rumored, had become a Secessionist. Wrong though that gossip was, the credulity with which it was received silhouetted his inner torment. Petigru never became a Secessionist, but neither did he cease being a Carolinian. Sometimes, in fact, he cheered southern victories. He conceded the brutality "the Federals" inflicted as they marched "through a hostile country." He began to refer to northern forces as "the enemy." And though he mourned the death of the old Union, he believed it could never be revived. Having "thought all along that the Gulf States, Virginia and the Carolinas would establish their independence," he continued to believe so. Yet in December 1862 he wrote Caroline that he still stood on Secession as he always had. It was a tragic mistake, albeit an irreversible one.[65]

As Petigru watched federal forces growing ever stronger while southern soldiers and civilians bled "at every pore," he increasingly sensed that the superiority of northern resources would determine the outcome. The new technology of ironclad naval vessels furnished one example. In March 1862 the sea battle between the ironclad *Monitor* and *Merrimac* inaugurated "a much greater Revolution than that of which Davis is at the head," one which "will render the strong still stronger and the weak, weaker still." But at year's end, although he believed peace was universally desired, Petigru had to admit that nobody was yet "willing to consent to the terms on which alone it can be had at present."[66] There was nothing he could do but watch the carnage, share the losses, and hope that peace would come at last.

Petigru did not live to see the peace for which he yearned. For the last ten years of his life he suffered from severe colds and bronchitis, which he threw off with ever-increasing difficulty. In the summer of 1861 he apparently experienced a myocardial infarction and then slipped into congestive heart failure. Driven to finish the code, he ignored his symptoms—constant fatigue, frequent rashes, wobbly legs, occasional dizziness, recurrent chills, and shortness of breath. After May 1862 he actually increased the strains on his aging body by commuting. Several days a week he made the fifty-mile round trip by rail between his rented house in Summerville and Charleston. The following winter he contracted severe bronchial congestion, which his wife attributed to riding on drafty trains.

Finally, in mid-February 1863, his body rebelled. He was too exhausted even to walk. He was too congested to sleep soundly. He lacked the will and the energy to leave Charleston after his last day of work. And so he stayed there, an invalid first in his sister Adele's townhouse and, when she left town, at the home of MacMillan King, Henry King's brother. Obviously unlikely to recover, he agreed on short notice to meet with the commission appointed to review his code. But when they arrived, he was too ill to discuss his final report. Clearly sensing that he was dying, he settled his private affairs as best he could. On February 22 he added a codicil to his will appointing his brother-in-law and former partner, Henry Lesesne, as his executor, since neither Caroline Carson nor Johnston Pettigrew could now serve.[67]

Lesesne undertook more than new legal responsibilities. A dedicated churchman, he urged Petigru to make at last the profession of faith he had heretofore avoided. He invited Stephen Elliott, the rector of St. Michael's, to visit this longtime vestryman of his parish. And Elliott pressed the dying man to acknowledge Christ's atonement for men's sins, assuring him that "it would be a comfort to all his friends if he would express that belief." But Petigru never did so explicitly. Rather, James Carson wrote his mother, his grandfather responded to the minister's assertion "with solemn emphasis, 'Yes, certainly,' and to all of the prayers he replied 'amen.' "[68]

Shortly thereafter, on March 9, 1863, just two months before his seventy-fourth birthday, James Petigru died. Jane North expressed the family's loss with eloquent simplicity: "Our rooftree has fallen."[69] But many others shared that loss. His friends lost the stalwart support, intellectual stimulation, and humor-sparked congeniality for which he was famous. Those whose politics differed from his lost a worthy opponent. The state bar lost its longtime tutor and guide. The community lost a citizen whose courage to differ was always marked by civility.

Two days later a long funeral procession followed Petigru's coffin from the King mansion, where he had died, to St. Michael's Church, in whose yard he was buried. Onlookers of all sorts and conditions watched as Charleston's most prominent and respectable men paid their final respects. In their ranks marched most of the city's merchants and bankers; many city and state officials, including judges and former state governors; erstwhile United States senators; and virtually all the Confederate military officers stationed in Charleston, led by their commanding general. But only a few saw Petigru's body placed, by his own request, between the graves of his sons Albert and Dan, symbols, respectively, of the hope and despair that had marked his life.[70]

The despair seemed to have triumphed when his code was first publicly debated. By then the war had ended, and legislators fought to define their state's future course while emotions created by war and revolutionary change pressed hard against old assumptions. In 1865 a legislature still similar in composition to the one that had commissioned Petigru to create the code rejected his work outright. Essentially they accepted Moses' report, which claimed that Petigru's code represented little more than one man's version of what the law should be. Thereafter the matter slept until, in 1872, a legislature dominated by Radical Republicans, three quarters of whom were African Americans, adopted a code largely based on Petigru's work but completely reorganized in form to make it more accessible to laypeople and somewhat revised in substance to make it more like the Vermont code with which Yankee-born Attorney General Daniel Corbin was most familiar.[71] By then, Franklin Moses, the father of the Radical Republican governor, was chief justice of the South Carolina Supreme Court; the courts on which David Wardlaw had once sat had been abolished; and Petigru's proposed amelioration of laws controlling the state's black population had been made irrelevant by emancipation and Reconstruction.

But however futile his political dissent, however limited the impact of his legal career, however flawed his personal relationships, taken altogether, the life of James Louis Petigru played out what philosopher Stuart Hampshire called the "virtues of innocence": "absolute integrity, gentleness, disposition to sympathy, a fastidious sense of honor, generosity, a disposition to gratitude."[72] In the conflicts they bred lay the ambiguity of his life and of the legends it spawned.

APPENDIXES

Petigru's caseload in South Carolina appeals courts
(cases reported and printed in *South Carolina Reports*, 1819–1860)

	Equity court		Law court		All appeals	
	Total	Cases won	Total	Cases won	Total	Cases won
1820s[a]	25	15 (60%)	50	31 (62%)	75	46 (61%)
1830s	64	44 (69%)	37	24 (65%)	101	68 (67%)
1840s	38	17 (45%)	50	32 (64%)	88	49 (56%)
1850s[b]	44	19 (43%)	47	25 (53%)	91	44 (48%)

[a] 1820s = 1819–29.
[b] 1850s = 1850–60.

Petigru's docketed appearances before the Charleston County
Court of Equity

	Total cases	Attorney for complainant	Attorney for defendant	Attorney for both parties	Total cases on the docket	Petigru's percentage of all cases on the docket
1842–46	358	147 (41%)	211 (59%)	0	1331	27
1847–51	449	169 (38%)	277 (62%)	3	1917	23
1852–56	290	89 (31%)	176 (61%)	25 (9%)	1586	18
1857–61	346	113 (33%)	180 (52%)	53 (15%)	2436	14

Nature of the cases Petigru handled in South Carolina appeals courts
(cases reported and printed in *South Carolina Reports*, 1819–1860)

	Debt		Trust and probate		Crime (including fraud)		Railroad, shipping, banks, corporations, wage labor		Contracts, commerce, real estate		Women's dower and property rights		Blacks, slave and free		Extent and limits of public authority		Other	
	Eq[a]	L[b]	Eq	L	Eq	L	Eq	L	Eq	L	Eq	L	Eq	L	Eq	L	Eq	L
1820s[c]	5	6	8	2	0	7	1	2	5	11	2	4	0	2	0	12	4	4
1830s	15	5	22	4	2	2	1	11	8	4	11	1	0	1	1	4	4	6
1840s	8	7	14	1	1	2	3	10	4	13	3	1	1	4	1	6	3	6
1850s[d]	4	14	21	2	0	3	5	10	2	7	3	1	3	3	3	4	3	4
Total	32	32	65	9	3	14	10	33	19	35	19	7	4	10	5	26	14	20

[a] Eq = Equity court.
[b] L = Law court.
[c] 1820s = 1819–29; includes Petigru's most active years as attorney general.
[d] 1850s = 1850–60.

NOTES

AAH	Alabama Department of Archives and History, Montgomery
BC	Bowdoin College, Brunswick, Maine
CC	College of Charleston, Charleston, South Carolina
CLS	Charleston Library Society, Charleston, South Carolina
DU	Duke University, Durham, North Carolina
EPFL	Enoch Pratt Free Library, Baltimore, Maryland
HL	Huntington Library, San Marino, California
HSP	Historical Society of Pennsylvania, Philadelphia
LC	Library of Congress, Washington, D.C.
MHS	Massachusetts Historical Society, Boston
NA	National Archives, Washington, D.C.
NCA	North Carolina Department of Cultural Resources, Division of Archives and History, Raleigh
SCA	South Carolina Department of Archives and History, Columbia
SCHS	South Carolina Historical Society, Charleston
UA	University of Alabama, University
UGa	University of Georgia, Athens
UNC	Southern Historical Collection, University of North Carolina, Chapel Hill
UR	University of Rochester, Rochester, New York
USC-A	University Archives, University of South Carolina, Columbia
USC-Car	South Caroliniana Library, University of South Carolina, Columbia

Chapter 1. The Legend

1. When Petigru died, on March 9, 1863, federal troops were in the vicinity of Folly Island, about twelve miles south of Charleston. Loyal National League of the State of New York, *The Sumter Anniversary, 1863. Opinions of Loyalists Concerning the Great Questions of the Times; Expressed in the Speeches and Letters of Prominent Citizens of All Sections and Parties on Occasion of the In-auguration of the Loyal National League in Mass Meeting in Union Square, New York on the 11th of April, 1863, the Anniversary of the Attack on Fort Sumter*

(New York: C. S. Westcott and Company, 1863). At this rally Francis Lieber offered three resolutions noticing Petigru's recent death and praising him. They were seconded by C. E. Detmold, a former Charlestonian and friend of Petigru (78–79). George Bancroft addressed the New York Historical Society on the occasion of Petigru's death, and Robert C. Winthrop addressed the Massachusetts Historical Society. See assorted newspaper clippings, Vanderhorst Papers, South Carolina Historical Society (hereafter SCHS).

2. Studies illuminating adult developmental psychology of contemporary white males include Daniel J. Levinson, *The Seasons of a Man's Life* (New York: Ballantine Books, 1978); Levinson, "Exploration in Biography: Evolution of the Individual Life Structure in Adulthood," in A. I. Rabin et al., eds., *Further Explorations in Personality* (New York: John Wiley and Sons, 1981), 44–85; George E. Vaillant, *Adaptation to Life* (Boston: Little, Brown, 1977); Jack Block, "Some Enduring and Consequential Structures of Personality," in Rabin et al., *Further Explorations;* and Robert W. White, *Lives in Progress* (1952; reprint, New York: Holt, Rinehart and Winston, 1975).

3. *Charleston Mercury,* March 19, 1863, quoting the minutes of the March 14 meeting of the Board of Directors of the Bank of Charleston; College of Charleston, Board of Trustees Minutes, typed copy, minutes of March 30, 1863, College of Charleston (hereafter CC); Charleston, S.C., Bar Association, *Memorial of the Late James L. Petigru. Proceeding of the Bar of Charleston, S.C., March 25, 1863* (New York: Richardson and Company, 1866), 52, 46–47.

4. Winfield Scott to Edwin M. Stanton, March 27, 1863, Petigru Correspondence, Library of Congress (hereafter LC); William T. Sherman to Caroline Carson, January 20, 1865, typed copy, Vanderhorst Papers, SCHS.

5. The gravestone inscription is in James Petigru Carson, *Life, Letters and Speeches of James Louis Petigru, the Union Man of South Carolina* (Washington, D.C.: W. H. Lowdermilk, 1920), 487. Among those who assisted Caroline Carson in drafting the epitaph were the historian George Bancroft; former speaker of the House of Representatives Robert C. Winthrop; the Reverend Dr. Orville Dewey; George Schuyler, a New York businessman; and Joseph H. Dukes, a New York lawyer who had apprenticed in Petigru's office; see Carson, *Life,* 477–85.

6. Caroline Carson to Edward Everett, [undated, except "Wednesday, 9th," 1863?], Vanderhorst Papers, SCHS; William J. Grayson, *James Louis Petigru. A Biographical Sketch* (New York: Harper and Brothers, 1866), 173; Joseph Blyth Allston, "Life and Times of James L. Petigru," clippings from *Charleston Sunday News,* 1899–1900, pasted in a scrapbook at the Charleston Library Society (hereafter CLS); Carson, *Life.*

7. Allston, "Life and Times," 21; [*Philadelphia?*] *Evening Express,* March 30, [1877], clipping, Vanderhorst Papers, SCHS.

8. Alexander Robert Lawton, *Annual Address before the American Bar Asso-*

ciation at Saratoga Springs, N.Y., August 9th, 1882 (Philadelphia: George E. Harris and Sons, 1883), 13, 19, 17, 34.

9. Ibid., 34.

10. Caroline Carson to Andrew J. Magrath, October 24, 1882; William A. Courtenay to Magrath, November 15, 1882; A. E. Harnisch to William A. Courtenay, July 2, 1883, all in microfiche, Courtenay Collection, SCHS.

11. Edward G. Mason, "A Visit to South Carolina in 1860," *Atlantic Monthly* 53 (February 1884): 245; Henry Holmes, Diary, 1898, microfiche pp. 95–97, CLS; James S. Cothran, "James Louis Petigru. An Essay Read to the Abbeville Literary Club at Mr. L. W. White's on the Night after the Full Moon in July 1883 . . . ," clippings, *Greenville Mountaineer*, December 2 and 5, 1903, microfiche, Courtenay Collection, SCHS.

12. Philippe Verner to Adele Allston, December 14, 1890, Allston Family Papers, SCHS. The portrait currently hangs in the portrait gallery of the South Carolina Supreme Court building.

13. "A Word Picture of Petigru. The Annual Oration before the University Law Class," *Charleston News and Courier*, April 1, 1891, clipping, Vanderhorst Papers, SCHS, reports the address; also see Joseph Daniel Pope, "James Louis Petigru," in William Draper Lewis, ed., *Great American Lawyers; the Lives and Influences of Judges and Lawyers Who Have Acquired a National Reputation and Have Developed the Jurisprudence of the United States. A History of the Legal Profession in America*, 8 vols. (Philadelphia: John C. Winston, 1907–1909), 4 (1908), 29–73; the middle quotation is from Lewis, ed., 4:51; the others are from the *News and Courier* report; see also Joseph Daniel Pope, *James Louis Petigru. An Address before the University Law Association of the University of South Carolina* (Charleston: Walker, Evans and Cogswell, 1891).

14. Pope, "James Louis Petigru," in Lewis, ed., 4:52. The monarchy issue is treated in the *Charleston Mercury*, June 18, 19, 20, 22, 1861; Petigru's refutation is in his letter to J. Johnston Pettigrew, June 24, 1861, Pettigrew Family Papers, Southern Historical Collection, University of North Carolina at Chapel Hill (hereafter UNC).

15. Dr. Grayson, Diary, March 8, 1919, in Arthur S. Link et al., eds., *The Papers of Woodrow Wilson* (Princeton: Princeton University Press, 1966–), 55:461–62. Robert Hayne, who died in 1839, was buried on the west side of the churchyard twenty-four years before Petigru was interred by its easternmost wall.

16. *Columbia State*, June 15, 1919. The newspaper apparently published an advance text, since the address was not actually delivered until June 16.

17. John P. Thomas, Jr., *James L. Petigru, Lawyer and Citizen. Address to the Joint Session of Georgia and South Carolina Bar Associations . . . May 30, 1919* (Columbia: The State Company, 1919), 21–22.

18. Ibid., 14.

19. "Do You Know Your Charleston?" *Charleston News and Courier*, September 29, 1930; "Old Home of James Louis Petigru with Two-Mile White Oak Avenue Recalled by Fragmentary Vestiges," *Columbia State*, January 31, 1937; "Badwell," *Raleigh News and Observer*, n.d., reprinted in the *News and Courier*, October 10, 1937.

20. Dubose Heyward, *Peter Ashley* (New York: Farrar and Rinehart, 1932), 20.

21. Rion McKissick, "Petigru," an address to the South Carolina Bar Association, April 21, 1936, printed in *Columbia State*, May 6, 1936. For Barnwell, see *State*, June 15, 1919.

22. Helen Hennig, *Great South Carolinians from Colonial Days to the Confederate War* (Chapel Hill: University of North Carolina Press, 1940), 328–29.

23. Tinsley E. Yarborough, *Passion for Justice. J. Waties Waring and Civil Rights* (New York: Oxford University Press, 1987), 102.

24. *Charleston News and Courier*, April 13, 1961.

25. Sally Edwards, *James Louis Petigru, 1789–1863* (n.p.: McCormick County Historical Commission, 1977), contains the quotations (3–4); see also Edwards, *The Man Who Said No* (New York: Coward-McCann, 1970).

26. The story of the Petigru Society and the University of South Carolina Law School comes from a series of interviews with the following people: attorneys Gedney H. Howe III, March 11, 1991; Robert Rosen, March 12, 1991; Ann Stirling, April 24, 1991, all of Charleston; President Harry Lightsey of the College of Charleston, March 6, 1991; Professor Lewis Burke, University of South Carolina Law School, February 12, 1991; and from the following documents, all in the personal files of Robert Rosen: Robert Rosen to Robert M. Figg, October 25, 1972, and July 31, 1973; Robert M. Figg to Robert Rosen, November 6, 1972; typed copy of "Report of the SBA Committee on Naming the New Law Building," November 15, 1972; USC Law School faculty, Minutes of the meeting of April 12, 1973; Robert Rosen to Joseph P. Riley, Jr., January 21, 1974; "Resolution" and Petition [ca. March 1974]; Dedication program, University of South Carolina Law Center, May 4, 1974; and de Rosset Myers to Robert Rosen, April 30, 1975. Claude Henry Neuffer, in an editor's note in 1982, observed, "Although the first two buildings housing the Law School on the University of South Carolina campus were named for [Petigru], the present imposing structure . . . is merely titled University Law Center" (*Names in South Carolina* 29 [Winter 1982]: 37). In 1994 that was still the case.

27. Lacy K. Ford, Jr., "James Louis Petigru: The Last South Carolina Federalist," in Michael O'Brien and David Moltke-Hansen, eds., *Intellectual Life in Antebellum Charleston* (Knoxville: University of Tennessee Press, 1986), 157, 174; and Ford, *The Origins of Southern Radicalism, 1800–1860* (New York: Oxford University Press, 1988), 173.

28. James Oscar Farmer, Jr., *The Metaphysical Confederacy. James Henley*

Thornwell and the Synthesis of Southern Values (Macon, Ga.: Mercer University Press, 1986), 26.

Chapter 2. Becoming a Lawyer

1. The general genealogical and family background that follows is largely drawn from James Petigru Carson, *Life, Letters and Speeches of James Louis Petigru, the Union Man of South Carolina* (Washington, D.C.: W. H. Lowdermilk, 1920), 1–27. For Revolutionary War and Confederation period (1775–1789) conditions generally in the South Carolina upcountry, see Richard M. Brown, *The South Carolina Regulators* (Cambridge: Harvard University Press, 1963); Rachel Klein, *Unification of a Slave State. The Rise of the Planter Class in the South Carolina Backcountry, 1760–1808* (Chapel Hill: University of North Carolina Press, 1990); Jerome J. Nadelhaft, *The Disorders of War. The Revolution in South Carolina* (Orono: University of Maine Press, 1981).

2. Klein, *Unification*, 48–57, 102–41; Nadelhaft, *Disorders*, 56–61, 127–33.

3. Klein, *Unification*, 14–34.

4. James Pettigrew, Will and Inventory, dated December 18, 1784, Ninety Six District, Abbeville, South Carolina, microfilm, South Carolina Department of Archives and History (hereafter SCA). The will was proved on August 14, 1789.

5. Klein, *Unification*, 152.

6. Carson, *Life*, 17–19; Joseph Blyth Allston, "Life and Times of James L. Petigru," CLS, 1–3.

7. Carson, *Life*, 5–10; Jean Louis Gibert, Inventory, December 21, 1773, Z:511–14, microfilm, South Carolina Probate Records, Abbeville District, SCA.

8. Carson, *Life*, 10, 14, 17.

9. Adele Allston, quoted in Allston, "Life and Times," 3.

10. Ibid., 2–3.

11. Petigru to Jane North, June 20, 1862, in Carson, *Life*, 453. Our treatment of the problem of alcoholism in the family here and elsewhere in this biography has been informed by a number of studies, including Stephanie Brown, *Treating Adult Children of Alcoholics: A Developmental Perspective* (New York: John Wiley and Sons, 1988), 138–47, 164–65; contemporary essays and dissertations dealing with alcohol: William Michel, "Essay on Wine Read to the Medical Society of South Carolina," *Carolina Journal of Medicine, Science, and Agriculture* 1 (1825): 20–31; Samuel H. Dickson, *Essay on Mania a Potu. Forming One of the Course of Lectures on the Theory and Practice of Medicine Delivered in the Medical College of the State of So[uth] Ca[rolina]* (Charleston: A. E. Miller, 1836); and the dissertations presented to faculty of the Medical College of South Carolina: Louis M. DeSaussure, "A Thesis on Mania a Potu" (1828 [1830?]); James E. B. Finley, "Dissertation on Mania a Potu" (1829); Robert

Oswald, "Mania a Potu" (1828); all in Waring Library, Medical University of South Carolina.

12. Carson, *Life*, 19.

13. When Petigru set a vacation course of study for his sixteen-year-old grandson, James Carson, he directed that he study penmanship and read Plutarch; Petigru to J. Johnston Pettigrew, November 29, 1861, Pettigrew Family Papers, UNC.

14. Waddel's intellectual heritage is discussed in Robert M. Calhoon, *Evangelicals and Conservatives in the Early South, 1740–1861* (Columbia: University of South Carolina Press, 1988), 80–84, which misnames him Joseph Waddel; also see James O. Farmer, Jr., *The Metaphysical Confederacy. James Henley Thornwell and the Synthesis of Southern Values* (Macon, Ga.: Mercer University Press, 1986), 94, 98.

15. Descriptions of Waddel's academy at Willington during Petigru's time there include Julius G. Campbell, "James Louis Petigru: A Rhetorical Study" (Ph.D. dissertation, University of South Carolina, 1980), 6, 7, 9; John P. Thomas, Jr., *James L. Petigru, Lawyer and Citizen. Address before the Joint Meetings of Georgia and South Carolina Bar Associations . . . May 30, 1919* (Columbia: State Company, 1919), 9; Colyer Meriwether, *History of Higher Education in South Carolina* (Washington, D.C.: Government Printing Office, 1889), 42–43; James L. Petigru, *An Oration Delivered before the Phi Kappa and Demosthenian Societies of the University of Georgia, August 6, 1846 . . .* (Athens: Southern Whig Office, 1846), 24; William J. Grayson, "Autobiography of William John Grayson," ed. Samuel Stoney, *South Carolina Historical Magazine* 49 (1948): 110.

16. Klein, *Unification*, 240–43, 266–67.

17. Carson, *Life*, 33; James S. Cothran, "James Louis Petigru. An Essay Read to the Abbeville Literary Club at Mr. L. B. White's on the Night after the Full Moon in July, 1883 . . . ," clippings, *Greenville Mountaineer*, December 2 and 5, 1903, microfiche, Courtenay Collection, SCHS.

18. Allston, "Life and Times," 2; Campbell, "Petigru," 10; Clariosophic Society, Minutes, 1808–9, University of South Carolina, University Archives (hereafter USC-A).

19. Robert Duncan Bass, ed., "The Autobiography of William John Grayson" (Ph.D. dissertation, University of South Carolina, 1933), i–xxiv; Daniel Hollis, *South Carolina College*, 2 vols. (Columbia: University of South Carolina Press, 1951), 1:40–96, 126.

20. Grayson, "Autobiography," 90; William J. Grayson, *James Louis Petigru. A Biographical Sketch* (New York: Harper and Brothers, 1866), 37–42.

21. Petigru to William Pettigrew, October 23, 1835, in Carson, *Life*, 178; Allston, "Life and Times," 2; Mary Boykin Chesnut, Diary, June 5, 1862, in C. Vann Woodward, ed., *Mary Chesnut's Civil War* (New Haven: Yale University Press,

1981), 366. In a letter to Margaret Pettigrew dated November 25, 1835 (typed copy, Petigru Letters, Gibbes Museum, Charleston, S.C.), Petigru wrote, "Our connection with this colony [of Petigru's grandfather] of New Bordeaux led to our name being written in the French fashion, and the tradition that it was originally French led us to adopt it." We have not verified the original of this letter.

22. Allston, "Life and Times," 3. The quotations are in Benjamin F. Perry, "Reminiscences of Public Men. James L. Petigru," *Nineteenth Century Magazine* (July 1870): 141; and Petigru to Robert F. W. Allston, March 21, 1859, R. F. W. Allston Papers, SCHS. Petigru's concern about deaths resulting from drunkenness is expressed in letters to Hugh Legaré, April 24, 1834, in Carson, *Life*, 138; and to Jane North, July 19, 1842, copy, Petigru Correspondence, LC.

23. Grayson, *Petigru*, 47.

24. Grayson, "Autobiography," 110; Carson, *Life*, 34.

25. Allston, "Life and Times," 3.

26. Carson, *Life*, 37–38; Martin L. Hurlbut to Jesse Appleton, May 9, 1812, Appleton Papers, Bowdoin College (hereafter BC); Beaufort College, Trustees' Minutes, microfilm minutes [1812], South Caroliniana Library, University of South Carolina (hereafter USC-Car). After the Revolution few Carolinians studied at the English Inns of Court. The Litchfield Law School, founded in 1784 and attended by John C. Calhoun, was far away in Connecticut. And although a few colleges in the late eighteenth and early nineteenth centuries, among them William and Mary, Harvard, and the Universities of Virginia, Pennsylvania, and Maryland, appointed professors of law, the overwhelming majority of aspiring lawyers read law with established attorneys, often as apprentice clerks; see Lawrence M. Friedman, *A History of American Law* (New York: Simon and Schuster, 1973), 278–82.

27. Jeffrey N. Lash, "The Reverend Martin Luther Hurlbut: Yankee President of Beaufort College, 1812–1814," *South Carolina Historical Magazine* 85 (1984): 308; Martin L. Hurlbut to Jesse Appleton, May 9, 1812, Appleton Papers, BC; Martin L. Hurlbut to Jedediah Morse, March 11, 1812, Yates-Snowden Collection, USC-Car.

28. James L. Petigru, Petition to Practice Law in the Courts of Equity of South Carolina, March 6, 1813, Court Records, Petitions to Practice Law, 1809–24, Court of Appeals in Equity, Record Group 0023, Series 002, SCA; Petigru to Francis Lieber, May 28, 1857, Francis Lieber Papers, Huntington Library (hereafter HL); Petigru to Robert F. W. Allston, September 8, 1852, R. F. W. Allston Papers, SCHS.

29. Carson, *Life*, 50–51; Allston, "Life and Times," 4; *Plutarch's Lives of Themistocles, Pericles, Aristides, Alcibiades, and Coriolanus, Demosthenes and Cicero, Caesar and Anthony in the Translation Called Dryden's, Corrected and Revised by Arthur Hugh Clough.* Harvard Classics, vol. 12 (New York: P. F.

Collier and Son, 1909, 1937), 84; James L. Petigru, *Oration Delivered on the Third Anniversary of the South Carolina Historical Society at Hibernian Hall . . . May 27, 1858* (Charleston: Walker, Evans and Company, 1858), 14.

30. John Belton O'Neall, *Biographical Sketches of the Bench and Bar of South Carolina,* 2 vols. (1859; reprint, Spartanburg, S.C.: Reprint Company, 1975), 1:80; Carson, *Life,* 52; Allston, "Life and Times," 4.

31. Allston, "Life and Times," 4; Grayson, *Petigru,* 71; O'Neall, *Bench and Bar,* 1:192; James L. Petigru [?], "Picture of Coosawhatchie," typed copy, UNC.

32. Petigru to Jane Postell, August 25, 1812, Vanderhorst Papers, SCHS; Carson, *Life,* 42–44; Grayson, *Petigru,* 62–79; Petigru to William Grayson, February 15, [1813], and October 18, 1815, Miscellaneous Manuscripts, SCHS, includes "On the Aloes."

33. Grayson, *Petigru,* 77–79, quotation at 78; Carson, *Life,* 58; Edward McCrady, *The History of South Carolina in the Revolution, 1780–1783* (New York: Macmillan, 1902), 99, 101, 150–51, 83, 557; Marriage Settlement, James L. Petigru and Jane Amelia Postell, August 22, 1816, Vanderhorst Papers, SCHS.

34. Carson, *Life,* 52, 59; Allston, "Life and Times," 4.

35. Petigru to Jane North, August 31, 1827, in Carson, *Life,* 75.

36. [George Bancroft], "Mr. Bancroft on James L. Petigru," *New York Evening Post,* May 6, 1863, clipping in Vanderhorst Papers, SCHS; Carson, *Life,* 293; Joseph D. Pope, "James Louis Petigru, 1789–1863," in William D. Lewis, ed., *Great American Lawyers . . . A History of the Legal Profession in America,* 8 vols. (Philadelphia: John C. Winston, 1908), 4:59.

37. Allston, "Life and Times," 5; O'Neall, *Bench and Bar,* 1:134; Charleston District Court of Common Pleas, Judgment Rolls, Bond, February 20, 1822, Record Group B1AE, Series 002, SCA; Petigru to Thomas Waties, June 29, 1824, Thomas Waties Papers, USC-Car.

38. Carson, *Life,* 76–77; Allston, "Life and Times," 5; Petigru to John G. North, July 18, 1819, and Petigru to James Carson, July 7, 1862, both in Allston, "Life and Times," 5, 44.

39. Petigru received eighty-eight votes for attorney general. His two rivals received forty and twenty-one votes each (*Charleston Courier,* December 10, 1822). He resigned as solicitor for the Southeastern District at the same time. See Petigru to the Legislature, December 3, 1822, Record Group 010, Series 017, SCA; Carson, *Life,* 63. For Petigru's work with the legislature and the executive branch, see, for example, "Report Respecting an Appropriation to Open Wappoo Cut," December 13, 1825, Record Group 010, Series 017; Petigru to J. B. I'On, President of the Senate, December 9, 1826; same to Henry Deas, President of the Senate, December 15, 1828, all in Record Group 010, Series 017, SCA; also Petigru to Stephen D. Miller, May 22, 1830, Stephen D. Miller Political and Plantation Papers, SCHS.

40. Charleston County, Records of the Court of General Sessions, Indictments and Subpoenas, 1830, passim, SCA.

41. *State* v. *William H. Taylor,* 2 McCord 483–92 (1823) (6 S.C. Reports 190–93), quotation at 486/191; *State* v. *Gulden,* 2 McCord 524–26 (1823) (6 S.C. Reports 206–7).

42. *Frederick Bennett and Richard Chitty ads the State,* Harper 503–8 (1828) (7 S.C. Reports 221–23). Of the remaining appeals cases, four involved some form of theft or receiving stolen goods: *State* v. *John Thomas,* 2 McCord 527–31 (1823) (6 S.C. Reports 207–8); *State* v. *Thomas Crosby,* Harper 90–91 (1824) (7 S.C. Reports 41); *State* v. *Antonio Larumbo,* Harper 183–84 (1824) (7 S.C. Reports 90); and *State* v. *Wright,* 4 McCord 358–63 (1827) (7 S.C. Reports 135–37). One involved forgery and another riot: *James Billis ads State,* 2 McCord 12–21 (1822) (6 S.C. Reports 5–9); and *State* v. *William Calder et alias,* 2 McCord 462–65 (1823) (6 S.C. Reports 182–83).

43. *James Stevens ads Treasurers,* 2 McCord 108–10 (1822) (6 S.C. Reports 42–43); *William Laval* v. *F. A. DeLiesseline,* 4 McCord 68–76 (1826) (7 S.C. Reports 26–29); *George W. Cross* v. *Anthony Gabeau and Benjamin F. Hunt,* 1 Bailey 211–14 (1829) (8 S.C. Reports 98–100).

44. *George Clark and Others ads Daniel Blake,* 3 McCord 179–83 (1825) (6 S.C. Reports 72–73); *Joseph Glover* v. *William Simmons, John Ramsay and Others, Com. of the Roads,* 4 McCord 67–68 (1826) (7 S.C. Reports 25–26).

45. *State* v. *Charles C. Chitty,* 1 Bailey Law 378–410 (1830) (8 S.C. Reports 173–87), quotations at 393/180 and 392/179, respectively.

46. *State* v. *William Mazyck,* 2 McCord 473–76 (1823) (6 S.C. Reports 186–87); *Theodore Gourdine ads The Heirs of Jesse Barino,* Harper 221–23 (1824) (7 S.C. Reports 99–100); *C. Patrick and C. J. Manigault* v. *Commissioners of Cross Roads on Charleston Neck,* 4 McCord 541–44 (1828) (7 S.C. Reports 201–2); *State at the Relation of Captain Martindale of the Charleston Neck Rangers* v. *J. H. Stevens and William Evans, Collectors of Militia Fines,* 2 McCord 32–38 (1822) (6 S.C. Reports 13–16); *Grier, Relator* v. *John Taylor, Governor etc.* 4 McCord 206–10 (1827) (7 S.C. Reports 78–79); and *State ex rel. Charles M. Gruber* v. *Samuel Champlin; The same* v. *Commissioners of Public Buildings,* 2 Bailey 220–24 (1831) (8 S.C. Reports 104–6).

47. *Mathew J. Payne ads Robert Robinson,* Harper 279–85 (1824) (7 S.C. Reports 123–26).

48. *Elkison* v. *Deliesseline,* Case No. 4366, 8 Federal Cases 493–98 (1823), quotation at 494. On the issue of the law's unconstitutionality, see "Philominus," in *Charleston Mercury,* September 5, 1823; also A. E. Kier Nash, "Negro Rights, Unionism, and Greatness on the South Carolina Court of Appeals: The Extraordinary Chief Justice John Belton O'Neall," *South Carolina Law Review* 21 (1969): 141–90; see also Paul Finkelman, "States Rights North and South in Antebellum America," in Kermit L. Hall and James W. Ely, Jr., eds., *An*

Uncertain Tradition: Constitutionalism and the History of the South (Athens: University of Georgia Press, 1989), 125–58, especially 131–33.

49. Alan F. January, "The First Nullification: The Negro Seamen's Acts Controversy in South Carolina, 1822–1860" (Ph.D. dissertation, University of Iowa, 1976), 153–54. The South Carolina Association was founded to prevent attempts at slave rebellion after the 1822 Denmark Vesey plot was discovered.

50. *State ex rel. Hon. William Johnson v. James C. Martindale et al.*, 1 Bailey 163–71 (1829) (8 S.C. Reports 77–80), quotation at 170/80.

51. Petigru to Joseph W. Allston, September 19, 1829, microfiche, Courtenay Collection, SCHS.

52. Thomas, *Petigru*, 18; South Carolina House of Representatives, Resolution to Appoint a Commission to Combine All Similar Laws on One Subject under a Single Law, December 20, 1825, Record Group 010, Series 016, SCA. On the reorganization of the state's equity courts, see Michael S. Hindus, *Prison and Plantation. Crime, Justice, and Authority in Massachusetts and South Carolina, 1767–1878* (Chapel Hill: University of North Carolina Press, 1980), 21–22; Donald J. Senese, "Building the Pyramid: The Growth and Development of the State Court System in Antebellum South Carolina," *South Carolina Law Review* 24 (1972): 365–66.

53. [James L. Petigru], "Court of Chancery," *Southern Review* 3 (1829): 63–77, quotation at 73.

54. Grayson, *Petigru*, 65–68; Allston, "Life and Times," 4; Petigru to Jane North, June 28, 1862, in Allston, 44.

55. Jack K. Williams, *Dueling in the Old South. Vignettes of Social History* (College Station: Texas A&M Press, 1980), 66–67; O'Neall, *Bench and Bar*, 2:436–40, quotation at 440; Allston, "Life and Times," 5. On Hunt's court tactics, see Petigru's comment in his letter to Joel R. Poinsett, January 25, 1822, Poinsett Papers, Historical Society of Pennsylvania (hereafter HSP). One case in which Petigru and Hunt were opposing counsel and which Petigru won hands-down was *William Aiken, Trustee v. Thomas Miller et al.*, Harper Equity 69–71 (1824) (21 S.C. Reports 29–30). Other cases that may have helped set the two attorneys at odds were *John L. North and Wife v. T. Drayton, Administrator of Glen Drayton*, Harper Equity 34–46 (1824) (21 S.C. Reports 14–19); and *Tabitha Singleton v. Eliza Elliott Bremar, Widow and Administratrix of F. Bremar, deceased*, Harper 201–14 (1824) (7 S.C. Reports 90–96), both of which Petigru won; and *Octavius Crips and Others v. Andrew Talvande*, 4 McCord 20–23 (1820) (7 S.C. Reports 8–9), which Hunt won.

56. Petigru to Jane Gibert Petigru, September 13, 1826, in Carson, *Life*, 72–73; Allston, "Life and Times," 5.

57. Carson, *Life*, 74; Louise Pettigrew, Will, [Proved] November 1826, Abbeville District, Wills, 2:164–65, transcript, Abbeville Public Library. For the consequences of clustered family tragedies in unstable home situations, see

Vincent D. Foley, *An Introduction to Family Therapy* (New York: Grune and Stratton, 1974), 87.

58. Allston, "Life and Times," 5.

59. Carson, *Life*, 75–76. For the Broad Street house, see the mortgage deed, May 16, 1828, Record Book W 9-300, Charleston County, Registry of Mesne Conveyance.

60. Harriette Petigru to Adele Allston, August 22, 1832, Allston Papers, SCHS; Petigru to [?], [ca. April 1832], typed fragment, Vanderhorst Papers, SCHS; Adele Allston to Robert F. W. Allston, January 17, 1840, Petigru to Adele Allston, December 21, 1858, Bessie Allston to Adele Allston, March 14, [1863], the last three in Allston Papers, SCHS.

61. The births of the four Petigru children and their mother's age at their births: married 1816 (age 21), Albert born 1818 (age 23), Caroline born 1820 (age 25), Daniel born 1822 (age 27), Susan born 1824 (age 29). Petigru held Badwell in trust to support both his father and an unmarried sister, Mary, who continued to live there.

62. For evidence of a miscarriage, see Charles Petigru to Adele Allston, May 2, 1832, Harriette Petigru to Adele Allston, June 10, 1832, Petigru to Adele Allston, July 10, 1832, and Jane Amelia Petigru to Adele Allston, September 20, 1832, all in Allston Papers, SCHS. On addiction, see Petigru to Jane North, August 4, 1835, copy, Petigru Correspondence, LC; and Jane Amelia Petigru to Henry Lesesne, May 10, 1863, Vanderhorst Papers, SCHS. The headaches had begun by 1827: Petigru to Jane North, August 31, 1827, Petigru Correspondence, LC; and the facial neuralgia in 1835: Petigru to John G. North, March 24, 1835, Vanderhorst Papers, SCHS.

63. See St. Michael's Protestant Episcopal Church, Vestry Book, 1824–69, typed copy, microfiche, SCHS, passim, for Petigru's service on the vestry. His pew purchase (for $600) is noted in [State of South Carolina], Legal Bill of Sale, June 15, 1829, Vanderhorst Papers, SCHS. For Petigru's dinner parties, see Margaret Hunter Hall, *The Aristocratic Journey: Being the Outspoken Letters of Mrs Basil Hall Written during a Fourteen-Month's Sojourn in America 1827–1828*, in Thomas D. Clark, ed., *South Carolina. The Grand Tour, 1780–1865* (Columbia: University of South Carolina Press, 1973), 143–44; William Ogilby, Journal, June 24 and August 1, 1830, SCHS; and Allston, "Life and Times," 20.

Chapter 3. Becoming a Politician

1. Jeffrey N. Lash, "The Reverend Martin Luther Hurlbut: Yankee President of Beaufort College, 1812–1814," *South Carolina Historical Magazine* 85 (1984): 313.

2. Rachel N. Klein, *Unification of a Slave State. The Rise of the Planter Class*

in the South Carolina Backcountry, 1760–1808 (Chapel Hill: University of North Carolina Press, 1990), 224–31.

3. William J. Grayson, *James Louis Petigru. A Biographical Sketch* (New York: Harper and Brothers, 1866), 84.

4. Brutus [Robert Turnbull], *The Crisis: Or, Essays on the Usurpations of the Federal Government* (Charleston: A. E. Miller, 1827); Petigru to Hugh Legaré, February 5, 1833, Miscellaneous Manuscripts, USC-Car.

5. James L. Petigru, *An Oration Delivered before the Washington Society on the Fourth July 1834* (Charleston: D. J. Dowling, 1834), quotation at 11; Petigru to William Elliott, August 31, 1825, copy, James L. Petigru Correspondence, LC.

6. Petigru to Hugh Legaré, [March 5, 1833], Miscellaneous Manuscripts, USC-Car; William W. Freehling, *Prelude to Civil War. The Nullification Controversy in South Carolina, 1816–1836* (New York: Harper and Row, 1968), 103, 213; Jane H. Pease and William H. Pease, "The Economics and Politics of Charleston's Nullification Crisis," *Journal of Southern History* 47 (1981): 350.

7. Marquis James, *The Life of Andrew Jackson*, part 2: *Portrait of a President* (Indianapolis: Bobbs-Merrill, 1937, 1938), 235–36. The exact wording varies; see, for example, Robert V. Remini, *The Life of Andrew Jackson* (New York: Harper and Row, 1988), 196–97.

8. *Charleston Courier*, July 7, 1830.

9. James Hamilton to William Preston, May 31, 1830, Miscellaneous Manuscript Collection, LC.

10. The only biography of Hamilton is Virginia L. Glenn, "James Hamilton, Jr., of South Carolina: A Biography" (Ph.D. dissertation, University of North Carolina, 1964).

11. James Hamilton to Stephen D. Miller, August 7, 1830, Chesnut-Miller-Manning Papers, SCHS.

12. James Hamilton to Martin Van Buren, May 27, 1830, and June 8, 1830, both microfilm, Series 2, Reel 9, Martin Van Buren Papers, LC; "Loans to Officers of Government, Members of Congress, and Editors of Newspapers," [1830–32], copy, microfilm, Reel 492, Adams Papers, Massachusetts Historical Society (hereafter MHS).

13. [Joel R. Poinsett to Andrew Jackson, October 23, 1830], draft, Poinsett Papers, HSP.

14. *Charleston Courier*, September 7, 1830.

15. *Charleston Mercury*, October 15, 1830; Petigru to [William J. Grayson?], [October] 1830; Joseph Blyth Allston, "Life and Times of James L. Petigru," 7, CLS; *Charleston Courier*, October 14 and December 16, 1830.

16. Petigru to Joel R. Poinsett, December 15, 1830, Poinsett Papers, HSP.

17. William C. Dukes, Journal and Diary, vol. 4, entry for July 4, 1831, microfilm, William Christopher Dukes Manuscripts, USC-Car.

18. James Hamilton to Stephen D. Miller, July 19, 1831, Chesnut-Miller-Manning Papers, SCHS.

19. Petigru to William Elliott, August 25, 1831, copy, Petigru Correspondence, LC.

20. Petigru to William Elliott, November 14, 1831, copy, Petigru Correspondence, LC; *Charleston Courier*, November 14 and December 8, 1831.

21. *The United States of America* v. *I. E. Holmes, Alexander Mazyck, and Thomas Gadsden* (1831), extensively reported in *Charleston Courier* and *Mercury*, September 1831, passim. The motion for judgment is in *United States . . .* v. *. . . Holmes [et al.]*, September Term, 1831, Justice Department, Attorney-General's Papers, Record Group 60, National Archives (hereafter NA).

22. *Charleston Courier*, September 7, 1831.

23. Lewis P. Jones, "William Elliott: South Carolina Non-Conformist," *Journal of Southern History* 17 (1951): 365.

24. South Carolina Legislature, "Journal of the House of Representatives," December 17, 15, and 12, 1831, microfilm, SCA.

25. *Charleston Mercury*, March 23 and 24, 1832; *The State of South Carolina* v. *A. Heyward et al.*, reported in the *Charleston Courier*, June 4, 1833.

26. Dumas Malone, *The Public Life of Thomas Cooper* (Columbia: University of South Carolina Press, 1961), 257–72, 286–335; Colyer Meriwether, *History of Higher Education in South Carolina* (Washington, D.C.: Government Printing Office, 1889), 156–60; Donald J. Senese, "Legal Thought in South Carolina, 1800–1860" (Ph.D. dissertation, University of South Carolina, 1970), 156–57.

27. [Petigru to William J. Grayson, 1831], in William J. Grayson, "Autobiography of William John Grayson," ed. Samuel Stoney, *South Carolina Historical Magazine* 49 (1948): 113.

28. Daniel Hollis, *South Carolina College*, 2 vols. (Columbia: University of South Carolina Press, 1951), 1:110–15; *Charleston Courier*, December 9, 1831; Petigru to William Elliott, November 4, 1831, copy, Petigru Correspondence, LC; William Elliott to Ann Elliott, December 5, 1831, in Beverly R. Scafidel, "The Letters of William Elliott" (Ph.D. dissertation, University of South Carolina, 1978), 280; South Carolina Legislature, "Journal of the House of Representatives," December 7, 1831, microfilm, SCA.

29. Malone, *Life of Thomas Cooper*, 355–62.

30. *Charleston Courier*, December 2 and 12, 1831. The resolution of endorsement is in the *Courier*, December 13, 1831. Petigru to William Drayton, November 28, 1834, in James Petigru Carson, *Life, Letters and Speeches of James Louis Petigru, the Union Man of South Carolina* (Washington, D.C.: W. H. Lowdermilk, 1920), 165.

31. *Charleston Courier*, January 5, 1832.

32. James Haig to Henry DeSaussure, April 28, 1832, Gilpin Papers, Poinsett Section, HSP. DeSaussure enclosed a copy of his letter for Congressman

Drayton's edification, in DeSaussure to William Drayton, May 4, 1832, Drayton Collection, HSP.

33. Petigru to Hugh Legaré, October 29, 1832, copy, Miscellaneous Manuscripts, USC-Car; *Charleston Courier*, June 14, 1832.

34. Petigru to Jane North, June 12, 1832, in Carson, *Life*, 87–88; *Charleston Mercury*, June 14, 1832; Stephen Elliott to William Elliott, July 27, 1830, Elliott-Gonzales Papers, UNC; *Mercury*, May 9, 1832. For Hamilton's hotly contested election, see *Mercury*, May 28, July 14, and November 29, 1832; also the *Charleston Courier*, August 6, September 12, and November 6, 1832.

35. Petigru to William Elliott, August 7, 1832, copy, Petigru Correspondence, LC; J. N. Barillon to John Seibels, August 29, 1832, Seibels Family Papers, USC-Car; Jacob Schirmer, Diary, September 2, 1832, SCHS; *Charleston Courier*, September 3, 1832.

36. *Charleston City Gazette*, September 15, 1832; John B. Grimball, Diary, October 5, 1832, UNC; Petigru to William Elliott, September 4, 1832, copy, Petigru Correspondence, LC.

37. *Charleston Mercury*, September 28, 1832; *Charleston City Gazette*, September 29, 1832.

38. Petigru to Hugh Legaré, October 29, 1832, in Carson, *Life*, 103–4; H. P. Holbrook to Edward Rutledge, [ca. October 13, 1832], fragment, Rutledge Family Papers, USC-Car; Petigru to Legaré, October 29, 1832.

39. *Charleston Courier*, October 11, 1832. In an election in which a few more than 2700 voters cast ballots for up to twelve of twenty-four candidates, the least number of votes to win was 1418; Petigru received 1315. Petigru to William Elliott, October 3, 1832, copy, Petigru Correspondence, LC.

40. Freehling, *Prelude to Civil War*, 260–64; Petigru to Hugh Legaré, December 21, 1832, Miscellaneous Manuscripts, USC-Car.

41. [James L. Petigru], *The Report of the Committee of the Convention of the Union and State Rights Party, Assembled at Columbia, 10th December, 1832. With Their Remonstrance and Protest* [1832]. The address to the people and the resolutions of the September 12, 1852, Union convention, which Petigru drafted, are in Carson, *Life*, quotations at 92 and 93.

42. Petigru, *Report of the Committee . . . 10th December, 1832*, 5.

43. Samuel Jackson to William True, December 14, 1832, Samuel C. Jackson Papers, USC-Car; Petigru to Hugh Legaré, December 21, 1832, Miscellaneous Manuscripts, USC-Car.

44. Petigru to Hugh Legaré, December 21, 1832, Miscellaneous Manuscripts, USC-Car; Andrew Jackson, *Correspondence of Andrew Jackson*, ed. John Spencer Bassett, 7 vols. (Washington, D.C.: Carnegie Institution, 1926–35), 4:502; Daniel Huger to William Drayton, December 17, 1832, Drayton Collection, HSP.

45. Remini, *Jackson*, 242; Joel Poinsett to Andrew Jackson, January 19, 1833,

microfilm, Series 1, Reel 42, Andrew Jackson Papers, LC; Petigru to Hugh Legaré, December 21, 1832, Miscellaneous Manuscripts, USC-Car; Freehling, *Prelude to Civil War*, 275–78.

46. Petigru to Hugh Legaré, December 21, 1832, Miscellaneous Manuscripts, USC-Car; Joel Poinsett to Andrew Jackson, January 16, 1833, microfilm, Series 1, Reel 42, Andrew Jackson Papers, LC; Mitchell King to Hugh Legaré, May 5, 1833, in Shirley C. Hughson, comp., "Letters of the Period of Nullification," copied extracts in bound manuscript volume, SCHS.

47. Petigru to William Elliott, September 20, 1832, copy, Petigru Correspondence, LC.

48. Mitchell King to Hugh Legaré, May 5, 1833, Mitchell King Papers, USC-Car; Grayson, *Petigru*, 157–58; Allston, "Life and Times," 14; Medical Society of South Carolina, Minutes, May 2, 5, 1831, Waring Medical Library, Medical University of South Carolina; Petigru to Hugh Legaré, July 15, 1833, Miscellaneous Manuscripts, USC-Car; King to Legaré, September 14, 1833, Yates-Snowden Collection, USC-Car.

49. Petigru to Hugh Legaré, July 15, 1833, Miscellaneous Manuscripts, USC-Car.

50. Henry Middleton to Harrison Gray Otis, July 25, 1833, Harrison Gray Otis Papers, MHS; Petigru to Adele Allston, September 3, 1833, in Allston, "Life and Times," 8.

51. Petigru to Adele Allston, September 3, 1833, in Allston, "Life and Times," 7.

52. Charles Petigru to Adele Allston, September 16, 1833, Allston Family Papers, SCHS.

53. *The State ex rel. James M'Daniel* v. *Thomas M'Meekin, Brig. Gen'l 6th Brigade So. Ca. Militia*, and *The State ex rel. Ed. M'Cready* v. *B. F. Hunt, Col. 16th Reg't So. Ca. Militia*, 2 Hill 1–71 (1834) (9 S.C. Reports 1–40). The entire test oath case is covered in *Book of Allegiance; or Appeals of South Carolina, on the Oath of Allegiance. Determined on the 24th of May, 1834* (Columbia: Telescope Office, 1834).

54. *Book of Allegiance*, 12.

55. *M'Cready* v. *Hunt*, at 64/36.

56. Ibid., at 69/39.

57. *Book of Allegiance*, 113–14.

58. Ibid., 114, 116.

59. Ibid., 117, 114, 120.

60. Ibid., 123, 121.

61. For O'Neall's opinion, see *Book of Allegiance*, 209–26; for Johnson, 226–48; for Harper, 248–82, quotation at 278.

62. Petigru to William Drayton, June 11, 1834, in Carson, *Life*, 141; Petigru to Hugh Legaré, August 1, 1834, Miscellaneous Manuscripts, USC-Car;

Petigru to Drayton, July 11, 1834, in Carson, *Life*, 153; Petigru to Legaré, September 16 and August 1, 1834, Miscellaneous Manuscripts, USC-Car; Petigru to Drayton, August 12, 1834, in Carson, *Life*, 157; "Looker On," in *Charleston Courier*, September 18, 1841.

63. Petigru to Hugh Legaré, September 16 and October 26, 1834, Miscellaneous Manuscripts, USC-Car.

64. Mitchell King to Hugh Legaré, May 5, 1833, in Hughson, "Letters," SCHS; Petigru to Legaré, April 24, 1834, Miscellaneous Manuscripts, USC-Car.

65. Petigru to Hugh Legaré, November 29, 1834, Miscellaneous Manuscripts, USC-Car.

66. The story of the final resolution of the oath crisis comes from Petigru to Hugh Legaré, December 15, 1834, in Carson, *Life*, 166–71; James Hamilton to Petigru, December 9, 1834, South Carolina Miscellany, Dalton Collection, Papers 1787–1934, Duke University (hereafter DU).

67. Petigru to James Chesnut, December 9, 1834, Williams-Chesnut-Manning Papers, USC-Car.

68. Donald J. Senese, "Building the Pyramid: The Growth and Development of the State Court System in Antebellum South Carolina," *South Carolina Law Review* 24 (1972): 368–69. The general problem of the South Carolina court system is summarized in Michael S. Hindus, *Prison and Plantation. Crime, Justice, and Authority in Massachusetts and South Carolina, 1767–1878* (Chapel Hill: University of North Carolina Press, 1980), 23–24.

69. Petigru to Hugh Legaré, May 31, 1835, Hugh Swinton Legaré Papers, USC-Car.

70. "Leaves from a Journal in Charleston, S.C.," copied from *Portland Advertiser* in *Charleston Courier*, May 2, 1833; William Ogilby, Journal, August 11, 1830, SCHS.

71. Alexander R. Lawton, *Annual Address before the American Bar Association at Saratoga Springs, N.Y., August 9th, 1882* (Philadelphia: George S. Harris and Sons, 1883), 22.

72. Benjamin F. Perry, "Reminiscences of Public Men. James L. Petigru," *Nineteenth Century Magazine* (July 1870): 140; *Charleston Mercury*, March 11, 1863; James M. Banner, Jr., "The Problem of South Carolina," in Stanley Elkins and Eric McKitrick, eds., *The Hofstadter Aegis: A Memorial* (New York: Alfred A. Knopf, 1974), 60–93.

Chapter 4. Becoming an Entrepreneur

1. James L. Petigru to Hugh Legaré, November 20, 1833, in James Petigru Carson, *Life, Letters, and Speeches of James Louis Petigru, the Union Man*

of South Carolina (Washington, D.C.: W. H. Lowdermilk, 1920), 127; Joseph Dukes to John Manning, July 10, 1839, Chesnut-Miller-Manning Papers, SCHS.

2. Petigru to Hugh Legaré, October 29, 1832, and August 1, 1834, Miscellaneous Manuscripts, USC-Car; Francis Lieber to [?], October 22, 1863, copy, Vanderhorst Papers, SCHS.

3. John J. Pringle et al., Petition, August 12, 1834, General Records of the Department of State, Letters of Application and Recommendation . . . Andrew Jackson, 1829–37, microfilm M-639, Roll 18, NA; Joel Poinsett to Charles Ingersoll, August 29, 1834, Charles Jared Ingersoll Correspondence, HSP; W. B. Bullock to John Forsythe, September 27, 1834, General Records, Department of State, Letters of Application and Recommendation . . . 1829–37, microfilm M-639, Roll 18, NA.

4. Petigru to Hugh Legaré, September 16, 1834, Miscellaneous Manuscripts, USC-Car. Earlier to William Drayton, however, after he noticed the unlikelihood of his own appointment, Petigru suggested Drayton as his first choice and Legaré as his second: Petigru to Drayton, August 12, 1834, in Carson, *Life*, 157–58.

5. Petigru to Hugh Legaré, October 26, 1834, Miscellaneous Manuscripts, USC-Car.

6. Petigru to Hugh Legaré, November 20, 1833, Miscellaneous Manuscripts, USC-Car.

7. Family letters throughout this period contain many references to Jane Amelia's poor health and frequent comments on the trials she caused to her family and relatives; see, for example, Jane Amelia Petigru to Adele Allston, April 23, 1834, R.F.W. Allston Papers, SCHS; Petigru to John G. North, March 24, 1835, Vanderhorst Papers, SCHS; Petigru to Jane North, May 18, 1836, James L. Petigru Correspondence, LC; same to same, October 27, 1836, Vanderhorst Papers, SCHS; Petigru to Robert F. W. Allston, November 30, 1837, and Louise Porcher to Adele Allston, June 24 and July 26, 1841, R. F. W. Allston Papers, SCHS; Petigru to Sue Petigru, January 14, 1842, copy, Petigru Correspondence, LC. Concerning her fear of dropsy, see Jane Amelia Petigru to Adele Allston, November 4, 1836, R. F. W. Allston Papers, SCHS; and Petigru to Jane North, February 27 and April 14, 1837, Vanderhorst Papers, SCHS.

8. Emma Huger to Adele Allston, September 1, [1835], R.F.W. Allston Papers, SCHS; Petigru to John North, September 28, 1835, Vanderhorst Papers, SCHS; Marion Gouverneur, *As I Remember. Recollections of American Society during the Nineteenth Century* (New York: D. Appleton, 1911), 98.

9. Caroline Petigru to Adele Allston, March 9, [1839], R. F. W. Allston Papers, SCHS.

10. Petigru to Jane North, July 10, 1837, copy, Petigru Correspondence, LC;

Petigru to Adele Allston, August 5, 1837, R. F. W. Allston Papers, SCHS; Petigru to Jane North, August 19, 1838, copy, Petigru Correspondence, LC.

11. Petigru to Hugh Legaré, February 17, 1836, Miscellaneous Manuscripts, USC-Car; Petigru to Jane North, May 21, 1839, copy, and April 14, 1837, copy, Petigru Correspondence, LC.

12. Petigru to Jane North, January 20, 1838, in Joseph Blyth Allston, "Life and Times of James L. Petigru," 9, CLS.

13. Petigru to Hugh Legaré, April 24, 1834, Miscellaneous Manuscripts, USC-Car; Petigru to Adele Allston, June 19, 1834, January 10, 1835, and June 22, 1835, R. F. W. Allston Papers, SCHS; Petigru to Jane North, August 4, 1835, copy, Petigru Correspondence, LC.

14. Harriette Lesesne to Adele Allston, January 8, 1838, R. F. W. Allston Papers, SCHS; Petigru to Jane North, May 21, 1839, copy, Petigru Correspondence, LC. Mary Petigru, however, had a somewhat less charitable view of Caroline's submissiveness toward her mother; see Mary Petigru to Adele Allston, March 8, [1839], R. F. W. Allston Papers, SCHS, in which she wrote, "Caroline's going out every night leaving her [mother] in such misery, is a bitter thing to her. She says Caroline's name will ring through the Town as one *who is most unnatural.*"

15. Petigru to Adele Allston, November 3, 1841, R. F. W. Allston Papers, SCHS; *Charleston Courier,* December 7, 1841.

16. Petigru to Adele Allston, August 30, 1836, R. F. W. Allston Papers, SCHS; Petigru to Jane North, July 10, 1837, copy, Petigru Correspondence, LC; Petigru to Adele Allston, April 27, 1838, R. F. W. Allston Papers, SCHS.

17. Petigru to Hugh Legaré, April 6, 1838, Miscellaneous Manuscripts, USC-Car.

18. Ibid.; Petigru to Hugh Legaré, May 7, 1838, Miscellaneous Manuscripts, USC-Car.

19. Jane Amelia Petigru to Mary Baber, September 9, 1840, Baber-Blackshear Collection, University of Georgia (hereafter UGa).

20. Dan's progress at Mount Saint Mary's College is from the official college records, courtesy of the college library and Professor Robert Olwell; see Robert Olwell to authors, May 13, 1991, in authors' possession. Professor Olwell delightfully summarized Dan's career: "From his grades it appears as if Daniel was a perfect 'Carolina Gentleman,' skilled at 'elocution' but of little distinction in the other arts and inclined to 'pout' in the face of failure." The Princeton material is from biographical data about Dan taken from faculty minutes in the Princeton University Archives; Petigru to William Elliott, October 1, 1840, Vanderhorst Papers, SCHS.

21. Susan Petigru King, in *Lily* (New York: Harper and Brothers, 1855), 119–20, speaks through the character of Alicia on the futility of southern women studying anything. For her own proclivities, see Sue Petigru to Adele Alls-

ton, August 28, [1835], Caroline Petigru to Adele Allston, November 19, 1838, Petigru to Adele Allston, September 9, 1839, Sue Petigru to Caroline Petigru, [1839–41?], and Elizabeth [Weston?] to Adele Allston, September 1, 1841, all in R. F. W. Allston Papers, SCHS; Allston, "Life and Times," 9. Sue Petigru turned much of her own experience into fiction later in her life; see especially "Crimes Which the Law Does Not Reach," in Susan Petigru King, *Sylvia's World. Crimes Which the Law Does Not Reach* (New York: Derby and Jackson, 1859), the first and second stories.

22. Jean H. Baker, *Mary Todd Lincoln. A Biography* (New York: W. W. Norton, 1989), 33; Petigru to Jane North, May 18, 1836, Vanderhorst Papers, SCHS; Petigru to John G. North, September 28, 1835, copy, Petigru Correspondence, LC.

23. Petigru to Hugh Legaré, February 14, 1838, Miscellaneous Manuscripts, USC-Car.

24. The trials and tribulations Petigru faced as an attorney frequently on the road may be sampled in Petigru to Adele Allston, July 10, 1832, and November 30, 1843, R. F. W. Allston Papers, SCHS; Petigru to John North, March 24, 1835, Vanderhorst Papers, SCHS; and Petigru to Jane North, April 4, 1836, in Carson, *Life*, 183.

25. Statistics on Petigru's caseload were assembled from the state appeals court decisions, 1816–63, compiled by a variety of reporters and confined to those likely to be of use to the legal profession. They are reprinted as *South Carolina Reports*, 27 vols. (St. Paul: West Publishing Company, 1916–21). Federal cases were located through the Lexus computerized law index. For a tabulation of state appeals court cases, see appendix A. Legal Document, [Admission to the Georgia Bar], January 24, 1833, Vanderhorst Papers, SCHS; William J. Grayson, *James Louis Petigru. A Biographical Sketch* (New York: Harper and Brothers, 1866), 141–42; Petigru to Jane North, December 17, 1838, copy, Petigru Correspondence, LC.

26. Petigru to Richard Singleton, February 8, 1836, Singleton Manuscripts, DU.

27. *Charleston Courier*, January 4, December 20, 1842, and May 3, 1843.

28. Petigru to Hugh Legaré, February 17, 1836, Miscellaneous Manuscripts, USC-Car; Fellowship Society, Charleston, Records, Minutes 1832–41, especially March 11, 1835, and March 8, 1837, microfilm, USC-Car; also *Charleston Mercury*, March 11, 1836, and March 16, 1838; College of Charleston, Board of Trustees, Minutes, 1831–41, passim, especially November 13, 1831, October 15, 1832, August [?], 1837, typed copy, CC.

29. Petigru to Hugh Legaré, May 31, 1835, Hugh Swinton Legaré Manuscripts, USC-Car; South Carolina College, Board of Trustees, Minutes, 1835–41, passim, microfilm, USC-Car.

30. James Louis Petigru, *Oration Delivered before the Thalian and Phi Delta*

Societies of Oglethorpe University, on Commencement Day, the 10th of November, 1841 (Milledgeville, Ga.: Grieve and Orme, 1841), 7–8, 5.

31. *Charleston Mercury,* March 7 and May 2, 1836; *Charleston Courier,* August 7, 1835, March 23, 1830, March 23, 1835; Carson, *Life,* 172; *Courier,* March 11, 1834; *Mercury,* September 8, 1837; George R. Locke to Joseph H. Lumpkin, March 5, 1852, enclosure, Lumpkin Papers, UGa.

32. Petigru to Jane North, June 13, 1832, copy, Petigru Correspondence, LC; Petigru to Hugh Legaré, September 16, 1834, Miscellaneous Manuscripts, USC-Car; Carson, *Life,* 102; Caroline Gilman to A. M. White, January 15, 1833, Caroline Howard Gilman Letters, SCHS.

33. [Petigru to William J. Grayson, ca. 1831], in William J. Grayson, "Autobiography of William John Grayson," ed. Samuel Stoney, *South Carolina Historical Magazine* 49 (1948): 113; Society for the Relief of Orphans and Widows of the Clergy of the Protestant Episcopal Church in South Carolina, Minute Books, 1824–62, Minutes for 1836, SCHS; *Charleston Mercury,* November 25, 1836.

34. *Charleston Mercury,* June 17, 1836; *Charleston Courier,* June 23 and 24, 1836; James Campbell to Joel Poinsett, August 27, 1836, Joel Poinsett Papers, HSP.

35. Petigru to Hugh Legaré, February 17, 1836, Miscellaneous Manuscripts, USC-Car; same to same, August 23 and 26, 1836, Petigru Correspondence, LC.

36. Alfred Huger to Joel Poinsett, August 27, 1836, Poinsett Papers, HSP; Petigru to Hugh Legaré, August 27 and September 6, 1836, Miscellaneous Manuscripts, USC-Car. For city election returns, see the *Charleston Mercury,* October 13, 1836; also Petigru to Jane North, October 27, 1836, Petigru Correspondence, LC.

37. Petigru to [Jane North?], January 3, 1837, Vanderhorst Papers, SCHS; Wylma Wates, "James L. Petigru and the Revolutionary War Widow: The Petition of Christiana Teulon," *South Carolina Historical Magazine* 86 (1985): 68–71; South Carolina Legislature, "Journal of the House of Representatives," December 2 and 12, 1836, microfilm, SCA; *Charleston Courier,* December 20, 1837; South Carolina Legislature, "Journal of the House of Representatives," December 4, 1837, December 13, 1836, and December 15, 1837, microfilm, SCA; South Carolina, *Statutes at Large,* ed. Thomas Cooper, David McCord et al., 14 vols. (Columbia: A. S. Johnson, 1840ff.), vol. 6, no. 2730.

38. South Carolina Legislature, "Journal of the House of Representatives," December 3, 7, 17, 1836, microfilm, SCA; *Charleston Courier,* December 13, 16, 18, 20, 1837; Petigru to Hugh Legaré, December 17, 1837, in Carson, *Life,* 193.

39. A convenient brief survey of the whole Jacksonian bank war is Robert V. Remini, *Andrew Jackson and the Bank War. A Study in the Growth of Presidential Power* (New York: W. W. Norton, 1967).

40. Petigru to Jane North, September 17, 1837, copy, Petigru Correspon-

dence, LC; *Charleston Courier*, December 4, 1837; James L. Petigru, "Speech of Mr. Petigru, on the Resolutions Reported by the Special Committee on the Currency—in the House of Representatives of South-Carolina, December [11], 1837," *Courier*, June 8, 1838.

41. South Carolina Legislature, "Journal of the House of Representatives," December 12, 1837, microfilm, SCA; *Charleston Courier*, December 14, 1837; Petigru to Jane North, December 20, 1837, copy, Petigru Correspondence, LC; Thomas Bennett to Joel Poinsett, [August 22], 1838, Poinsett Papers, HSP; Petigru to Hugh Legaré, September 10, 1838, in Carson, *Life*, 200.

42. George Bryan to John Pendleton Kennedy, October[?] 26, 1838, John Pendleton Kennedy Papers, George Peabody Department, Enoch Pratt Free Library (hereafter EPFL); Albert Case to Gideon Welles, April 24, 1840, Miscellaneous Manuscripts, USC-Car; Petigru to [William Preston Barbecue Committee], August 31, 1840, *Charleston Courier*, September 2, 1840; Petigru to William Elliott, December 11, 1834, Vanderhorst Papers, SCHS; Petigru to William Elliott, August 21, 1841, and October 6, 1841, copies, Petigru Correspondence, LC.

43. [Petigru to William Grayson, ca. 1851], in Grayson, "Autobiography," 113; Petigru to Hugh Legaré, November 20, 1833, Miscellaneous Manuscripts, USC-Car; Grayson, *Petigru*, 137; Chatham County, Georgia, Registry of Deeds, Deed Books 2P:285–86 (1830), 2T:34–35 (1834), and 2V:489–90 (1838). For Petigru's various mortgages on the property, see Deed Books 2P:277–84 (1830), 2U:170–71, and 349–51 (1836). The manuscript "Purchase of Nigs," Vanderhorst Papers, SCHS, is a fragment, possibly by Joseph Blyth Allston, detailing Petigru's holdings in slaves in 1831–33 and their cost. If accurate, Petigru's slaves (ca. 125) were worth approximately $36,000; see Allston, "Life and Times," 8.

44. Petigru to Adele Allston, November 16, 1832, R. F. W. Allston Papers, SCHS; Petigru to William Drayton, May 23, 1834, in Carson, *Life*, 140; Petigru to Hugh Legaré, September 16, 1834, and October 26, 1834, Miscellaneous Manuscripts, USC-Car; Petigru to Jane North, December 24, 1835, copy, Petigru Correspondence, LC.

45. *By-Laws of the South Carolina Canal and Rail Road Company* ([Charleston]: J. S. Burges, [1834]), 7; Petigru to Jane North, October 27, 1836, copy, Petigru Correspondence, LC; *Charleston Mercury*, October 21, 1836; *Charleston Courier*, January 21, 1834, and January 20, 1835; *Mercury*, January 19, 1836; *Wotherspoon et al. v. The Bank of the State of South Carolina*, Speers Equity 488–95 (1844) (25 S.C. Reports 203–6); *Bank of the State of South Carolina v. James Rose and Others*, 1 Richardson Equity 292–96 (1845) (22 S.C. Reports 137–39); *The Bank of the State of South Carolina v. James B. Campbell, James Rose and Others*; and *James Rose and Others v. The Bank of the State of South Carolina, James B. Campbell and Others*, 2 Richardson Equity 179–92 (1846)

(25 S.C. Reports 80–86); *The Executors of Haslett et al.* v. *Wotherspoon et al.*, 1 Strobhart Equity 209–57 (1847) (26 S.C. Reports 103–33).

46. Samuel Gaillard Stoney, *The Story of South Carolina's Senior Bank. The Bank of Charleston, Mother of the South Carolina National Bank of Charleston* (Charleston: The Bank, 1955), passim; William H. Pease and Jane H. Pease, *The Web of Progress: Private Values and Public Styles in Boston and Charleston, 1828–1843* (1985; reprint, Athens: University of Georgia Press, 1991), 47; Petigru to Hugh Legaré, May 31, 1835 (continued June 5), Legaré Papers, USC-Car.

47. Petigru to Hugh Legaré, May 31, 1835, (continued June 5), Legaré Papers, USC-Car.

48. Bank of Charleston, *Proceedings of the Annual Meeting . . . "Monthly Condition of the Bank"* (Charleston: A. E. Miller, 1842); *Charleston Mercury*, February 6, 1837; Bank of Charleston, *Proceedings of the Stockholders . . . at a Public Meeting, Held . . . on Monday, the Thirtieth January, 1837 . . . for the Purpose of Considering the Expediency of Increasing the Capital of the Bank to Four Millions of Dollars . . .* (Charleston: A. E. Miller, 1837), 8–12, 14–16.

49. *Charleston Mercury*, February 18, 22, and 23, 1837; Jacob F. Schirmer, Diary, July 8, 1837, SCHS; Petigru to Jane North, July 10, 1837, copy, Petigru Correspondence, LC.

50. *State v. Bank of Charleston*, Dudley Equity 187–208 (1838) (10 S.C. Reports 78–87).

51. Convention of Banks of the City of Charleston, *Minutes . . . Held on the 3d and 6th of Feb. 1841, to Consider the Act of the Legislature, Passed at the Last Session; with the Opinions of the Solicitors of Each Bank* (Charleston: A. E. Miller, 1841), 11–12, 17.

52. Henry Bailey to Armistead Burt, May 7, 1841, Armistead Burt Papers, DU; *The State v. The Bank of Charleston*, 2 McMullens 439–53 (1842) (11 S.C. Reports 184–89).

53. *Charleston Courier*, March 10, 1842; Bank of Charleston, *Proceedings of the Stockholders* [1842] (Charleston: A. E. Miller, 1842), 7; *Charleston Mercury*, June 3 and 5, 1843.

54. Grayson, *Petigru*, 137; jotted note about financial obligations of James Petigru, 1842, Petigru Papers, LC; Charleston County Deed Books U9:530, V10:122, O10:105, Registry of Mesne Conveyance, Charleston, South Carolina; Charleston Bar Association, *Memorial of the Late James L. Petigru. Proceedings of the Bar of Charleston, S.C., March 25, 1863* (New York: Richardson and Company, 1866), 26.

55. On the background of land speculation, see John H. Moore, *The Emergence of the Cotton Kingdom in the Old Southwest. Mississippi, 1770–1860* (Baton Rouge: Louisiana State University Press, 1988), 16–19. James Hamilton to J. H. Hammond, October 19, 1840, Hammond Papers, LC; jotted note, 1842, Petigru Papers, LC.

56. Petigru to [Jane North?], [ca. 1837] and January 25, 1839, in Allston, "Life and Times," 8, 9; Petigru to Jane North, September 17, 1837, in Carson, *Life*, 190; Petigru to Hugh Legaré, January 9, 1839, Miscellaneous Manuscripts, USC-Car; James L. Petigru, "Liability and Principal," [June 1842], Petigru Papers, LC. A dollar in 1842 was worth roughly twelve times as much as a 1990 dollar.

57. Petigru to Jane North, May 21, 1839, copy, Petigru Correspondence, LC. Petigru sold the Savannah plantation land and buildings for $25,000, and one-half of the slaves (61) for $29,550: Chatham County, Georgia, Deed Books 2W:292–93; Petigru to Jane North, May 21, 1839, and December 17, 1838, copies, Petigru Correspondence, LC; same to same, August 17, 1839, in Allston, "Life and Times," 9; Petigru to Dr. Baber, October 29, 1842, Baber-Blackshear Collection, UGa.

58. Petigru to Hugh Legaré, October 5, 1839, James L. Petigru Papers, USC-Car; Petigru to Adele Allston, November 3, 1841, R. F. W. Allston Papers, SCHS; Petigru to Hugh Legaré, April 6, 1838, and January 19, 1842, Miscellaneous Manuscripts, USC-Car.

59. Petigru to Hugh Legaré, January 19, 1842, Miscellaneous Manuscripts, USC-Car; James L. Petigru, Fair Copy of Liabilities, June 30, 1842, H. W. Conner, Bank of Charleston, to Petigru, July 1, 1842, James Rose, South Western Rail Road Bank, to Petigru, July 19, 1842, Petigru to Jane North, July 19, 1842, copy, and receipt, South Western Rail Road Bank, December 6, 1842, all in Petigru Correspondence, LC; J. Johnston Pettigrew to [James C. Johnston?], December 27, 1853, Pettigrew Family Papers, UNC.

Chapter 5. Practicing Law

1. *Hamilton* v. *Hamilton*, 2 Richardson Equity 355–94 (1845) (25 S.C. Reports 161–79).

2. Petigru to Jane North, May 20, 1845, in Joseph Blyth Allston, "Life and Times of James L. Petigru," 10, CLS; Petigru to Tom Petigru, May 20, 1845, copy, Petigru Correspondence, LC.

3. J. Johnston Pettigrew to [James C. Johnston?], December 27, 1853, Pettigrew Family Papers, UNC.

4. For Petigru's generosity to clients and friends, see, for example, Petigru to S. S. Farrar, June 16, 1854, draft, Petigru Correspondence, LC; Alfred Huger to Petigru, April 28, 1857, Alfred Huger Papers, Letterpress Book, DU; "M." to Petigru, January 19, 1863, in James Carson, *Life, Letters, and Speeches of James L. Petigru, the Union Man of South Carolina* (Washington, D.C.: W. H. Lowdermilk, 1920), 467. Caroline Carson remained a constant drain on her father; see Adele Allston to Ben Allston, November 4, 1856, R. F. W. Allston Papers, SCHS; and Jane North to Caroline Pettigrew, July 14, [1859], Pettigrew Family Papers, UNC. Petigru also purchased a house for J. Johnston

Pettigrew to provide him the requisite property necessary to qualify for political officeholding; see J. Johnston Pettigrew to William Pettigrew, December 28, 1856, cited in Clyde N. Wilson, Jr., *Carolina Cavalier. The Life and Mind of James Johnston Pettigrew* (Athens: University of Georgia Press, 1990), 79. For bond and land holding, see Memorandum: Georgia Bonds, August 5, 1856, Petigru Correspondence, LC; Charleston County, Registry of Mesne Conveyance, Deed Books O13:557, W13:65, V13:13, V12:235, C10:246–47, O11:314, and Z13:436; and Petigru to R. J. Davant, January 31, 1855, Petigru and King, Letterbooks, microfilm, R514, USC-Car. The quotations are in Petigru to Adele Allston, August 31, 1850, R. F. W. Allston Papers, SCHS; and Petigru to Decima Heyward, February 1, 1856, Petigru and King, Letterbooks, microfilm, R514, USC-Car.

5. R. G. Dun & Company, Credit Ledgers, South Carolina, 1:409, October 1855, R. G. Dun Collection, Baker Library, Harvard University Graduate School of Business Administration. Petigru's income compares reasonably with the $18,000–$23,000 the most notable lawyers in Charleston and other American cities received in the years when Petigru first began to practice law; see Anton-Hermann Chroust, *The Rise of the Legal Profession in America*, 2 vols. (Norman: University of Oklahoma Press, 1965), 2:87–89; Allston, "Life and Times," 30. For samples of Petigru's legal fees, see Petigru to R. H. Wilde, January 4, 1843, Petigru Correspondence, LC; Petigru to A. J. Miller, April 17, 1855, Petigru and King to R. J. Davant, April 8, 1858, and Petigru to J. Caldwell, June 28, 1860, all in Petigru and King, Letterbooks, microfilm, R514 and R515, USC-Car; see also T. Pinckney Huger to Langdon Cheves II, March 21, 1860, Langdon Cheves Papers, SCHS; the quotation is cited in Allston, "Life and Times," 26.

6. Statistics on Petigru's caseload were assembled from the state appeals court decisions, 1816–63, compiled by a variety of reporters and selected by them as likely to be of use to the legal profession. They are reprinted as *South Carolina Reports* (St. Paul: West Publishing Company, 1916–). See appendix A for a tabulation of state appeals court cases.

7. Charleston County, Court of Equity, Records 1842–61, SCA; see appendix B for tabulation.

8. Petigru to W. F. DeSaussure, April 24, 1858, Petigru and King, Letterbooks, microfilm, R514, USC-Car; Charleston County, Court of Equity, Records 1842–61, SCA; see appendix B for tabulation.

9. The burial vault issue is outlined in Petigru to Henry Middleton, August 27, 1850, and November 17, 1851, Petigru to J. W. Hayne, July 16, 1851, J. W. Hayne to Henry Middleton, November 18, 1851, and Magnolia Cemetery Company, Title Deed to cemetery lot, to Henry Middleton, March 31, 1852, recorded by Secretary of State, March 18, 1857, all in Cheves-Middleton Business Papers, SCHS. Numerous letters in Petigru and King, Letterbooks,

microfilm, R514, USC-Car, speak to Petigru's concern for compromise or arbitration; see letters at June 16 and 24, July 24, and December 14, 1854, July 13 and September 12, 1855, July 3, 1856, January 25, 1858, January 29, 1859, and January 28, 1861; also see Petigru to Ann Cunningham, August 25, 1860, Pickens Manuscripts, DU.

10. For the DeSaussure-Heyward contretemps, see Petigru to William Elliott, December 9 and 14, 1854, Vanderhorst Papers, SCHS, quotation in the latter letter; Petigru to William Heyward, February 20, 1855, and enclosure [plan for a compromise settlement]. For another potential duelling issue, see Petigru to A. R. Taft, June 2, 1854, and Petigru to S. S. Farrar, June 5 and October 14, 1854, Petigru and King, Letterbooks, microfilm, R514, USC-Car. For the *Morse* case, see Petigru to Jane North, November 8, 1853, in Allston, "Life and Times," 27.

11. James L. Petigru, "Oration . . . Delivered at Fort Moultrie, Sullivan's Island, on the 28th June, 1844," *Charleston Courier*, July 4, 1844; James L. Petigru, *An Oration, Delivered before the Phi Kappa and Demosthenian Societies of the University of Georgia, August 6, 1846 . . .* (Athens: Southern Whig Office, 1846), 12.

12. *John B. Irving v. George Robertson; James S. Shingler v. Same*, 6 Richardson 236–37 (1853) (16 S.C. Reports 94); James L. Petigru, *Oration Delivered on the Third Anniversary of the South Carolina Historical Society, at Hibernian Hall . . . May 27, 1858* (Charleston: Walker, Evans and Company, 1858), 5.

13. Petigru to Benjamin Perry, August 24, 1842, Benjamin F. Perry Papers, Alabama Department of Archives and History (hereafter AAH). The comment about J. Johnston Pettigrew, the young colleague, is in Carson, *Life*, 457 (no other source given).

14. Ulrich B. Phillips, *History of Transportation in the Eastern Cotton Belt* (1908; reprint, New York: Octagon Books, 1968), 160, 179; Samuel M. Derrick, *Centennial History of South Carolina Railroad* (Columbia: State Company, 1930), 196; Lacy K. Ford, Jr., *Origins of Southern Radicalism. The South Carolina Upcountry, 1800–1860* (New York: Oxford University Press, 1988), 221, 242, 266. Chief among the legal historians who have argued a major shift in law to accommodate the new economic interests of the nineteenth-century northern states are William E. Nelson, *Americanization of the Common Law. The Impact of Legal Change on Massachusetts Society, 1760–1830* (Cambridge: Harvard University Press, 1975); and Morton J. Horwitz, *The Transformation of American Law* (Cambridge: Harvard University Press, 1977).

15. The complexities of the *Pell-Ball* case that follow are treated in the various appeals court reports; see *Ferris Pell and Mary Anna, his wife . . . v. E. O. Ball and T. Waring . . .*, Speers Equity 48–87 (1843) (25 S.C. Reports 21–37); *Ferris Pell et ux. et al. v. Executors of Hugh Swinton Ball et al.*, Speers Equity 518–532 (1844) (25 S.C. Reports 215–21); *Ferris Pell and Wife et al. v. Executors*

of H. S. Ball et al., 1 Richardson Equity 361–89 (1845) (25 S.C. Reports 168–81).

16. Legaré's dramatic speech is reported in Alexander R. Lawton, *Address before the American Bar Association at Saratoga Springs, N.Y., August 9th, 1882* (Philadelphia: George S. Harris and Sons, 1883), 31.

17. The ins and outs of the *Cheves* case and the family disputes that accompanied it may be followed in various letters and documents of the collections given and at the dates indicated: Langdon Cheves Papers (Personal and Business Papers), SCHS: July 21 and December 21, 1857, March 14, April 4, May 13, and 25, 1858, February 13, 1859, January 17, 23, 25, and 26, and February 3 and 5, 1860; also Petigru and King, Letterbooks, microfilm, R514, USC-Car: May 17 and November 13, 1858; and *Langdon Cheves, Executor v. Charles F. Haskell and Others*, 10 Richardson Equity 534–50 (1859) (29 S.C. Reports 175–201).

18. Petigru to Langdon Cheves, January 25, 1860, Langdon Cheves Papers, SCHS.

19. Petigru and King to Langdon Cheves, February 5, 1860, Langdon Cheves Papers, SCHS.

20. *Daniel E. Huger, Jr., and Others v. Isabella I. Huger and Others*, 9 Richardson Equity 217–43 (1857) (28 S.C. Reports 75–85); Petigru to Daniel E. Huger, June 2, 1860, Petigru and King, Letterbooks, microfilm, R515, USC-Car.

21. Petigru to Daniel E. Huger, Jr., June 13 and 19, 1860, Petigru and King, Letterbooks, microfilm, R515, USC-Car.

22. Petigru to Dr. D. H. Trezevant, March 24, 1858, and Petigru to Charles Prioleau, June 20, 1862, both in Petigru and King, Letterbooks, microfilm R514 and R515, USC-Car. There is on both reels extensive correspondence with the various Trezevant heirs and London solicitors from 1854 through 1862; see Petigru and King, Letterbooks, at September 25, October 17, December 15, 1854; March 10, 1855; January 8 and 11, March 12, June 9 and 10, July 16, November 18, 1856; January 13, February 4, December 14 and 23, 1857; April 3, 5, 7, and 9, 1858; January 29, April 14, June 16, July 21 and 27, 1859; March 16, 21, and 28, October 23, 1860; and June 20, October 23, November 17, December 12, 1862.

23. For steamship cases, see *Administrators of William Patton v. John Magrath and W. P. Brooks*, Dudley 159–64 (1838) (10 S.C. Reports 67–69; *Jane Patton, Administratrix, and A. Kennedy and J. Foster, Administrators of William Patton, Deceased, v. John Magrath and J. P. Brooks*, Rice 162–70 (1839) (10 S.C. Reports 69–72); *R. C. Swindler, Survivor v. Hilliard & Brooks*, and *P. P. Chambers & Co. v. The Same*, 2 Richardson 286–314 (1846) (13 S.C. Reports 115–26). For railroad cases, see *F. & J. Bradford v. The South Carolina R. R. Company*, and *Others v. The Same*, 7 Richardson 201–15 (1854) (28 S.C. Reports 79–84); *Wardlaw, Walker & Burnsides v. South Carolina Railroad Company*, and *Gardelle & Daigle v. The Same*, 11 Richardson 337–42 (1858) (17 S.C. Reports 114–16); Horwitz, *Transformation of American Law*, 192–95, 202–5.

24. The discussion that follows is from *Louisville, Cincinnati, and Charleston R. R. Co., Plaintiffs in Error* v. *Thomas W. Letson, Defendant,* 43 U.S. (1844) 497–549.

25. Ibid., 508. Not surprisingly, Petigru ignored the possible alternatives of *in rem* proceedings in the courts of the diverse states in which members of the corporation, and the corporation itself, held property because it would have benefited the railroad and run at odds to his client's interests. A court eager to extend federal jurisdiction over corporations specifically validated Petigru's approach.

26. Ibid., 510.

27. *The State ex rel. A. Ottolengui et al. vs G. V. Ancker et al. Report of the Evidence and Arguments of Counsel. By a Member of the Charleston Bar* (Charleston: Samuel Hart, 1844), 31.

28. William J. Grayson, *James Louis Petigru. A Biographical Sketch* (New York: Harper and Brothers, 1866), 153–54; Ford, *Origins of Southern Radicalism,* 315–18.

29. George Dewitt Brown, "A History of the Blue Ridge Railroad, 1852–1874" (M.A. Thesis, University of South Carolina, 1967), 50–56. The convolutions of the *Bangs* case may be followed in numerous letters in Petigru and King, Letterbooks, microfilm, R514 and R515, 1854–61, USC-Car.

30. Petigru and King to Thomas R. R. Cobb, May 4, 1857; same to same, January 11, 1857; same to H. H. Hunt, February 16, 1857; Petigru to Messrs. Law, Barton, and Lovell, February 17, 1857, all in Petigru and King, Letterbooks, microfilm, R514, USC-Car.

31. Petigru to William Henry Seward, May 2, 1857, William Henry Seward Papers, University of Rochester (hereafter UR). To satisfy the diversity principle for cases brought in federal courts, this case was not brought in South Carolina, the state in which the Blue Ridge Rail Road was situated.

32. Petigru and King to Law, Barton, and Lovell, July 3, 1857, Petigru and King Letterbooks, microfilm, R514, USC-Car.

33. Petigru and King to W. J. Gould, July 13, 1857, Petigru and King, Letterbooks, microfilm, R514, USC-Car; *Savannah Republican,* n.d., copied in *Charleston Courier,* September 28, 1858; *Marietta Patriot,* n.d., quoted in *Courier,* September 25, 1858.

34. Petigru to Thomas R. R. Cobb, June 8, 1860, Petigru and King, Letterbooks, microfilm, R515, USC-Car.

35. J. Johnston Pettigrew to James Johnston, February 5, 1849, Hayes Collection, UNC.

36. J. Johnston Pettigrew to Robert F. W. Allston, November 21, 1852, R. F. W. Allston Papers, SCHS.

37. Petigru to Robert F. W. Allston, July 5, 1850; J. Johnston Pettigrew to Robert F. W. Allston, November 21, 1852, both in R. F. W. Allston Papers, SCHS.

38. From the memories of Joseph D. Pope, in Allston, "Life and Times," 25.

39. Quoted in Carson, *Life*, 56–57.

40. Petigru to Benjamin F. Perry, July 7, 1856, Benjamin Franklin Perry Papers, AAH.

41. Petigru to R. Welsman, June 23, 1859, Petigru and King, Letterbooks, microfilm, R515, USC-Car; Petigru to John H. Bryan, January 8, 1861, John H. Bryan Collection, North Carolina Department of Cultural Resources, Division of Archives and History (hereafter NCA); John Belton O'Neall, *Biographical Sketches of the Bench and Bar of South Carolina*, 2 vols. (1859; reprint, Spartanburg, S.C.: Reprint Company, 1975), 2:39. The declining standards for admission to the South Carolina bar may have shaped some of Petigru's impatience with his colleagues, who were as well the pool from which judges and chancellors were drawn. In 1796, three years' experience as a legal clerk was required for admission to the bar if the candidate was a college graduate, four years if he was not. By 1812 the only requirements were a good character and having lived for twenty-one years. By 1829 Charleston's recorder (municipal judge) had already detected a decline in standards; see Donald Joseph Senese, "Legal Thought in South Carolina, 1800–1860" (Ph.D. dissertation, University of South Carolina, 1970), 57–67.

42. Petigru to Jane North, July 5, 1845, in Carson, *Life*, 243; J. Johnston Pettigrew to James Johnston, June 10, 1853, Hayes Collection, UNC; Charles Warren, *History of the Harvard Law School and of Early Legal Conditions in America*, 3 vols. (New York: Lewis Publishing Company, 1908), 2:175; O'Neall, *Biographical Sketches*, 2:450 and 1:i.

43. Petigru to Sue Petigru King, November 27 and December 10, 1845, and November 22, 1847, copies, Petigru Correspondence, LC, quotations in December 10 letter.

44. Georgia, Senate Journal (November 1847), 71; Petigru to Jane North, January 6, 1843, and December 27, 1847, in Allston, "Life and Times," 16; Petigru to Tom Petigru, December 27, 1847, and Petigru to Jane North, November 19, 1838, copies, Petigru Correspondence, LC; Petigru to Jane North, January 5, 1849, in Allston, 16.

45. Franklin H. Elmore to Joshua Bates, May 3, 1849, in Franklin H. Elmore, President of the Bank of the State of South Carolina, Special Report in Reply to a Senate Resolution on Concerns Expressed by Baring Brothers and Company . . . , Record Group 0010, Series 017, SCA; Petigru to Franklin H. Elmore, December 13 and 18, 1849, Franklin Harper Elmore Papers, UNC.

Chapter 6. Pursuing Justice

1. Louise Porcher to Adele Allston, May 1849, R. F. W. Allston Papers, SCHS.

2. Joseph D. Pope, "James Louis Petigru," in William Draper Lewis, ed., *Great American Lawyers; the Lives and Influence of Judges and Lawyers Who Have Acquired a National Reputation and Have Developed the Jurisprudence of the United States*, 8 vols. (Philadelphia: John C. Winston, 1907–9), 4:58–59; Joseph Blyth Allston, "Life and Times of James L. Petigru," 25, CLS.

3. Robert F. W. Allston to Adele Allston, November 30, 1842, R. F. W. Allston Papers, SCHS. Family and business correspondence from the 1840s and 1850s contains numerous references to Petigru's poor health.

4. Business correspondence during the 1850s is filled with references to Petigru's increasing forgetfulness and his tendency to make mistakes. He was all too aware of his failing, writing to his sister in 1857 that he needed to have some mechanism to help him remember: "In fact, such help is becoming more necessary for me every day" (Petigru to Jane North, May 26, 1857, in Allston, "Life and Times," 31). The quotations in the text, in order, are from Petigru to Mrs. J. R. Valk, December 16, 1859, Petigru and King, Letterbooks, microfilm, R515, USC-Car; Petigru to Adele Allston, February 9, 1855, R. F. W. Allston Papers, SCHS; Petigru and King to J. Dyson, May 13, 1854, Petigru and King, Letterbooks, microfilm, R514, USC-Car; Alexander R. Lawton, *Annual Address before the American Bar Association at Saratoga Springs, N.Y., August 9th, 1882* (Philadelphia: George S. Harris and Sons, 1883), 15.

5. Petigru to Hugh Legaré, November 20, 1833, Miscellaneous Manuscripts, USC-Car; Petigru to R. H. Wilde, November 13, 1843, Gratz Collection, HSP.

6. Petigru to Stephen Watson, July 17, 1857, Petigru and King, Letterbooks, microfilm, R514, USC-Car. Huger died in 1854, Hamilton in 1857, Gilman in 1857, and Fraser in 1860.

7. Petigru to Jane North, June 17, 1859, in Allston, "Life and Times," 32; Adele Allston to Ben Allston, May 1, 1856, and Mary Petigru to Adele Allston, September 5, [1859], both in R. F. W. Allston Papers, SCHS.

8. Petigru to Jane North, November 27, 1849, in Allston, "Life and Times," 19; Jane North to Adele Allston, March 22, 1850, and Louise Porcher to Adele Allston, July 11, 1850, both in R. F. W. Allston Papers, SCHS.

9. Petigru to Adele Allston, August 23, 1850, R. F. W. Allston Papers, SCHS.

10. J. Johnston Pettigrew to [James Johnston?], June 22, 1855, Pettigrew Family Papers, UNC. Petigru family correspondence is full of references to everyday doings at Badwell and to Petigru's hopes and dreams for the farm over the years.

11. Basil Manly to A. Bowie, April 2?, 1857, copy, Manly Family Papers, University of Alabama (hereafter UA); William J. Rorabaugh, *The Alcoholic Republic. An American Tradition* (New York: Oxford University Press, 1979), 233.

12. Mary Petigru to Adele Allston, January 5, 1855, and Jane North to Adele Allston, December 28, 1854, both in R. F. W. Allston Papers, SCHS; Petigru to Jane North, July 10, 1837, copy, Petigru Correspondence, LC; Mary Petigru to

Adele Allston, June 29, [1857], and Petigru to Adele Allston, February 9, 1855, both in R. F. W. Allston Papers, SCHS.

13. Thomas Petigru's career is summarized in John DeCamp, *Reply of Com[mander] John DeCamp, to Aspersions upon His Character Contained in an Article Published in the* Charleston Mercury, *of November 6, 1855, Entitled "Commander Thomas Petigru and the Naval Board"* (1856), 9; also "Memorial of Thomas Pettigru, [sic]," in *Charleston Courier*, February 26, 1856.

14. Petigru to Jane North, April 17, 1849, in Allston, "Life and Times," 18; Petigru to William Henry Seward, February 16, 1850, William Henry Seward Papers, UR. The story of Thomas Petigru's trials and tribulations is drawn largely from DeCamp, *Reply*, passim.

15. Petigru to Adele Allston, August 31, 1850, R. F. W. Allston Papers, SCHS.

16. Petigru to Benjamin F. Perry, October 2, 1855, Benjamin Franklin Perry Papers, AAH.

17. Petigru's campaign against the navy on behalf of Tom is outlined in Petigru to Jane North, April 22, 1851, June 11, [1852] [misdated 1849], and December 27, 1855, all in Allston, "Life and Times," 21, 23, 29; Petigru to Alfred Huger, May 31, 1852, Vanderhorst Papers, SCHS; J. Johnston Pettigrew to William S. Pettigrew, October 6, 1855, Pettigrew Family Papers, UNC; and Petigru to Hamilton Fish, December 16, 1855, Hamilton Fish Papers, LC.

18. Jane North to Adele Allston, March 6, 1856, R. F. W. Allston Papers, SCHS; Petigru to Mary Anne Petigru, March 11, 1857, in James Petigru Carson, *Life, Letters, and Speeches of James Louis Petigru, the Union Man of South Carolina* (Washington, D.C.: W. H. Lowdermilk, 1920), 322–23; Petigru to William P. Miles, March 6, 1858, William P. Miles Papers, UNC.

19. *Smith* v. *Croom*, 7 Fla. 81–107 (1857).

20. Petigru to Adele Allston, April 4, 1857, R. F. W. Allston Papers, SCHS.

21. See appendix A for a tally of the cases Petigru won in South Carolina appeals courts.

22. A slashing attack on the entire South Carolina judicial system appeared in Edward J. Pringle, "The Judiciary System of South Carolina," *Southern Quarterly Review*, n.s., 2 (1850): 464–86.

23. John Belton O'Neall, *Biographical Sketches of the Bench and Bar of South Carolina* 2 vols. (1859; reprint, Spartanburg, S.C.: Reprint Company, 1975), 1:163–64.

24. Petigru to Hugh Legaré, May 13, 1843, Miscellaneous Manuscripts, USC-Car.

25. James Louis Petigru, *Oration Delivered before the Charleston Library Society at Its First Centennial Anniversary, June 13th, 1848* (Charleston: J. B. Nixon, 1848), 17.

26. Petigru to J. H. Robert, June 25, 1855, Petigru to Charles Hammond, May 10, 1854, Petigru and King to E. Waterman, July 21, 1855, all in Petigru

and King, Letterbooks, microfilm, R514, USC-Car. It may be indicative that half of Petigru's appeal cases in the 1850s involving issues that Horwitz included within the category of economically driven transformations of the law were heard in equity court, whereas only two of the nine that dealt with traditional economic complaints were. It may have been that chancellors' willingness to make law in cases not customarily associated with equity proceedings provided a way to resist pressures to change common law practice; see Morton J. Horwitz, *The Transformation of American Law* (Cambridge: Harvard University Press, 1977), 164–65.

27. Petigru to Hon. H. Chipman, March 22, 1855, and Petigru to Susan Wood, May 27, 1857, both in Petigru and King, Letterbooks, microfilm, R514, USC-Car; Petigru to Jane North, February 27, 1855, in Allston, "Life and Times," 28.

28. William R. Johnson, in *Schooled Lawyers: A Study in the Clash of Professional Cultures* (New York: New York University Press, 1978), noted the prevalence of apprenticeship as "a formal mode of legal training in the nineteenth century" involving "extended legal training . . . by the practitioners themselves who selected, advised and sponsored those young men who desired to become lawyers" (52). Petigru to Mary Baber, November 20, 1848, Baber-Blackshear Collection, UGa; William P. Starke to Francis Lieber, February 7, 1846, Francis Lieber Papers, HL. From 1825 until 1860, Petigru sponsored 30 of the 280 attorneys who petitioned to practice in the South Carolina Court of Appeals in Law. In his endorsements of the applicants he stated that 28 of them had read law in his office. Petitions to Practice Law, 1825–59, Court of Appeals, Court of Appeals in Law, SCA.

29. Petigru to William Pettigrew, October 23, 1835, in Carson, *Life*, 176–77.

30. Jane North to Adele Allston, December 21, 1843, R. F. W. Allston Papers, SCHS; Petigru to Susan P. King, October 9, 1847, in Carson, *Life*, 259; Carson, *Life*, 281; Louise Porcher to Adele Allston, [ca. 1849], and Adele Allston to Benjamin Allston, December 7, 1849, both in R. F. W. Allston Papers, SCHS.

31. Petigru to Jane North, February 7, 1849, in Allston, "Life and Times," 17. For a biography of J. Johnston Pettigrew, see Clyde N. Wilson, *Carolina Cavalier. The Life and Mind of James Johnston Pettigrew* (Athens: University of Georgia Press, 1990); for his intellectual prowess, see especially 144–45.

32. J. Johnston Pettigrew to James C. Johnston, May [29] [misdated 28], 1849, Hayes Collection, UNC; Petigru to Charles Pettigrew, August 2, 1849, Pettigrew Family Papers, UNC.

33. J. Johnston Pettigrew to W. S. Pettigrew, July 8, 1853, same to James C. Johnston, December 6, 1853, and same to W. S. Pettigrew, January 1 [?], 1854, all in Pettigrew Family Papers, UNC.

34. Petigru to Jane North, October 5, 1855, in Carson, *Life*, 315.

35. On Jane Amelia's mesmerism, see Petigru to Jane North, May 20, 1845,

in Allston, "Life and Times," 10; also Petigru to Sue King, December 10, 1845, copy, Petigru Correspondence, LC.

36. Jane North to Adele Allston, February 18, 1850, R. F. W. Allston Papers, SCHS.

37. Louise Porcher to Adele Allston, October 15, 1849, R. F. W. Allston Papers, SCHS; J. Johnston Pettigrew to James C. Johnston, January 4, 1853, Pettigrew Family Papers, UNC; Petigru to Sue King, August 21, 1849, Vanderhorst Papers, SCHS; Petigru to Jane North, June 29, 1852, in Allston, "Life and Times," 24.

38. On the couple's mutual reticence, see Jane Petigru to Henry Lesesne, August 7, 1854, Vanderhorst Papers, SCHS; and Petigru to Sue Petigru, December 17, 1842, copy, Petigru Correspondence, LC. For Petigru's innocent pleasure in the company of interesting women, see Robert F. W. Allston to Adele Allston, March 1, 1852, and Jane North to Adele Allston, August 10, 1854, both in R. F. W. Allston Papers, SCHS. On Petigru's obstinacy, see Jane Amelia Petigru to William P. Miles, July 7, 1860, William P. Miles Papers, UNC. The tensions in the marriage are reflected in many family letters of the 1840s and 1850s; see, for instance, Louise Porcher to Adele Allston, July 11, 1850, and June 9, 1854, and Mary Petigru to Adele Allston, August 8, [1854], all in R. F. W. Allston Papers, SCHS; J. Johnston Pettigrew to W. S. Pettigrew, June 14, 1853, Pettigrew Family Papers, UNC.

39. Caroline Carson to James Carson, June 25, [1878], Vanderhorst Papers, SCHS; Louise Porcher to Adele Allston, June 18, 1842, R. F. W. Allston Papers, SCHS; Petigru to Thomas Petigru, December 8, 1846, same to Jane North, April 17, 1849, in Allston, "Life and Times," 13, 18; Petigru to Adele Allston, December 16, 1851, R. F. W. Allston Papers, SCHS.

40. Petigru to Robert F. W. Allston, June 4, 1845, R. F. W. Allston Papers, SCHS; Petigru to Sue King, July 15, 1845, and Petigru to Jane Amelia Petigru, October 6, 1845, both in Vanderhorst Papers, SCHS; Louise Porcher to Adele Allston, June 27, [1850], October 5, 1850, October 15, 1849, and January 20, 1850, all in R. F. W. Allston Papers, SCHS.

41. Letters between Jane North, Louise Porcher, and Adele Allston alluding to Caroline Carson's unhappy marriage during 1849 and 1850 culminate in explicit discussions of that marriage in Louise Porcher to Adele Allston, October 15, 1849, and January 20, 1850, and Petigru to Adele Allston, December 16, 1851, all in R. F. W. Allston Papers, SCHS.

42. Louise Porcher to Adele Allston, October 16, 1854, R. F. W. Allston Papers, SCHS.

43. J. Johnston Pettigrew to William S. Pettigrew, December 28, 1856, Pettigrew Family Papers, UNC; "Schedule of the Estate of William A. Carson," [n.d. but ca. 1860–61], Vanderhorst Papers, SCHS.

44. Louise Porcher to Adele Allston, January 9, [1845], and Sue King to Adele Allston, January 28, 1846, R. F. W. Allston Papers, SCHS; Deed Books,

Q:14–20, W11:275–83, F13:159 and 347, Charleston County, Registry of Mesne Conveyence.

45. References to the tense daughter-parent relations are many; see, for example, Petigru to Adele Allston, February 6, 1843, R. F. W. Allston Papers, SCHS; Petigru to Sue King, July 8, 1846, Vanderhorst Papers, SCHS; Louise Porcher to Adele Allston, [n.d., ca. 1849], and Harriette Lesesne to Adele Allston, July 22, 1853, both in R. F. W. Allston Papers, SCHS; Petigru to Susan King, November 18, 1853, and January 12, 1858, Vanderhorst Papers, SCHS, quotations in the last letter.

46. The most comprehensive treatment of South Carolina's legal and judicial treatment of women from 1750 to 1830 is Marylynn Salmon, *Women and the Law of Property in Early America* (Chapel Hill: University of North Carolina Press, 1986). Jane H. Pease and William H. Pease, *Ladies, Women, and Wenches: Choice and Constraint in Antebellum Charleston and Boston* (Chapel Hill: University of North Carolina Press, 1990), 90–114, deals, though less systematically, with women's legal position between 1830 and 1860. Glenda Riley, *Divorce: An American Tradition* (New York: Oxford University Press, 1991), 34–84, gives an overview of the evolution of American divorce laws from 1790 to 1875. For separation cases, see Petigru to John William Wallace, October 31, 1856, Petigru and King to Thomas Waring, March 13, 1855, and to Messrs. Browne and Porter, October 15, 1856, all in Petigru and King, Letterbooks, microfilm R514, USC-Car.

47. *V. M. Converse by Next Friend v. A. L. Converse*, 9 Richardson Equity 535–71 (1856) (28 S.C. Reports 192–205), is a full report of the case; quotation from Adele Allston to Della Allston, March 2, 1854, R. F. W. Allston Papers, SCHS.

48. Petigru to A. P. Butler, June 23, 1855, and Petigru to F. I. Moses, June 23, 1855, both in Petigru and King, Letterbooks, microfilm, R514, USC-Car.

49. *Converse v. Converse*, 536/193. The details that follow are from this case.

50. Ibid., 540/194.

51. Ibid., 570/205.

52. Ibid., 562/202, 571/205. Marylynn Salmon, "Women and Property in South Carolina: The Evidence from Marriage Settlements, 1730–1830," *William and Mary Quarterly*, 3d ser., 39 (October 1982): 674, asserts that generally "judges in equity did everything in their power to protect women," a point also made in her *Women and the Law of Property*, 75–76, 104–6.

53. Petigru to W. F. DeSaussure, December 27, 1856, Petigru and King, Letterbooks, microfilm, R514, USC-Car.

54. The diabolical appellation is in Petigru to John B. Moore, February 18, 1857. The final settlement was thrashed out in 1857; see Petigru to J. B. Moore, January 12, 19, 28, and February 18, 1857, Petigru to F. I. Moses, January 19, 1857, and Petigru to W. M. Anderson, February 18, 1857, all in Petigru and King, Letterbooks, microfilm, R514, USC-Car.

55. Summaries of the case are in Carson, *Life*, 291–92, which includes Peti-

gru's report to Jane North, January 8, [1853] [misdated 1852]; and Allston, "Life and Times," 26, which quotes Petigru's letter to Jane North, November 16, 1852, about the case.

56. Allston, "Life and Times," 25. Allston was present at the hearing.

57. Petigru and King to John Winberg, November 16, 1854, same to John Phillips, November 30, 1854, same to Kohlsaat and Brothers, December 9, 1854, and same to Julia Winberg, December 14, 1854, all in Petigru and King, Letterbooks, microfilm, R514, USC-Car.

58. Marriage Settlement, James L. Petigru and Jane Amelia Postell, August 22, 1816, Vanderhorst Papers, SCHS; United States Census, South Carolina, Charleston District, 1840 and 1850, microfilm manuscript census, NA.

59. On slave purchases, see Allston, "Life and Times," 21, 22; and Jane Petigru to Henry Lesesne, July 29, 1857, Bill of Sale, January 8, 1857, Petigru to Sue King, September 5, 1859, all in Vanderhorst Papers, SCHS; for Sammy, see Allston, 33; for slave discipline, see Petigru to Jane North, February 7, 1849, June 16, 1856, and October 10, 1857, all in Allston, 17, 30, and 31.

60. Allston, "Life and Times," 6; Petigru to Jane North, June 13, 1832, copy, Petigru Correspondence, LC; Francis Lieber, Notebook on Slavery (1845), HL; and Allston, "Life and Times," 21, deal with emancipating slaves. Richard De Treville in the *Smalle* case strongly implied that Petigru was an abolitionist, see p. 144. *William Fountain, Administrator de bonis non cum testamento annexo of Frederick Kohne, Deceased, Appellant v. William Ravenel*, 58 U.S. 369–99 (1854); J. Johnston Pettigrew to James C. Johnston, October 27, 1853, Hayes Collection, UNC. The Wardlaw quotation is in Friedman, *History of American Law*, 198. For the action of South Carolina courts in cases involving slaves, see A. E. Keir Nash, "A More Equitable Past? Southern Supreme Courts and the Protection of the Ante-Bellum Negro," *North Carolina Law Review* 48 (1970): 197–242; and Nash, "Negro Rights, Unionism, and Greatness on the South Carolina Court of Appeals: The Extraordinary Chief Justice John Belton O'Neall," *South Carolina Law Review* 21 (1969): 141–90, quotation at 172.

61. James Louis Petigru, *Oration Delivered before the Thalian and Phi Delta Societies of Oglethorpe University, on Commencement Day, the 10th of November, 1841* (Milledgeville, Ga.: Grieve and Orme, 1841), 4–5. Race ideas and Nott's particular views are discussed in Reginald Horsman, *Race and Manifest Destiny. The Origins of American Racial Anglo-Saxonism* (Cambridge: Harvard University Press, 1981), 48–52, 128–33, and 151–55.

62. Petigru to Jane North, December 29, 1847, in Allston, "Life and Times," 16.

63. *Charleston Mercury*, July 14, 17, 1849; Robert F. Durden, "The Establishment of Calvary Episcopal Church for Negroes in Charleston," *South Carolina Historical Magazine* 65 (1964): 70–72; *Mercury*, July 16, 1849; Jacob Frederick Schirmer, Diary, July 13, 14, 1849, SCHS.

64. Petigru to Susan King, July 12, 1849, in Carson, *Life*, 278; Allston, "Life and Times," 21. Allston misattributed the quotation of Petigru to the Saturday night mob at the church rather than to the Monday morning crowd at city hall.

65. *Charleston Courier*, July 21, 24 (first quotation), 1849; *Charleston Mercury*, August 3, 1849; Petigru to Robert F. W. Allston, August 21, 1849, R. F. W. Allston Papers, SCHS.

66. *Charleston Courier*, November 14, 1849; John B. Adger, *My Life and Times, 1810–1899* (Richmond: Presbyterian Committee of Publications, 1899), 173.

67. The laws restricting emancipation can be found in South Carolina, *Statutes at Large*, ed. Thomas Cooper, David McCord et al., 14 vols. (Columbia: A. S. Johnson, 1840ff.), vol. 7, no. 2236, and vol. 11, no. 2836. The convolutions of the Broad slave issue are contained in *The State v. John J. Singletary, Rebecca Rhame, and Others*, Dudley 220–23 (1838) (10 S.C. Reports 92–93); *Rebecca Rhame v. James Ferguson and John R. Dangerfield*, Rice 196–203 (1839) (10 S.C. Repots 83–86); and *Jane De Hay ads Ferguson and Dangerfield*, 2 McMillan 228–30 (1842) (11 S.C. Reports 96–97).

68. W. McLain [American Colonization Society] to Petigru, February 28, 1854, Vanderhorst Papers, SCHS; Petigru to Theodore Gaillard, June 2, 1850, Petigru and King, Letterbooks, microfilm, R514, USC-Car.

69. *F. A. Ford Escheator ex rel. J. Ferguson v. Starling J. Dangerfield*, 8 Richardson Equity 95–111 (1856) (28 S.C. Reports 33–39). The development of this final chapter of the Broad slaves is covered in extensive correspondence in Petigru and King, Letterbooks, especially June, July, and November 1854, and October and December 1855, microfilm, R514, USC-Car; Petigru and King to C. H. Simonton, July 14, 1854, and Petigru and King to Theodore Gaillard, August 20, 1855, both in the Letterbooks, R514. "An Act to Vest the Title of the State in Certain Escheated Property in Certain Persons Therein Mentioned," Act no. 4237, South Carolina, *Statutes at Large*, 12:363–64, awarded Broad's slaves to Theodore Gaillard. James S. Dangerfield was awarded the Broad plantation in Act no. 4313, South Carolina, *Statutes at Large*, 12:495–96. For the final disposition of the Broad slaves to Liberia, see Petigru and King to Randolph Mott, February 23 and March 19, 1857, and Petigru to J. S. Mustian, December 31, 1857, all in the Letterbooks, R514. In a separate case similar to that of the Broad slaves, Petigru tried to defend a will and trust arrangement made by a shiftless drunkard in order to prevent the return of a mulatto family to very real rather than nominal slavery; see *Carsten Vose Adm. of Josiah Dangerfield v. R. S. H. Hannahan*, 10 Richardson 465–73 (1857) (17 S.C. Reports 157–60).

70. For the Wigg story, see Petigru to Robert Habersham, April 16, 1857, May 8, 1857, and to John Postell, November 11, 1857, all in Petigru and King, Letterbooks, microfilm, R514, USC-Car.

71. Philip Hamer, "British Consuls and the Negro Seamen's Acts, 1850–1860," *Journal of Southern History* 1 (1935): 141–56; Alan F. January, "The First Nullification: The Negro Seamen's Acts Controversy in South Carolina, 1822–1860" (Ph.D. dissertation, University of Iowa, 1976), 339–50.

72. *Charleston Mercury*, December 15, 1851.

73. Petigru to William Mathew, March 26, 1851, Great Britain, Foreign Office, General Correspondence United States of America, Series 2, 5/551.

74. Ibid.; Hamer, "British Consuls," 156–57.

75. F. C. Adams (pseud.), *Manuel Pereira: Or the Sovereign Rule of South Carolina with Views of Southern Laws, Life, and Hospitality* (Washington, D.C.: Buell and Blanchard, 1853), 168–69, 272–73; *Ex Parte Manuel Pereira*, 6 Richardson 149–50 (1853) (16 S.C. Reports 59–60), quotation at 150/60. The revision of 1835 is in South Carolina, *Statutes at Large*, vol. 6, no. 2653.

76. *Reuben D. Roberts v. Jeremiah D. Yates*, 20 Federal Cases (1853), Case No. 11,919, 937–38 (16 Law Reports 49). The case is summarized in the *Charleston Courier* and the *Charleston Mecury*, April 22, 1853; also in January, "The First Nullification," 358–59.

77. *Charleston Mercury*, April 22, 1853.

78. *Charleston Courier*, June 20, 1853; Laura A. White, "The South in the 1850s as Seen by British Consuls," *Journal of Southern History* 1 (1935): 34–35; Hamer, "British Consuls," 166; January, "The First Nullification," 71–388.

79. *Charleston Daily Standard*, December 1, 4, 1854; Adams, *Manuel Pereira*, 169ff.; William J. Grayson, *James Louis Petigru. A Biographical Sketch* (New York: Harper and Brothers, 1866), 155–56; Allston, "Life and Times," 28.

80. Petigru to Jane North, December 2, 1854, in Allston, "Life and Times," 28.

81. *Charleston Daily Standard*, December 4, 1854.

82. Ibid.

83. The quotations are from Petigru to Jane North, December 2, 1854, in Allston, "Life and Times," 28; Petigru to William Elliott, December 14, 1854, Vanderhorst Papers, SCHS.

84. *Charleston Daily Standard*, December 4, 1854; Petigru to William Elliott, December 14, 1854, Vanderhorst Papers, SCHS.

85. Petigru to Mercy Smalle, January 14, 24, and February 11, 1856; quotations in January 14 letter and in Petigru to O. P. Williams, March 20, 1856, all in Petigru and King, Letterbooks, microfilm, R514, USC-Car.

86. Several recent essays have argued that southern law differed from law in the antebellum North: David J. Bodenhamer and James W. Ely, Jr., "Regionalism and the Legal History of the South," in Bodenhamer and Ely, eds., *Ambivalent Legacy. A Legal History of the South* (Jackson: University of Mississippi Press, 1984), 3–29; Kermit L. Hall and James W. Ely, Jr., "The South and the American Constitution," in Hall and Ely, eds., *An Uncertain Tradition. Constitutionalism and the History of the South* (Athens: University of

Georgia Press, 1989), 3–16; William M. Wiecek, " 'Old Times There Are Not Forgotten': The Distinctiveness of the Southern Constitutional Experience," in Hall and Ely, eds., *Uncertain Tradition*, 159–98; and Paul Finkelman, "Exploring Southern Legal History," *North Carolina Law Review* 64 (1985):77–116. The feoffment case was *Dehon* v. *Redfern* (1838) cited in Friedman, *History of American Law*, 207.

Chapter 7. Enduring War

1. Charleston, S.C., Bar Association, *Memorial of the Late James L. Petigru. Proceedings of the Bar of Charleston, S.C., March 25, 1863* (New York: Richardson and Company, 1866), 4.

2. The South Carolina Historical Society was organized, and Petigru elected president, on June 2, 1855: *Charleston Courier*, June 4, 1855. He was elected to the Massachusetts Historical Society on February 14, 1861: Massachusetts Historical Society, *Proceedings . . . 1860–1862* (Boston: The Society, 1862), 147. On the collection and publication of documents during Petigru's presidency, see "The South Carolina Historical and Genealogical Magazine," *South Carolina Historical Magazine* 31 (1930): 1; see also Petigru to A. Crottet, June 26, 1860, Petigru and King, Letterbooks, microfilm, R515, USC-Car.

3. James Louis Petigru, *Oration Delivered on the Third Anniversary of the South Carolina Historical Society, at Hibernian Hall . . . May 27, 1858* (Charleston: Walker, Evans and Company, 1858), 15.

4. James L. Petigru, "Oration of James L. Petigru, Esq., Delivered at Fort Moultrie, Sullivan's Island, on the 28th June, 1844," *Charleston Courier*, July 4, 1844.

5. Ibid.; James L. Petigru, *Semi-Centennial Celebration of the South-Carolina College; Consisting of the Baccalaurate Address by the President of the College and the Semi-Centennial Oration by James L. Petigru* (Charleston: Walker and Evans, 1855), 13; Petigru to David L. Swain, March 4, 1861, Walter B. Clark Papers, NCA.

6. *City Council of Charleston* v. *S. A. Benjamin*, 2 Strobhart 508–36 (1847) (14 S.C. Reports 237–49), at 511/239.

7. Ibid., at 520/242. Daniel Webster had similarly argued in *Vidal et al.* v. *Philadelphia* (1844) that "all, all, proclaim that Christianity, general, tolerant Christianity, Christianity independent of sects and parties, that Christianity to which the sword and the fagot are unknown, general, tolerant Christianity, is the law of the land"; quoted in Perry Miller, *The Life of the Mind in America from the Revolution to the Civil War* (London: Victor Gollancz, 1966), 200.

8. *City Council of Charleston* v. *S. A. Benjamin*, at 526/245.

9. On Petigru's fear both of *aristoi* and of *demos* and his faith in the virtuous republican middle, see his *Oration Delivered before the Charleston Library*

Society at Its First Centennial Anniversary, June 13th, 1848 (Charleston: J. B. Nixon, 1848). Caroline Carson summarized her father's position by saying that he "was essentially conservative but a thorough republican. The majority of the Roman republic was always in his mind. But to *Demus* he never bent" (Caroline Carson to Edward Everett, October 31, 1863, Vanderhorst Papers, SCHS). The quotations are in Petigru to William Henry Seward, February 16, 1850, William Henry Seward Papers, UR; and J. Johnston Pettigrew to William Pettigrew, August 15, 1853, Pettigrew Family Papers, UNC.

10. Petigru to Hugh Legaré, March 5 and July 15, 1833, in James Petigru Carson, *Life, Letters, and Speeches of James L. Petigru, the Union Man of South Carolina* (Washington, D.C.: W. H. Lowdermilk, 1920), 122, 125; James Louis Petigru, *An Oration Delivered before the Washington Society, on the Fourth July, 1834* (Charleston: D. J. Dowling, 1834), 15–16. Lacy K. Ford, Jr., "Inventing the Concurrent Majority: Madison, Calhoun, and the Problem of Majoritarianism in American Political Thought," *Journal of Southern History* 60 (1994): 19–58, illuminates parallel concerns.

11. Benjamin Perry, quoted in Lillian Kibler, *Benjamin Perry. South Carolina Unionist* (Durham: Duke University Press, 1946), 82; Robert F. W. Allston to Adele Allston, December 10, 1842, R. F. W. Allston Papers, SCHS. During his unsuccessful race in 1844 for the governorship, Allston wrote his wife, "I would give the average of any 10 negroes I own if your brother thought with me now. In a certain event I shall have constant need of the best legal advice, from a sound orthodox Constitutional lawyer" (Robert F. W. Allston to Adele Allston, December 6, 1844, R. F. W. Allston Papers, SCHS).

12. On the attorney generalship, see Petigru to Jane North, July 26, 1850, Vanderhorst Papers, SCHS; also Louise Porcher to Adele Allston, [August 10, 1850], R. F. W. Allston Papers, SCHS. For the South Carolina federal district attorney appointment, see Petigru to Millard Fillmore, November 3, 1850, Fillmore Papers, Buffalo and Erie County Historical Society; and Petigru to Millard Fillmore, November 9, 1850, General Records, Department of State, Record Group 59, microfilm M-873, Roll 67, NA; Millard Fillmore to J. C. Chamberlain, April 4, 1863, typescript, Vanderhorst Papers, SCHS; J. Johnston Pettigrew to James C. Johnston, March 28, 1853, Pettigrew Family Papers, UNC.

13. John Barnwell, *Love of Order: South Carolina's First Secession Crisis* (Chapel Hill: University of North Carolina Press, 1982), especially 139–79; Petigru to Daniel Webster, [December 6, 1850], Webster Papers, LC, in Charles Wiltsie, ed., Papers of Daniel Webster, microfilm edition (Ann Arbor: University Microfilms, in collaboration with Dartmouth College, 1971).

14. Petigru to Francis Lieber, March 1, 1852, Francis Lieber Papers, HL.

15. Petigru to Jane North, July 17, 1852, in Joseph Blyth Allston, "Life and Times of James L. Petigru," 24, CLS; Petigru to Josiah J. Evans, June 23,

1854, Petigru and King, Letterbooks, microfilm, R514, USC-Car; Petigru to William P. Miles, March 6 and December 31, 1858, William P. Miles Papers, UNC.

16. Kibler, *Perry*, 6; Petigru to Benjamin F. Perry, December 8, 1860, Benjamin F. Perry Papers, AAH.

17. Petigru to Alfred Huger, September 5, 1860, and Petigru to Edward Everett, October 28, 1860, copies, Petigru Correspondence, LC.

18. Steven A. Channing, *Crisis of Fear. Secession in South Carolina* (New York: Simon and Schuster, 1970), passim, especially 246–47; Kibler, *Perry*, 345–46; Lillian A. Kibler, "Unionist Sentiment in South Carolina in 1860," *Journal of Southern History* 4 (1938): 363–64; Petigru to Sue King, November 10, 1860, Vanderhorst Papers, SCHS; Allston, "Life and Times," 35, 36; George S. Bryan to John P. Kennedy, December 1860, John Pendleton Kennedy Papers, EPFL; Mary Boykin Chesnut, Diary, June 1861, in C. Vann Woodward, ed., *Mary Chesnut's Civil War* (New Haven: Yale University Press, 1981), 71.

19. Petigru to Jane North, November 20, 1860, in Carson, *Life*, 362; Joseph D. Pope, quoted in Allston, "Life and Times," 35; Petigru to Edward Everett, January 26, 1861, Petigru Correspondence, LC.

20. Petigru, "Oration . . . 28th June, 1844"; Petigru to Jane North, January 9, 1861, in Allston, "Life and Times," 35.

21. Petigru to Jane North, January 16 and 29, 1861, and February 13, 1861, all in Allston, "Life and Times," 36.

22. Petigru to Willie Carson, March 2, 1861, Petigru Correspondence, LC; Petigru to Jane North, March 7 and 26, 1861, in Allston, "Life and Times," 37, 38.

23. Daniel W. Crofts, *Reluctant Confederates: Upper South Unionists in the Secession Crisis* (Chapel Hill: University of North Carolina Press, 1989), 285; Jeffrey W. Lash, "Stephen Augustus Hurlbut: A Military and Diplomatic Politician, 1815–1882" (Ph.D. dissertation, Kent State University, 1980), 22–23, 56, and note 61; Petigru to J. Johnston Pettigrew, March 25, 1861, copy, Pettigrew Papers, NCA, original in Pettigrew Family Papers, UNC.

24. Petigru to N. P. Gignilliat, April 13, 1861, and Petigru to David L. Swain, April 26, 1861, Petigru and King, Letterbooks, microfilm, R515, USC-Car.

25. George S. Bryan to John P. Kennedy, [pre–June 16, 1861], John Pendleton Kennedy Papers, EPFL; Petigru to J. Johnston Pettigrew, June 24, 1861, copy, Pettigrew Papers, NCA.

26. Petigru to Jane North, December 24, 1860, in Allston, "Life and Times," 35; Petigru to Caroline Carson, July 17, 1861, Vanderhorst Papers, SCHS; same to same, February 7, 1862, and January 18, 1862, both in Petigru Correspondence, LC.

27. William Howard Russell, *My Diary North and South* (1863; reprint, Philadelphia: Temple University Press, 1988), 91–92, 101; Lacy K. Ford, Jr.,

"James Louis Petigru: The Last South Carolina Federalist," in Michael O'Brien and David Moltke-Hansen, eds., *Intellectual Life in Antebellum Charleston* (Knoxville: University of Tennessee Press, 1986), 157, 174; Ford, *The Origins of Southern Radicalism. The South Carolina Upcountry, 1800–1860* (New York: Oxford University Press, 1988), 173; James Oscar Farmer, Jr., *The Metaphysical Confederacy. James Henley Thornwell and the Synthesis of Southern Values* (Macon, Ga.: Mercer University Press, 1986), 26; Richard W. Singleton to Petigru, August 6, 1844, Vanderhorst Papers, SCHS; Petigru to Jane North, February 4, 1861, in Allston, "Life and Times," 36; Petigru to General P. G. T. Beauregard, March 30, 1861, Miscellaneous Manuscripts, USC-Car; and Carson, *Life*, 379, all speak of the guests at the Petigrus' dinner table. Also see Mary Chesnut, Diary, June 12, 1862, 379; Plowden Weston to Adele Allston, March 17, 1863, R. F. W. Allston Papers, SCHS; Charleston Bar Association, *Memorial of . . . James L. Petigru*, 25; Benjamin F. Perry, "Reminiscences of Public Men," *Nineteenth Century Magazine* (July 1870): 141. Caroline Carson had sent her older son, William, to Europe in 1859 to be educated for a career in business. And even though he stayed with his mother in New York on his return in 1863, his absence from the South was not a political statement.

28. Petigru to Sue King, September 30, 1861, copy, Petigru Correspondence, LC; Petigru to Jane North, March 2, 1862, in Allston, "Life and Times," 42. On the isolation that Petigru felt, see, for example, Bessie Allston, Diary, October 30, 1865, in Elizabeth W. Allston Pringle, *Chronicles of "Chicora Wood"* (New York: Scribners, 1922), 298; Adele Allston to Mrs. Hunter, May 15, 1861, draft/copy, R. F. W. Allston Papers, SCHS; Petigru to Caroline Carson, February 7, 1862, Vanderhorst Papers, SCHS; and Harriette Lesesne to Adele Allston, April 14, 1861, R. F. W. Allston Papers, SCHS. For Jane North's shift, see Jane North to Adele Allston, December 29, 1860, R. F. W. Allston Papers, SCHS; and Jane North to James Carson, June 5, 1861, Vanderhorst Papers, SCHS; Petigru to Jane North, February 5, 1862, in Allston, "Life and Times," 42.

29. For examples of Petigru's sense of financial responsibility for Caroline Carson, see Petigru to Caroline Carson, February 7, 1862, Petigru Correspondence, LC; same to Charles Prioleau, June 20, 1862, Petigru and King, Letterbooks, microfilm R515, USC-Car; Caroline Carson to Petigru, June 17, 1862, and Petigru to Caroline Carson, February 6, 1863, both in Vanderhorst Papers, SCHS. For his obligations as grandfather, see Petigru to Caroline Carson, December 21, 1861, James Carson to Caroline Carson, February 20, 1862, both in Vanderhorst Papers, SCHS; Petigru to Jane North, January 29, 1862, in Allston, "Life and Times," 41; Petigru to J. Johnston Pettigrew, October 21, 1862, Pettigrew Family Papers, UNC; and Petigru to Caroline Carson, January 20 and December 16, 1862, Petigru Correspondence, LC.

30. Petition for Petigru's appointment to the United States Supreme Court, MS dated March 4, 1862, signed by Horace Binney, Hamilton Fish, William C.

Bryant, et al., SCHS. The petition was sent to President Lincoln by Alfred Pell on March 17, 1862. Other supporting letters include Benjamin Ogle Taylor to Alfred Pell, March 14, 1862, and William M. Evarts to Abraham Lincoln, November 22, 1862, all in Application Files for Supreme Court Candidates Who Were Not Commissioned, 1853–88, Department of Justice Records, Record Group 60, NA.

31. Petigru to Jane North, July 31, 1861, in Allston, "Life and Times," 38; Petigru to Robert F. W. Allston, December 1, 1861, R. F. W. Allston Papers, SCHS; Petigru to Jane North, November 14, 1861, in Allston, 40.

32. Petigru to Benjamin F. Perry, March 22, 1861, Benjamin F. Perry Papers, AAH; Petigru to Caroline Carson, August 22, 1861, in Carson, *Life*, 391.

33. Confederate States of America, *The Statutes at Large of the Provisional Government of the Confederate States of America, from the Institution of the Government February 8, 1861, Inclusive . . .* (Richmond: R. M. Smith, 1864; photoreproduction, Indian Rocks Beach, Fla.: D & S Publishers, 1970), 151 (May statute), 201–6 (August statute); the quotations are from sections 1 and 2 of the August statute. Also see Petigru to David Swain, September 27, 1861, Walter Clark Papers, NCA.

34. *Charleston Courier*, October 8, 1861.

35. Ibid.

36. Ibid.; [Louise Porcher to Adele Allston, October 1861], R. F. W. Allston Papers, SCHS.

37. Alfred Huger to Petigru, October 10, 1861, Letterpress books, Alfred Huger Papers, DU; James L. Petigru, [Argument Against the Sequestration Act], in Carson, *Life*, 401–9, quotation at 405.

38. Petigru, Argument, 406.

39. Confederate States of America, *Statutes at Large*, 261–62.

40. Petigru to J. Johnston Pettigrew, November 29, 1861, Pettigrew Family Papers, UNC; Petigru to Jane North, October 16, 1861, in Allston, "Life and Times," 39. Petigru's continuing action against the sequestration laws can be followed in several of his letters: to Jane North, March 12, 1862, in Allston, 42; to Caroline Carson, October 14, 1862, in Carson *Life*, 458; to G. M. Coffin, February 7, 1862, J. L. Manning, July 23, 1862, and R. H. Lowndes, October 7, 1862, all in Petigru and King, Letterbooks, microfilm, R515, USC-Car; to G. Didier, December 28, 1862, and to Caroline Carson, February 6, 1863, both in Petigru Correspondence, LC; and see also Carson, *Life*, 401.

41. Carson, *Life*, 388–89; Lash, "Stephen Augustus Hurlbut," 130. Only William spelled his name Hurlbert.

42. The first, second, and fourth quotations are in Petigru to Sue King, July 24, 1861, copy, Petigru Correspondence, LC; the third is in Petigru to Caroline Carson, July 5, 1861, in Carson, *Life*, 387.

43. Petigru to Sue King, October 7, 1861, copy, Petigru Correspondence, LC; Carson, *Life*, 394.

44. Petigru to Jane North, October 30, 1861, in Allston, "Life and Times," 34; Mary Petigru to Adele Allston, December 27, 1860, R. F. W. Allston Papers, SCHS.

45. Petigru to Jane North, October 29, 1860, and January 29, 1861, in Allston, "Life and Times," 34 and 36; Charleston, South Carolina, Tax Assessor, Assessment Books, 1863, SCA; Petigru to Francis Lieber, February 11, 1851, Francis Lieber Papers, HL.

46. A. V. Wylie to Petigru, January 20, 1860, Petigru to A. V. Wylie, January 24, 1860, and Petigru, Memorandum of questions put to Julia Alexander, n.d., all in Vanderhorst Papers, SCHS.

47. On the early codification movement, see Donald J. Senese, "Legal Thought in South Carolina, 1800–1860" (Ph.D. dissertation, University of South Carolina, 1970), 222–25; Ford, "Petigru," 167–68, 172–73; [James L. Petigru], "Court of Chancery," review article, *Southern Review* 3 (1829): 63–77.

48. South Carolina, *Statutes at Large*, ed. Thomas Cooper, David McCord et al., 14 vols. (Columbia: A. S. Johnston, 1840ff), 12:589–90, 649–51; South Carolina Legislature, *Report of Certain Members of the Commission on Petigru's Code of the Statute Law of South Carolina . . .* (Columbia: F. G. DeFontaine and Company, 1864), [3]; South Carolina Senate, "Journal," December 20, 1859, p. 141, microfilm, SCA; Petigru to R. B. Boyleston, January 7, 1862, Petigru and King, Letterbooks, microfilm, R515, USC-Car. For a summary of earlier compilations of South Carolina law, see James W. Ely, Jr., "American Independence and the Law: A Study of Post-Revolutionary South Carolina Legislation," *Vanderbilt Law Review* 26 (1973): 939–40, n. 2.

49. For Petigru's first report on the codification, see [James L. Petigru], *Portion of the Code of Statute Law of South Carolina. Submitted to the General Assembly as Required by A. A., 1859 . . .* (Charleston: Evans and Cogswell, 1860). For Wardlaw's response, see David L. Wardlaw to Samuel McGowan, December 10, 1860, Samuel McGowan Papers, USC-Car.

50. Wardlaw to McGowan, December 10, 1860, Samuel McGowan Papers, USC-Car.

51. Petigru to Jane North, December 19, 1861, in Allston, "Life and Times," 41.

52. On the slow progress of the codification, see, for example, Petigru's letters to Jane North, in Allston, "Life and Times": June 15, 1860, 33; October 16, 1860, 34; October 29, 1860, 34; and October 30, 1861, 39; also his letters to Caroline Carson: July 5, 1861, August 22, 1861, and November 23, 1861, Petigru Correspondence, LC; also Petigru to Robert F. W. Allston, December 1, 1861, R. F. W. Allston Papers, SCHS; Petigru to David Risley, January 17, 1862, Petigru Correspondence, LC; Henry D. Lesesne to Caroline Pettigrew July 5, 1862, and Petigru to J. Johnston Pettigrew, November 30, 1862, both in Pettigrew Family Papers, UNC.

53. South Carolina Legislature, "Report of the Commission on the Code," MS, December 2, 1864, SCA, passim. This is the majority report. The quotation is from the minority report: South Carolina Legislature, *Report of Certain Members of the Commission . . .* , 5.

54. Charleston County, South Carolina, Court of General Sessions, Dockets 1859–63, SCA; Petigru to Jane North, January 16 and February 4, 1861, in Allston, "Life and Times," 36; Petigru and King to H. W. Litler, January 6, 1862, Petigru and King, Letterbooks, microfilm, R515, USC-Car; and Petigru to Caroline Carson, April 17, 1862, Petigru Correspondence, LC; Charleston, South Carolina, Tax Assessor, Assessment Books, 1861, 1862, 1863, microfilm, SCA; Petigru to Jane North, November 20, 1861, in Allston, "Life and Times," 40. The virtual cessation of court business is noted in numerous letters in the Petigru and King Letterbooks; see, for example, at November 14, 1860, February 15 and December 26, 1861, January 20 and 29, February 7, March 26, and July 28, 1862, Petigru and King, Letterbooks, microfilm, R515, USC-Car; also Petigru to J. Johnston Pettigrew, November 20, 1862, Pettigrew Family Papers, UNC.

55. Petigru to Caroline Carson, April 17, 1862, Petigru Correspondence, LC; Petigru to Benjamin F. Perry, March 22, 1861, Benjamin F. Perry Papers, AAH; Petigru to J. Johnston Pettigrew, October 6, 1862, Pettigrew Family Papers, UNC; Petigru to Jane North, February 19, 1863, copy, Petigru Correspondence, LC; Jane Petigru to [James Carson], May 28, 1861, Vanderhorst Papers, SCHS; Petigru to Caroline Carson, November 23, 1861, Petigru Correspondence, LC; Jane North to Adele Allston, September 23, 1862, R. F. W. Allston Papers, SCHS.

56. Petigru to Caroline Carson, December 13 and 21, 1861, Petigru Correspondence, LC; same to same, December 31, 1861, Vanderhorst Papers, SCHS; Petigru to J. Johnston Pettigrew, November [December] 15, 1861, Pettigrew Family Papers, UNC; Petigru to Adele Allston, December 18, 1861, R. F. W. Allston Papers, SCHS; Petigru to Jane North, December 13 and 16, 1861, in Allston, "Life and Times," 40, 41.

57. Petigru to Caroline Carson, December 31, 1861, Vanderhorst Papers, SCHS; Petigru to Robert F. W. Allston, December 20, 1861, and Petigru to Adele Allston, January 25, 1862, both in R. F. W. Allston Papers, SCHS; Petigru to Jane North, December 19, 1861, in Carson, *Life*, 423.

58. Petigru to Messrs. DeSaussure and Blanding, February 25, 1859, Petigru and King, Letterbooks, microfilm, R514, USC-Car; Petigru to Caroline Carson, December 21, 1861, Petigru to Sue King, March 6, 1862, copy, Petigru to Caroline Carson, April 17, 1862, all in Petigru Correspondence, LC.

59. Petigru to Caroline Carson, June 18, 1862, Petigru Correspondence, LC.

60. Petigru to Caroline Carson, July 4, 1862, Petigru Correspondence, LC; Petigru to Adele Allston, October 31, 1862, R. F. W. Allston Papers, SCHS.

61. Petigru to Caroline Carson, January 8, 1863, in Carson, *Life*, 466; Petigru to Adele Allston, January 9, 1863, R. F. W. Allston Papers, SCHS; James Carson to Caroline Carson, January 6, 1863, Vanderhorst Papers, SCHS, reported that Jane Amelia Petigru, having opened a letter to Dan from a Miss McDowel, found the salutation "dear husband" and, supposing it possible that they were secretly married, invited McDowel to come forward openly as his wife and be received into the family. Apparently McDowel never answered her letter; Petigru to Jane North, April 9, 1862, in Allston, "Life and Times," 43.

62. Petigru to W. H. Trapman, July 7, 1862, Petigru and King, Letterbooks, microfilm, R515, USC-Car; Petigru to Jane North, June 4, 1862, in Allston, "Life and Times," 43.

63. Mary Petigru to Adele Allston, November 18, [1861], R. F. W. Allston Papers, SCHS; Petigru to Caroline Carson, March 18, 1862, Petigru Correspondence, LC; Petigru to Jane North, March 19, 1862, in Allston, "Life and Times," 42.

64. Petigru to Caroline Carson, May 10, 1862, and June 18, 1862, also Petigru to William Elliott, May 6, 1862, copy, all in Petigru Correspondence, LC; Petigru to Jane North, July 16, 1862, in Allston, "Life and Times," 45.

65. Caroline Carson to Petigru, November 26, [1862], Vanderhorst Papers, SCHS; Petigru to J. Johnston Pettigrew, October 21, 1862, Pettigrew Family Papers, UNC; Petigru to Atkinson, Pilgrim, and Philips, October 27, 1862, and Petigru to James Carson, February 9, 1863, Petigru Correspondence, LC; Petigru to Jane North, February 19, 1862, in Allston, "Life and Times," 42; Petigru to Caroline Carson, December 16, 1862, Petigru Correspondence, LC.

66. Petigru to Jane North, June 18, 1862, copy, and Petigru to Caroline Carson, March 18, 1862, Petigru Correspondence, LC; Petigru to Charles K. Prioleau, December 12, 1862, Petigru and King, Letterbooks, microfilm, R515, USC-Car.

67. Henry Lesesne to Jane North, February 25, 1863, Pettigrew Family Papers, UNC; [Henry Lesesne?], "Memr. of Mr. Petigru's Last Days," MS, Vanderhorst Papers, SCHS.

68. Henry Lesesne to Jane North, February 25, 1863, Pettigrew Family Papers, UNC; James Carson to Caroline Carson, March 28, [1863], Vanderhorst Papers, SCHS.

69. [Mary N. Allston] to J. Johnston Pettigrew, March 22, [1863], Pettigrew Family Papers, UNC.

70. *Charleston Courier*, March 11, 1863; John Berkley Grimball, Diary, March 10, 1863, in *South Carolina Historical Magazine* 56 (1955): 213; James Carson to Caroline Carson, March 28, [1863], Vanderhorst Papers, SCHS.

71. South Carolina Senate, "Report of the Committee on the Judiciary on a Resolution from the House in Relation to the Code Prepared by the Late James L. Petigru," MS [1865], SCA, recommended in effect that it was "in-

expedient" to adopt the code at the time; also see Carson, *Life*, 359; Senese, "Legal Thought," 400–403. The information on Daniel Corbin is courtesy of Professor Lewis Burke, University of South Carolina School of Law, interview with the authors, February 12, 1991.

72. Philip Lopate, quoting Stuart Hampshire, "Can Innocence Go Unpunished?" *New York Times Book Review,* March 11, 1990, 10.

BIBLIOGRAPHIC ESSAY

Each of the three book-length biographies of James L. Petigru is useful to modern readers, though more as a source book than an insightful interpretation of its subject. William J. Grayson, *James Louis Petigru. A Biographical Sketch* (New York: Harper and Brothers, 1866), is the reminiscence of a forty-five-year friendship that began when the author and his subject were college classmates. Joseph Blyth Allston's life-and-letters biography of his uncle by marriage was published serially in the *Charleston Sunday News* (1899–1900) and then compiled as a scrapbook, "Life and Times of James L. Petigru," whose original is in the Charleston Library Society. It is largely an edited transcription of family letters, many of which have since been lost. Both it and James Petigru Carson's biography of his grandfather, *Life, Letters, and Speeches of James Louis Petigru, the Union Man of South Carolina* (Washington, D.C.: W. H. Lowdermilk, 1920), though filiopietistic in nature, contain quite accurate renditions of letters, read against the originals that still exist. Consequently, when original letters are not available, it is reasonably safe to rely on the published versions.

Of the Petigru letters still extant in manuscript, most, including many not published in either Allston or Carson as well as many of the handwritten or typed copies made for their work, are in the South Carolina Historical Society as parts of the Vanderhorst Papers and R. F. W. Allston Papers and in the collection of James L. Petigru Correspondence in the Library of Congress. The South Caroliniana Library of the University of South Carolina holds most of Petigru's letters to Hugh Legaré written during the nullification controversy as part of its Miscellaneous Manuscripts Collection and an extensive record of Petigru's outgoing professional correspondence in the Petigru and King Letterbooks, 1854–63. It also houses, in addition to many collections in which there are scattered Petigru items, the most complete collection of Petigru's printed speeches, though the South Carolina Historical Society also has many of these. Finally, the Pettigrew Family Papers in the Southern Historical Collection at the University of North Carolina at Chapel Hill and the North Carolina State Archives contain numerous letters by and about Petigru. Most of his incoming letters either burned in his home in the 1861 fire that destroyed it or were lost while his legal papers were stored in a Columbia building used as a barracks for Union soldiers at the end of the Civil War. His remaining outgoing letters are widely scattered in the papers of those with whom he corresponded.

Several articles published in the 1980s treat specific aspects of Petigru's life. The most soundly researched is Lacy K. Ford, Jr., "James Louis Petigru: The Last South Carolina Federalist," in Michael O'Brien and David Moltke-Hansen, eds., *Intellectual Life in Antebellum Charleston* (Knoxville: University of Tennessee Press, 1986), 152–85. The others are all by Lyon G. Tyler: "James Louis Petigru: Freedom's Champion in a Slave Society," *South Carolina Historical Magazine* 83 (1982): 272–86; "Prisoners All—The Slave and James Louis Petigru," *Proceedings of the South Carolina Historical Association* (1980): 55–72; and "God and Mr Petigru: Episcopal Attitudes toward Faith and Doctrine in Antebellum South Carolina," *Historical Magazine of the Protestant Episcopal Church* 52 (1983): 229–43.

There are relatively few modern biographies of those with whom Petigru was most closely associated. There are two about his colleague and intimate friend of the 1820s and 1830s, Hugh Legaré: Linda Rhea, *Hugh Swinton Legaré: A Charleston Intellectual* (Chapel Hill: University of North Carolina Press, 1934), is a traditional narrative. Michael O'Brien, *A Character of Hugh Legaré* (Knoxville: University of Tennessee Press, 1985), is largely confined to Legaré's ideas and intellectual accomplishments. Lillian Kibler, *Benjamin F. Perry. South Carolina Unionist* (Durham: Duke University Press, 1946), portrays the life and world of a close political associate from 1830 to 1860. And Clyde N. Wilson, *Carolina Cavalier. The Life and Mind of James Johnston Pettigrew* (Athens: University of Georgia Press, 1990), is a romantic and highly sympathetic portrayal of Petigru's cousin and special protégé.

Biographies of other South Carolina political figures who shaped Petigru's life include Jon Wakelyn, *The Politics of a Literary Man, William Gilmore Simms* (Westport, Conn.: Greenwood Press, 1973); Archie Vernon Huff, Jr., *Langdon Cheves of South Carolina* (Columbia: University of South Carolina Press, 1977); and Drew Gilpin Faust, *James Henry Hammond and the Old South. A Design for Mastery* (Baton Rouge: Louisiana State University Press, 1982). Of the many biographies of John C. Calhoun, the most recent is John Niven's *John C. Calhoun and the Price of Union* (Baton Rouge: Louisiana State University Press, 1988). The only biography of James Hamilton, Jr., is Virginia Louise Glenn, "James Hamilton, Jr., of South Carolina: A Biography" (Ph.D. dissertation, University of North Carolina, 1964), which is available on microfilm.

A spate of books trace South Carolina politics and economics during Petigru's life. Among the most useful in reconstructing his world are Peter A. Coclanis, *The Shadow of a Dream. Economic Life and Death in the South Carolina Low Country, 1670–1920* (New York: Oxford University Press, 1989); Jerome J. Nadelhaft, *The Disorders of War. The Revolution in South Carolina*

(Orono: University of Maine Press, 1981); Rachel N. Klein, *Unification of a Slave State. The Rise of the Planter Class in the South Carolina Backcountry, 1760–1808* (Chapel Hill: University of North Carolina Press, 1990); William W. Freehling, *Prelude to Civil War. The Nullification Controversy in South Carolina, 1816–1836* (New York: Harper and Row, 1965); Michael O'Brien and David Moltke-Hansen, eds., *Intellectual Life in Antebellum Charleston* (Knoxville: University of Tennessee Press, 1986); William H. Pease and Jane H. Pease, *The Web of Progress. Private Values and Public Styles in Boston and Charleston, 1828–1843* (1985; reprint, Athens: University of Georgia Press, 1991); Lacy K. Ford, Jr., *Origins of Southern Radicalism. The South Carolina Upcountry, 1800–1860* (New York: Oxford University Press, 1988); John Barnwell, *Love of Order: South Carolina's First Secession Crisis* [1850–1852] (Chapel Hill: University of North Carolina Press, 1982); Steven A. Channing, *Crisis of Fear. Secession in South Carolina* (New York: Simon and Schuster, 1970); E. Milby Burton, *The Siege of Charleston, 1861–1865* (Columbia: University of South Carolina Press, 1970). Microfilms of the *Charleston Courier* and *Mercury* are the basic sources for following any event day by day.

The key issues in the antebellum evolution of American law and legal practice are explored in Maxwell Bloomfield, *American Lawyers in a Changing Society, 1776–1876* (Cambridge: Harvard University Press, 1976); Charles M. Cook, *The American Codification Movement. A Study in Antebellum Legal Reform* (Westport, Conn.: Greenwood Press, 1981); Lawrence M. Friedman, *A History of American Law* (New York: Simon and Schuster, 1972); Fletcher M. Green, *Constitutional Development in the South Atlantic States, 1776–1860. A Study in the Evolution of Democracy* (1930; reprint New York: W. W. Norton, 1966); Kermit L. Hall, *The Magic Mirror: Law in American History* (New York: Oxford University Press, 1989); Morton J. Horwitz, *The Transformation of American Law, 1780–1860* (Cambridge: Harvard University Press, 1977); and Jamil Zainaldin, *Law in Antebellum Society: Legal Change and Economic Expansion* (New York: Alfred A. Knopf, 1983).

The most comprehensive study of antebellum South Carolina legal structures and practices is Michael S. Hindus, *Prison and Plantation. Crime, Justice, and Authority in Massachusetts and South Carolina, 1767–1878* (Chapel Hill: University of North Carolina Press, 1980). Donald J. Senese gives an excellent narrative description in his "Building the Pyramid: The Growth and Development of the State Court System in Antebellum South Carolina, 1800–1860," *South Carolina Law Review* 24 (1972): 357–79. Some of the essays in Herbert A. Johnson, ed., *South Carolina Legal History* (Spartanburg: Reprint Company, 1980), provide useful material on South Carolina law. Essays that pose questions about how and why southern law differed from northern appear in David J. Bodenhamer and James W. Ely, Jr., eds., *Ambivalent Legacy. A Legal History of the South* (Jackson: University of Mississippi Press, 1974); and in Kermit L. Hall and James W. Ely, Jr., eds., *An Uncertain Tradition: Constitutionalism and the History of the South* (Athens: University of Georgia Press, 1989). Paul Finkelman, "Exploring Southern Legal History," *North Carolina Law Review* 64 (1985): 77–116, provides an excellent historiographical survey of the current state of southern legal history.

Illuminating a special phase of Petigru's practice are Senese, "The Free Negro and the South Carolina Courts, 1790–1860," *South Carolina Historical Magazine* 68 (1967): 130–53; and A. E. Kier Nash, "Negro Rights, Unionism and Greatness on the South Carolina Court of Appeals: The Extraordinary Chief Justice John Belton O'Neall," *South Carolina Law Review* 21 (1969): 141–90. The background for Petigru's wartime practice is accessible in William M. Robinson, Jr., *Justice in Grey. A History of the Judicial System of the Confederate States of America* (1941; reprint, New York: Russell and Russell, 1968). Particularly useful for understanding domestic and probate law and the legal treatment of women's property nationally are Norma Basch, *In the Eyes of the Law: Women, Marriage, and Property in Nineteenth-Century New York* (Ithaca: Cornell University Press, 1982); and Michael Grossberg, *Governing the Hearth: Law and Family in Nineteenth-Century America* (Chapel Hill: University of North Carolina Press, 1985). South Carolina practice is well explored in John E. Crowley, "Family Relations and Inheritance in Early South Carolina," *Histoire Sociale/Social History* 17 (1984): 35–57; Marylynn Salmon, *Women and the Law of Property in Early America* (Chapel Hill: University of North Carolina Press, 1986); and Jane H. Pease and William H. Pease, *Ladies, Women, and Wenches: Choice and Constraint in Antebellum Charleston and Boston* (Chapel Hill: University of North Carolina Press, 1990), 90–114. Finally, opinions of the South Carolina appeals courts of sufficient lasting interest to be printed are compiled most conveniently in *South Carolina Reports* (St. Paul: West Publishing Company, 1917–), vol. 8–29.

Our understanding of adult male developmental patterns has been shaped by Daniel J. Levinson, *The Seasons of a Man's Life* (New York: Ballantine Books, 1978), and his "Exploration in Biography: Evolution of the Individual Life Structure in Adulthood," in A. I. Rabin et al., eds., *Further Explorations in Personality* (New York: John Wiley and Sons, 1981), 44–85; and by George E. Vaillant, *Adaptation to Life* (Boston: Little, Brown, 1977). Also helpful were Jack Block, "Some Enduring and Consequential Structures of Personality," in Rabin et al., *Further Explorations;* and Robert W. White, *Lives in Progress* (1952; reprint, New York: Holt, Rinehart and Winston, 1975). For understanding the Petigru family dynamics, James L. Framo, *Explorations in Marital and Family Therapy: Selected Papers* (New York: Springer, 1982), especially his 1970 essay on "Symptoms from a Family Transactional Viewpoint"; and James C. Hansen and Luciano L'Abate, *Approaches to Family Therapy* (New York: Macmillan, 1982), were most helpful. Three books on the families of alcoholics illuminated problems within the Pettigrew/Petigru family: Stephanie Brown, *Treating Adult Children of Alcoholics: A Developmental Perspective* (New York: John Wiley and Sons, 1988); Michael Elkin, *Families under the Influence. Changing Alcoholic Patterns* (New York: W. W. Norton, 1984); and Peter Steinglass et al., *The Alcoholic Family* (New York: Basic Books, 1987).

INDEX